PRAISE FOR *GRIEF COUNSELING AND GRIEF THERAPY*

"The fourth edition of this book retains all the theoretical strengths and clinical wisdom of past editions, while incorporating emerging theories and cutting-edge research. It is required reading for any counselor, educator, or researcher who wishes to understand grief."

—**Kenneth J. Doka,** PhD, *Professor, The Graduate School, The College of New Rochelle; Senior Consultant, The Hospice Foundation of America*

"[If] you knew Worden's work and his writings previously, you'll find an enhanced book with a much broader and challenging perspective than his previous editions. If you are not familiar with Bill Worden, then it is time to begin."

—**Ben Wolfe,** MEd, LICSW, *Fellow in Thanatology, Program Manager/Grief Counselor, St. Mary's Medical Center's Grief Support Center, Duluth, MN; Past President, Association for Death Education and Counseling*

"This book challenges how we conceptualize the experience of grief and the process of mourning, it informs how we assess those experiencing problems in adjusting to loss, and it guides our treatment approaches. I can't think of a thing Worden has missed."

—**Stephen Fleming,** PhD, *Department of Psychology, Faculty of Health, York University, Toronto, Ontario, Canada*

"Simply stated, you will not find a better book to guide you in assisting people struggling with the myriad of issues following a death."

—**Donna L. Schuurman,** EdD, CT, *Executive Director, The Dougy Center for Grieving Children & Families*

Praise for Earlier Editions

"This book is the 'Bible' for those involved in the field of bereavement work. . . . It is a straightforward, tightly focused, practical, soundly reasoned, compact working text."

—**William M. Lamers, Jr.,** MD, *The Lamers Medical Group*

"[Worden] has again provided mental health professionals with a superb guide describing specific . . . procedures that may be helpful in working with bereaved clients undergoing normal or abnormal grief reactions . . . [An] extremely practical book and an invaluable resource."

—***Contemporary Psychology,*** now known as ***PsyCritiques***

J. William Worden, PhD, ABPP, is a fellow of the American Psychological Association and holds academic appointments at the Harvard Medical School and at the Rosemead Graduate School of Psychology in California. He is also co-principal investigator of the Harvard Child Bereavement Study, based at Massachusetts General Hospital. Recipient of five major NIH grants, his research and clinical work over 40 years have centered on issues of life-threatening illness and life-threatening behavior.

His professional interests led him to become a founding member of the Association of Death Education and Counseling and the International Work Group on Death, Dying, and Bereavement. A pioneer in the hospice movement in the United States, Dr. Worden was on the advisory board for the first hospice in the United States in Branford, Connecticut, as well as the Hospice of Pasadena, California. He has been a consultant to various research projects across the United States, including "Women and HIV" for Columbia University, "Assisted Suicide and End-of-Life Decisions" for the American Psychological Association, and "Fathers' Experience With Pediatric End of Life Care" for the University of California, San Francisco. He served for 7 years on the national board of the American Cancer Society and is active in the society at the state and local levels.

Dr. Worden has lectured and written on topics related to terminal illness, cancer care, and bereavement. He is the author of *Personal Death Awareness* and *Children & Grief: When a Parent Dies*, and is coauthor of *Helping Cancer Patients Cope. Grief Counseling & Grief Therapy: A Handbook for the Mental Health Practitioner* has been translated into 11 foreign languages and is widely used around the world as the standard reference on the subject. Dr. Worden's clinical practice is in Laguna Niguel, California.

Grief Counseling and Grief Therapy

A Handbook for the Mental Health Practitioner

FOURTH EDITION

J. William Worden, PhD, ABPP

SPRINGER PUBLISHING COMPANY

New York

Springer Publishing Company, LLC
11 West 42nd Street
New York, NY 10036
www.springerpub.com

Acquisitions Editor: Sheri W. Sussman
Production Editor: Julia Rosen
Cover design: Mimi Flow
Composition: Apex CoVantage
Book cover photo: Celestino Garcia

11 12/ 9 8 7 6

Library of Congress Cataloging-in-Publication Data

Worden, J. William (James William)
  Grief counseling and grief therapy : a handbook for the mental health practitioner /
J. William Worden. — 4th ed.
      p. ; cm.
  Includes bibliographical references and index.
  ISBN 978-0-8261-0120-4 (alk. paper)
  1. Grief therapy.   2. Mental health counseling.   I. Title.
  [DNLM: 1. Counseling—methods.   2. Grief.   3. Psychotherapy—methods.
WM 55 W924g 2008]
  RC455.4.L67W67   2008
  616.89'14—dc22   2008016551

Printed in the United States of America by Bang Printing.

To my children, Michael and Karin
And my grandchildren, Abigail Ann and Andrew William
May these thoughts be helpful to you one day.

Grieving allows us to heal, to remember with love rather than pain.
It is a sorting process.
One by one you let go of things that are gone
and you mourn for them.
One by one you take hold of the things that have become a part of
who you are and build again.
—Rachael Naomi Remen

Happiness has gone out of our lives;
Grief has taken the place of our dances.
—Lamentations 5

Contents

ix

Preface

Twenty-five years have passed since the first edition of *Grief Counseling & Grief Therapy* was published. In these 25 years there have been a number of challenges and changes to the field. Some have challenged the effectiveness of grief counseling, while others have suggested that it can have a negative effect on some mourners. Is grief counseling unnecessary, ineffective, and harmful? I want to address these issues in this edition of the book.

Still others have wanted to challenge the tasks of mourning by suggesting that they are nothing other than stages of mourning, and that this stage theory of mourning is passé. This belief is based on a limited understanding of the task model and a failure to keep abreast of its development through the earlier editions of the book.

Others support the task of mourning idea but put their own spin on how and when these tasks should be accomplished. For example, the dual process of mourning approach of Schut and Stroebe covers the tasks but does so in an oscillating fashion. Doka, Corr, and Rando have each increased the number of tasks and come up with an alternative model.

I still believe that the task model is a useful way to think about the process of mourning, but I have modified it and made some changes in this edition of the book. Readers will notice that the mediators of mourning now has its own chapter. These mediators affect how the tasks are adapted to or not. While bereavement is a universal phenomenon, the experience of grief is not. These mediators account for much of this individual difference.

Task III has been reformulated as "adjusting to a *world* without the deceased" and has been divided into three subtasks: external, internal, and spiritual tasks. These subtasks were included in the third edition, but some apparently missed this, so I have tried to make this emphasis clearer and link it with current research findings, including those having to do with meaning making.

Readers of earlier editions will understand how task IV has evolved from its original conceptualization of "emotionally withdrawing from the deceased so that emotional energy can be reinvested in other relationships." This early Freudian notion gave way to object relations thinking, where the task involved "keeping the deceased in one's life but emotionally relocating the deceased so that one can move forward with one's life." Currently, a good definition of this fourth task, which is supported by research on continuing bonds, would be: "To find an enduring connection with the deceased in the midst of embarking on a new life." Select a definition that makes the most sense to you in understanding your personal loss experience as well as in understanding what is going on with your clients. I do think that a fourth task is needed to round out one's overall adaptation to the loss. Incidentally, I prefer to use the word "adaptation" rather than words like "recovery" or "resolution."

Special acknowledgments are due a number of people who assisted me with this project. I would like to thank Robert Cochran for his help in tracking down the vast amount of recent literature. My appreciation is also extended to Karin Worden, Jim Monahan, Carlos Canales, Sharon Hsu, and Jason Smith for their assistance, and Sheri W. Sussman, vice president, Editorial, at Springer Publishing Company, who has added her wisdom and encouragement for all four editions of this book.

The professionals in the Worden group, which meets monthly for support and supervision, have inspired me and clarified my thinking. These include Dennis Bull, Ann Goldman, Linda Grant, Bill Hoy, Annette Iverson, Michael Meador, Ron Ritter, Barbara Smith, and Stephanie Thal. And, as always, my family and friends provided important emotional support.

Introduction

Over the 25 years since the first edition of this book was written, there have been a number of new concepts introduced into the field of grief, loss, and bereavement. Before we get into the content of this fourth edition, I would like to highlight some that I believe are worth noting. Many of these appeared during the past 10 years, and some of these I discuss in more detail in the book. Although tempted to put these into the top 10 in order of importance as the E-Channel does, I will merely list them. They are all important.

WHAT IS THE NATURE OF COMPLICATED BEREAVEMENT?

For years, most of those working with complicated mourning and grief therapy have used terms like "chronic grief," "delayed grief," and "exaggerated grief" to delineate the diagnosis of those with complicated bereavement or complicated mourning. In fact, some of these concepts were defined by consensus when Beverly Raphael and Warwick Middleton (1990) did a survey to determine which terms were the most frequently used by leading therapists in the field. Although there was a surprising degree of consensus, the problem is that complicated grief is a V code in the *DSM,* and V code diagnoses do not qualify for third-party payment through insurance carriers.

1

Another problem has been the lack of precise definitions of these terms, which makes rigorous research of them difficult. The easiest solution has been to do research using well-defined pathological entities like depression, anxiety, and somatization, for which there are good standardized measures. Although these clinical entities may be part of the mourner's experience, they clearly are not measures of grief. There were a few measures of grief like the Texas Revised Grief Inventory and the Hogan Grief Reaction Checklist, but most were normed on a clinical population.

Beginning with the work of Holly Prigerson and Mardi Horowitz, there has been a 10-year-plus attempt to come up with a diagnosis of complicated grief that would be acceptable to go into the *DSM-V*, scheduled for release in 2010. Such a diagnosis would make insurance money available for the treatment of patients with this diagnosis and would make research funds available for further investigation on this clinical entity. Details on this diagnosis and its development can be found in chapter 5.

DISENFRANCHISED GRIEF

This term, coined by Ken Doka and further developed by Attig (2004), has been an important addition to the field. Although Doka's first volume came out in 1989, he updated the concept in a second volume that came out in 2002. Disenfranchised grief refers to losses in the mourner's life of relationships that are not socially sanctioned. A classic example would be the death of someone with whom the mourner is having an affair. If this affair is not widely known, the mourner will not be invited to participate in the funeral rituals and may not receive the social support that many people find helpful after a death. Alternate lifestyles may not be socially sanctioned, and the friend or lover may be ostracized by the dead person's family. There are numerous other examples of disenfranchised grief and there are suggestions in this book for reenfranchising some of these losses to aid the mourner in adapting to the loss.

Aaron Lazare (1979), an early colleague at Massachusetts General Hospital, talked about two kinds of loss that are directly related to this concept of disenfranchised grief. *Socially negated losses* are those losses that society treats as non-losses. Examples of this would be pregnancy losses either spontaneous or induced. The second kind of loss related to disenfranchised grief would be *socially unspeakable losses.* These are specific losses about which the mourner has a difficult time talking. Common examples would be deaths by suicide and death by AIDS. Both of these losses carry some stigma in the broader society. One intervention that can be helpful to those experiencing these types of losses can be assisting them in talking about them and exploring their thoughts and feelings about the death. Reenfranchising suggestions for these types of losses can be found in chapter 7 of this volume.

CONTINUING BONDS

Attachments to the deceased that are maintained rather than relinquished have been called continuing bonds. This is not an entirely new concept. Shuchter and Zisook (1988) noted that widows in their seminal studies in San Diego maintained a sense of their loved one's presence for several years after the death. In the Harvard Child Bereavement Study, Silverman, Nickman, and I observed ongoing connections with the dead parent among a large number of these bereaved children. For most it was a positive experience; for some it was not. The book by Klass, Silverman, and Nickman titled *Continuing Bonds: New Understandings of Grief* (1996) pulled together information from our study and several others to promote the notion that people stay connected with the deceased rather than emotionally withdrawing, as was the notion promoted by Freud.

This new concept was not embraced by all and questions soon arose as to whether continuing bonds can be adaptive for some and maladaptive for others? Are continuing bonds actually associated with a healthy ongoing life? A lot of this controversy is based on the lack of good research evidence for the efficacy of continuing bonds. As more research is done, some of these questions will be resolved. Essentially, the questions center around five main issues: (1) What types of bonds are the most helpful in the adaptation to loss? These would include objects from the deceased (linking and transitional objects, keepsakes), a sense of the deceased's presence, talking to the deceased, introjecting the deceased's beliefs and values, taking on characteristics of the deceased, and the like. (2) For whom are continuing bonds helpful, and for whom are they not? This necessitates the identification of subgroups of mourners; the concept should not be applied to everyone. One promising approach to this is to look at the mourner's attachment style in relationship to the deceased. In the case of anxious attachments that can lead to chronic grief, holding onto the deceased may not be adaptive. Some mourners need to relinquish and move on (Stroebe & Schut, 2005). (3) In what time frame are continuing bonds the most adaptive and when are they less adaptive—closer to the loss, farther from the loss? (Field, Gao, & Paderna, 2005). (4) What is the impact of religious and cultural differences on maintaining healthy bonds? This would include beliefs and rituals that promote a connection and memorialization of the deceased in various societies. (5) What is the relationship between maintaining a continuing bond with the deceased and relocating the deceased, which is an important part of Worden's fourth task of mourning? More on bonds can be found in chapter 2.

MEANING MAKING

Meaning reconstruction and meaning making, concepts introduced and promoted by Robert Neimeyer, have been an important emphasis in the field over the past 10 years. He sees meaning reconstruction as the central process faced by bereaved individuals. This reconstruction is primarily accomplished through the use of narratives or life stories. When unanticipated or incongruous events such as the death of a loved one occur, a person needs to redefine the self and relearn ways to engage with the world without the deceased. The person cannot return to a pre-loss level of functioning but learns how to develop a meaningful life without the deceased loved one. This is central to my third task of mourning, in which the mourner must learn to adjust to a world without the deceased. Death can challenge one's assumptions about the world (spiritual adjustments) and one's personal identity (internal adjustments). Bereaved individuals have serious questions such as: "What will my life look like now?" "What did the deceased's life mean?" "How can I feel safe in a world such as this?" and "Who am I now that this death has occurred?" (Neimeyer, Prigerson, & Davies, 2002).

I think it is important to note, however, that some deaths do *not* challenge personal meaning making in any fundamental way. Davis and colleagues (2000) conducted research on two different bereaved populations and found that 20%–30% of the bereaved individuals appeared to function well without engaging in the process of meaning making. Of those who searched for meaning, fewer than half of the individuals found it even over a year after the death. Those who did find meaning, however, were better adjusted than those who searched and didn't find it, but, interestingly, for some the quest to understand continued even after meaning was found.

Neimeyer (2000), commenting on the Davis research, makes note that the majority in the studies were struggling with meaning making and these should be helped with this process. But, he cautions the counselor about initiating this process if it does not occur spontaneously. He concludes his comments with an important distinction: meaning making is a process, not an outcome or achievement. The meanings associated with death loss are constantly revised. We see this clearly in our work with bereaved children, who, as they age and pass through new developmental stages, ask: "What would my parent be like now?" and "What would our relationship be like now that I am graduating college, getting married, etc?" (Worden, 1996). More on meaning making as a task of mourning can be found in chapter 2.

RESILIENCE

When Phyllis Silverman and I studied 125 parentally bereaved children over a 2-year period after the death, we noted that children fell into one of three groups. The first was the group of children (approximately 20%) who were not doing well during the 2 years after the death. Since our research grant came from the NIMH for a study intended to identify bereaved children at-risk and prevent problem outcomes, this group became a major focus of our study. Could we identify at-risk children early after the loss so that early intervention might be offered to prevent later negative sequelae from the death? However, we also noticed a second smaller group of children who seemed to be doing very well, and we identified them as resilient children. Their academic performance, social life, communication about the deceased, self-worth, sense of control, and healthy identification with the dead parent were all on the high side. The third and largest group was "making do" during the first 2 years of bereavement (Silverman, 2000; Worden, 1996).

Thanks to the work of George Bonanno (2004), we have begun to look at resilient bereaved individuals. These are people who adapt well to the loss and are not in need of either counseling or therapy. I think this focus is overdue.

In Arizona, Irwin Sandler, Sharlene Wolchik, and Tim Ayers (2008) have added to our thinking on resilience. Like myself, they prefer the term "adaptation" to "recovery." Those mourners who make a good or effective adaptation to the loss have made a "resilient adaptation." Sandler's group has identified both risk and protective factors in their study of parentally bereaved children and their families that lead to a good (resilient) or a less good adaptation to the loss. By focusing on positive as well as negative outcomes, a resilient approach goes beyond the more narrow focus of pathological outcomes. It is interesting that the risk and protective factors found in Arizona families are similar to those Silverman and I found in the Harvard study. Multiple factors at both the individual and social environmental levels are at work here, so Sandler's group calls their theory a *contextual framework on adaptation.* Individuals are seen as nested within families, which are in turn nesting within communities and cultures. This fairly new research and thinking on resilience in bereavement holds promise for our understanding of grief and loss. More on this can be found in chapter 3.

TRAUMA AND GRIEF

Like depression and grief, trauma and grief share many of the same behavioral features. A number of articles discuss how they are similar and how they are different. There are some, like Rando, Horowitz, and Figley, who would subsume all grief under trauma, but I find this a stretch. I prefer the model offered by Stroebe, Schut, and Finkenauer (2001), which makes the following three distinctions: The first is *trauma without bereavement*. Here the person experiences a traumatic event that gives rise to trauma symptoms leading to a diagnosis of posttraumatic stress disorder or acute stress disorder, mostly depending on the time frame. Other symptoms of depression and anxiety may lead to a comorbid diagnosis. In this first distinction the traumatic event has not led to any deaths and the person is dealing with one or more of the classic trauma symptoms (intrusion, avoidance, hyperarousal) without bereavement. *Bereavement without trauma* is the second distinction. Here the person has experienced the death of a loved one without experiencing trauma symptoms associated with the event. If there are complications after the loss, one of the complicated mourning categories would apply to this complication. The third category could be called *traumatic bereavement*. Here the person experiences a death and there is something about the death itself (often violent deaths) or something about the person's experience of the death (often related to an insecure attachment or conflicted relationship with the deceased) that gives rise to symptoms associated with trauma.

Two questions emerge in any discussion of traumatic bereavement. First, which is the most important in defining traumatic bereavement—the circumstances of the death or the reaction of the mourner? Second, in the treatment of traumatic bereavement, which symptoms should be addressed first—the trauma symptoms or the grief symptoms? Traumatic stress interferes with grief over loss; grief interferes with trauma mastery (Rando, 2003). Many believe that the trauma symptoms must be dealt with first before the grief can be addressed.

There have always been people who have been exposed to violent deaths, but the number of violent events seems to have increased during the past 10 years. The recent rash of school shootings as well as September 11, 2001, illustrate the pervasiveness of violence in our society. Such violent events will continue to expose more people to both trauma and bereavement. We need more research on grief and trauma, including research on which interventions are most effective. We need to educate the media that interventions done in the days following school shooting are *not* grief counseling but rather crisis intervention, and there are major differences between the two in goals and techniques.

Let me conclude this introduction with something that causes me concern—the failure of both clinicians and researchers to recognize the uniqueness of the grief experience. Even though the mourning tasks apply to all death losses, how a person approaches and adapts to these tasks can be quite varied. A one-size-fits-all approach to grief counseling or grief therapy is very limiting.

When I was a graduate student at Harvard, Professor Gordon Allport had a strong impact on my thinking. Allport (September 1957, lecture notes) would tell students that "Each man is like *all* other men; each man is like *some* other men; and each man is like *no* other man." Allport was affirming his longtime professional interest in individual differences—an interest that led to his collaboration with Robert White on the longitudinal case studies of men called *Lives in Progress* (1952). These studies affirm both the similarity and uniqueness of each person.

If we were to translate Allport's dictum into the field of bereavement, we would say, "Each person's grief is like *all* other people's grief; each person's grief is like *some* other person's grief; and each person's grief is like *no* other person's grief." Over the last 25 years we have tended to lose sight of the uniqueness of the grief experience in our clinical and research undertakings. I always liked Alan Wolfelt's idea of "companioning" the bereaved individual. In this approach the counselor comes alongside the mourner and they share their experiences in a way that can be helpful for both. I worry that in our rush to formulate a *DSM* diagnosis for complicated (traumatic) grief, we may focus too much on "Each person's grief is like *some* other person's grief" and lose sight of the uniqueness of grief, the fact that each person's grief is like *no* other person's grief. I have affirmed in each edition of this book that every person's experience of grief is unique to him or her, and people's experiences shouldn't be saddled with the term "abnormal grief." I much prefer the term "complicated mourning," which affirms some kind of difficulty in the mourning process that brings the person to the attention of the mental health worker.

Affirmation of the uniqueness of grief is not a new emphasis in the field of bereavement. Colin Parkes (2002) said, "From the start, Bowlby and I recognized that there was a great deal of individual variation in the response to bereavement and that not everybody went through these phases in the same way or at the same speed" (p. 380).

An interesting affirmation of the uniqueness and subjective quality of grief comes from an fMRI study of grief by Gundel, O'Connor, Littrell, Fort, and Lane (2003). After investigating the grief experience in the brains of eight women, they concluded that grief is mediated by a distributed neural network that subserves a number of neural processes affecting various parts of the brain and its functions, including affect processing, mentalizing, memory retrieval, visual imagery, and autonomic regulation. This neural network may account for the unique, subjective quality of grief, and this finding provides new leads in our quest to understand the health consequences of grief and the neurobiology of attachment.

I believe that the mediators of mourning outlined in detail in chapter 3 hold the key to understanding individual differences in the mourning experience—the adaptation to loss from death.

I said in the first edition of this book 25 years ago that I don't believe that we need to establish a new profession of grief counselors. I still believe this. D. M. Reilly (1978), a social worker, says, "We do not necessarily need a whole new profession of . . . bereavement counselors. We do need more thought, sensitivity, and activity concerning this issue on the part of the existing professional groups, that is, clergy, funeral directors, family therapists, nurses, social workers, and physicians" (p. 49). To this Lloyd (1992) adds, "Skills in working with grief and loss remain core essential tools for professionals who are not necessarily specialist counselors" (p. 151). I agree with this. What I want to do in this book is address those of you in these traditional professions who are already in a position to extend care to the bereaved and have the knowledge and skills required to do effective intervention and, in some cases, preventive mental health work.

REFERENCES

Attig, T. (2004). Disenfranchised grief revisited: Discounting hope and love. *Omega, 49,* 197–215.

Bonanno, G. A. (2004). Loss, trauma, and human resilience. *American Psychologist, 59,* 20–28.

Davis, C., Wortman, C., Lehman, D., & Silver, R. (2000). Searching for meaning in loss: Are clinical assumptions correct? *Death Studies, 24,* 497–540.

Doka, K. (Ed.). (1989). *Disenfranchised grief: Recognizing hidden sorrow.* Lexington, MA: Lexington Books.

Doka, K. (2002). *Disenfranchised grief: New directions, challenges, and strategies for practice.* Champaign, IL: Research Press.

Field, N. P., Gao, B. I., & Paderna, L. (2005). Continuing bonds in bereavement: An attachment theory based perspective. *Death Studies, 29,* 277–299.

Gundel, H., O'Connor, M. F., Littrell, L., Fort, C., & Lane, R. D. (2003). Functional neuroanatomy of grief: An fMRI study. *American Journal of Psychiatry, 160,* 1946–1953.

Klass, D., Silverman, P., & Nickman, S. (Eds.). (1996). *Continuing bonds: New understandings of grief.* Washington, DC: Taylor & Francis.

Lazare, A. (1979). *Outpatient psychiatry: Diagnosis and treatment.* Baltimore: Williams and Wilkins.

Lloyd, M. (1992). Tools for many trades: Reaffirming the use of grief counseling by health, welfare and pastoral workers. *British Journal of Guidance and Counselling, 20,* 150–163.

Neimeyer, R. (2000). Searching for the searching of meaning: Grief therapy and the process of reconstruction. *Death Studies, 24,* 541–558.

Neimeyer, R., Prigerson, H. G., & Davies, B. (2002). Mourning and meaning. *American Behavioral Scientist, 46,* 235–251.

Parkes, C. M. (2002). Grief: Lessons from the past, visions for the future. *Death Studies, 26,* 367–385.

Rando, T. A. (2003). Public tragedy and complicated mourning. In M. Lattanzi-Licht & K. Doka (Eds.), *Living with grief: Coping with public tragedy* (pp. 263–274). New York: Brunner-Routledge.

Raphael, B., & Middleton, W. (1990). What is pathologic grief? *Psychiatric Annals, 20,* 304–307.

Reilly, D. M. (1978). Death propensity, dying, and bereavement: A family systems perspective. *Family Therapy, 5,* 35–55.

Sandler, I., Wolchik, S., & Ayers, T. (2008). Resilience rather than recovery: A contextual framework on adaptation following bereavement. *Death Studies, 32,* 59–73.

Shuchter, S. R., & Zisook, S. (1988). Widowhood: The continuing relationship with the dead spouse. *Bulletin Menninger Clinic, 52,* 269–279.

Silverman, P. R. (2000). *Never too young to know: Death in children's lives.* New York: Oxford University Press.

Stroebe, M. S., & Schut, H. (2005). To continue or relinquish bonds: A review of consequences for the bereaved. *Death Studies, 29,* 477–494.

Stroebe, M. S., Schut, H., & Finkenauer, C. (2001). The traumatization of grief: A conceptual framework for understanding the trauma-bereavement interface. *Israel Journal of Psychiatry and Related Sciences, 38,* 185–201.

White, R. W. (1952). *Lives in progress.* New York: Holt, Rinehart, & Winston.

Worden, J. W. (1996). *Children & grief: When a parent dies.* New York: Guilford Press.

Attachment, Loss, and the Experience of Grief

ATTACHMENT THEORY

Before one can fully comprehend the impact of a loss and the human behavior associated with it, one must have some understanding of the meaning of attachment. There is considerable writing in the psychological and psychiatric literature as to the nature of attachments—what they are and how they develop. One of the key figures and primary thinkers in this area is the late British psychiatrist John Bowlby. He devoted much of his professional career to the area of attachment and loss and wrote several substantial volumes as well as a number of articles on the subject.

Bowlby's attachment theory provides a way for us to conceptualize the tendency in human beings to create strong affectional bonds with others and a way to understand the strong emotional reaction that occurs when those bonds are threatened or broken. To develop his theories, Bowlby casts his net wide and includes data from ethology, control theory, cognitive psychology, neurophysiology, and developmental biology. He takes exception to those who believe that attachment bonds between individuals develop only in order to have certain biological drives met, such as the drive for food or the drive for sex. Citing Lorenz's work with animals and Harlow's work with young monkeys, Bowlby (1977a) points to the fact that attachment occurs in the absence of the reinforcement of these biogenic needs.

Bowlby's (1977b) thesis is that these attachments come from a need for security and safety; they develop early in life, are usually directed toward a few specific individuals, and tend to endure throughout a large part of the life cycle. Forming attachments with significant others is considered normal behavior not only for the child but for the adult as well. Bowlby argues that attachment behavior has survival value, citing the occurrence of this behavior in the young of almost all species of mammals. But he sees attachment behavior as distinct from feeding and sexual behavior.

Attachment behavior is best illustrated by the young animal and the young child, who, as they grow, leave the primary attachment figure for increasingly long periods of time to search an ever-widening radius of their environment. But they always return to the attachment figure for support and safety. When the attachment figure disappears or is threatened, the response is one of intense anxiety and strong emotional protest. Bowlby suggests that the child's parents provide the secure base of operation from which to explore. This relationship determines the child's capacity to make affectional bonds later in life. This is similar to Erik Erikson's (1950) concept of basic trust: through good parenting, the individual sees himself as both able to help himself and worthy of being helped should difficulties arise. Obvious pathological aberrations can develop in this pattern. Inadequate parenting can lead people either to form anxious attachments or to form very tenuous attachments, if any at all (Winnicott, 1953). Various attachment styles can be found in chapter 3.

If the goal of attachment behavior is to maintain an affectional bond, situations that endanger this bond give rise to certain very specific reactions. The greater the potential for loss, the more intense and the more varied these reactions are. "In such circumstances, all the most powerful forms of attachment behavior become activated— clinging, crying, and perhaps angry coercion. . . . When these actions are successful, the bond is restored, the activities cease and the states of stress and distress are alleviated" (Bowlby, 1977a, p. 429). If the danger is not removed, withdrawal, apathy, and despair then ensue.

Animals demonstrate this behavior as well as humans. In *The Expression of Emotions in Man and Animals*, written during the latter part of the 19th century, Charles Darwin (1872) described the ways in which sorrow is expressed by animals as well as by children and adult human beings. Ethologist Konrad Lorenz (1963) has described this grief-like behavior in the separation of a greylag goose from its mate:

> The first response to the disappearance of the partner consists in the anxious attempt to find him again. The goose moves about restlessly by day and night, flying great distances and visiting places where the partner might be found, uttering all the time the penetrating trisyllable long-distance call. . . . The searching expeditions are extended farther and farther and quite often the searcher itself gets lost, or succumbs to an accident. . . . All the objective observable characteristics of the goose's behavior on losing its mate are roughly identical with human grief. (Lorenz, 1963, quoted in Parkes, 2001, p. 44)

There are many other examples of grieving in the animal world. Several years ago there was an interesting account about dolphins in the Montreal zoo. After one of the dolphins died, its mate refused to eat, and the zookeepers had the difficult, if not impossible, task of keeping the surviving dolphin alive. By not eating, the dolphin was exhibiting manifestations of grief and depression akin to human loss behavior.

Psychiatrist George Engel, speaking at the psychiatric grand rounds at Massachusetts General Hospital, described a case of bereavement in great detail. This case sounded typical of the kinds of reactions that you would find in a person who has lost a mate. Later in his lecture, after reading a lengthy newspaper account of this loss, Engel revealed that he was describing the behavior of an ostrich that had lost her mate!

Because of the many examples in the animal world, Bowlby concludes that there are good biological reasons for every separation to be responded to in an automatic, instinctive way with aggressive behavior. He also suggests that irretrievable loss is not taken into account, and that in the course of evolution, instinctual equipment developed around the fact that losses are retrievable and the behavioral responses that make up part of the grieving process are geared toward reestablishing a relationship with the lost object (Bowlby, 1980). This biological theory of grief has been influential in the thinking of many, including that of British psychiatrist Colin Murray Parkes (Parkes, 1972; Parkes & Stevenson-Hinde, 1982; Parkes & Weiss, 1983). Other prominent attachment theorists include Mary Ainsworth (1978) and Mary Main (Main & Hesse, 1990). The mourning responses of animals show what primitive biological processes are at work in humans. However, there are features of grieving specific only to human beings, and these normal grief reactions are described in this chapter.

There is evidence that all humans grieve a loss to one degree or another. Anthropologists who have studied other societies, their cultures, and their reactions to the loss of loved ones report that whatever the society studied, in whatever part of the world, there is an almost universal attempt to regain the lost loved object and/or there is the belief in an afterlife where one can rejoin the loved one. In preliterate societies, however, bereavement pathology seems to be less common than it is in more civilized societies (Parkes, Laungani, & Young, 1997; Rosenblatt, Walsh, & Jackson, 1976).

IS GRIEF A DISEASE?

George Engel (1961) raised this interesting question in a thought-provoking essay published in *Psychosomatic Medicine*. Engel's thesis is that the loss of a loved one is psychologically traumatic to the same extent that being severely wounded or burned is physiologically traumatic. He argues that grief represents a departure from the state of health and well-being, and just as healing is necessary in the physiological realm in order to bring the body back into homeostatic balance, a period of time is likewise needed to return the mourner to a similar state of psychological equilibrium. Therefore, Engel sees the process of mourning as similar to the process of healing. As with healing, full function, or nearly full function, can be restored, but there are also incidents of impaired function and inadequate healing. Just as the terms "healthy" and "pathological" apply to the various courses in the physiological healing process, Engel argues that these same terms may be applied to the courses taken by the mourning process. He sees mourning as a course that takes time until restoration of function can take place. How much functional impairment occurs is a matter of degree (Engel, 1961). Rather than using terms like "restoration" and "recovery," I prefer to use the term "adaptation": some people make a better adaptation to the loss while others make a less good adaptation. In chapter 5 we will look at complicated mourning, where individuals are not making an adequate adaptation to the loss.

Before we look at the characteristics of normal grief, it would be useful to look at three terms that are often used interchangeably: grief, mourning, and bereavement. For purposes of common understanding, in this book I am using the term "grief" to indicate the *experience* of one who has lost a loved one to death. Grief is a term that can be applied to other losses, but this book primarily addresses losses due to death. "Mourning" is the term applied to the *process* that one goes through in adapting to the death of the person. "Bereavement" defines the loss to which the person is trying to adapt.

NORMAL GRIEF

Normal grief, also referred to as uncomplicated grief, encompasses a broad range of feelings and behaviors that are common after a loss.[1] One of the earliest attempts to look at normal grief reactions in any systematic way was done by Erich Lindemann (1944) when he was chief of psychiatry at Massachusetts General Hospital.

In the Boston area there are two Catholic colleges well known for their football rivalry. Back in the fall of 1942, they met for one of their traditional Saturday encounters. Holy Cross beat Boston College, and after the game many people went to Coconut Grove, a local nightclub, to celebrate. During the revelries, a busboy lit a match while trying to change a lightbulb and accidentally set a decorative palm tree on fire. Almost immediately, the whole nightclub, which was packed beyond its legal capacity, was engulfed in flames. Nearly 500 people lost their lives in that tragedy.

Afterward, Lindemann and his colleagues worked with the family members who had lost loved ones in that tragedy, and from these data and others he wrote his classic paper, "The Symptomatology and Management of Acute Grief" (1944). From his observations of 101 recently bereaved patients he discovered similar patterns, which he described as the pathognomic characteristics of normal or acute grief:

1. Somatic or bodily distress of some type
2. Preoccupation with the image of the deceased
3. Guilt relating to the deceased or circumstances of the death
4. Hostile reactions
5. The inability to function as one had before the loss

In addition to these five, he described a sixth characteristic exhibited by many patients: they appeared to develop traits of the deceased in their own behavior.

There are many limitations to Lindemann's study. Some of these have been outlined by Parkes (2001), who points out that Lindemann does not present figures to show the relative frequency of the syndromes described. Lindemann also neglects to mention how many interviews he had with the patients, and how much time had passed between the interviews and the date of the loss. Nevertheless, this remains an important and much cited study.

What is of particular interest to me is that the bereaved we see today at Massachusetts General Hospital exhibit behaviors very similar to those described by Lindemann more than 60 years ago. In a large number of people undergoing an acute grief reaction, we find some or most of the following phenomena. Because the list of normal grief behaviors is so extensive and varied, I have placed them under four general categories: feelings, physical sensations, cognitions, and behaviors. Anyone counseling the bereaved needs to be familiar with the broad range of behaviors that falls under the description of normal grief.

Feelings

Sadness

Sadness is the most common feeling found in the bereaved and really needs little comment. This feeling is not necessarily manifested by crying behavior, but often it is. Parkes and Weiss (1983) conjecture that crying is a signal that evokes a sympathetic and protective reaction from others and establishes a social situation in which the normal laws of competitive behavior are suspended. Some mourners have a fear of sadness, especially the fear of its intensity (Taylor & Rachman, 1991). It is not uncommon to hear a person say, "I lost it at the funeral." Still others try to block sadness through excessive activity only to discover that the sadness comes out at night. Not allowing the sadness to be experienced, with or without tears, can frequently lead to complicated mourning (see chapter 5).

Anger

Anger is frequently experienced after a loss. It can be one of the most confusing feelings for the survivor and as such is at the root of many problems in the grieving process. A woman whose husband died of cancer said to me, "How can I be angry? He didn't want to die." The truth is that she was angry at him for dying and leaving her. If the anger is not adequately acknowledged, it can lead to complicated mourning.

This anger comes from two sources: from a sense of frustration that there was nothing one could do to prevent the death, and from a kind of regressive experience that occurs after the loss of someone close. You may have had this type of regressive experience when you were a very young child on a shopping trip with your mother. You were in a department store and suddenly you looked up to find that she had disappeared. You felt panic and anxiety until your mother returned, whereupon, rather than express a loving reaction, you hauled off and kicked her in the shins. This behavior, which Bowlby sees as part of our genetic heritage, symbolizes the message "Don't leave me again!"

In the loss of any important person there is a tendency to regress, to feel helpless, to feel unable to exist without the person, and then to experience the anger that goes along with these feelings of anxiety. The anger that the bereaved person experiences needs to be identified and appropriately targeted toward the deceased in order to make a healthy adaptation. However, it often is handled in other less effective ways, one of which is displacement, or directing it toward some other person and often blaming him or her for the death. The line of reasoning is that if someone can be blamed, then that person is responsible and, hence, the loss could have been prevented. People may blame the physician, the funeral director, family members, an insensitive friend, and frequently God. "I feel cheated but am confused not knowing who cheated me. God showed me something so precious and takes it away. Is this fair?" queried one widow.

One of the riskiest maladaptations of anger is the posture of turning the anger inward against the self. In a severe case of retroflected anger, the person may be down on him- or herself and could develop severe depression or suicidal behavior. A more psychodynamic interpretation of this retroflected anger response was given by Melanie Klein (1940), who suggests that the "triumph" over the dead causes the bereaved person to turn his or her anger against him- or herself or direct it outward toward others nearby.

Guilt and Self-Reproach

Guilt and self-reproach—over not being kind enough, over not taking the person to the hospital sooner, and the like—are common experiences of survivors. Usually the guilt is manifested over something that happened or something that was neglected around the time of the death, something that may have prevented the loss. Most often the guilt is irrational and mitigates through "reality testing." There is, of course, the possibility of real guilt, where the person has indeed done something to cause the death. In these cases, interventions other than reality testing would be called for.

Anxiety

Anxiety in the survivor can range from a light sense of insecurity to a strong panic attack, and the more intense and persistent the anxiety, the more it suggests an abnormal grief reaction. Anxiety comes primarily from two sources. First, fear the survivor will not be able to take care of him- or herself on their own and frequently comment "I won't be able to survive without him." Second, anxiety relates to a heightened sense of personal death awareness—the awareness of one's own mortality heightened by the death of a loved one (Worden, 1976). Carried to extremes, this anxiety can develop into a full-blown phobia. The well-known author C. S. Lewis (1961) knew this anxiety and said after losing his wife, "No one ever told me that grief felt so like fear. I am not afraid, but the sensation is like being afraid. The same fluttering in the stomach, the same restlessness, the yawning. I keep on swallowing" (p. 38).

Loneliness

Loneliness is a feeling frequently expressed by survivors, particularly those who have lost a spouse and who were used to a close day-to-day relationship. Even though very lonely, many widows will not go out because they feel safer in their homes. "I feel so all alone now," said one widow who had been married for 52 years. "It's been like the world has ended," she told me 10 months after her husband's death. Stroebe, Stroebe, Abakoumkin, and Schut (1996) distinguish between emotional loneliness and social loneliness. Social support can help with social loneliness but does not mitigate against emotional loneliness due to a broken attachment. The latter can only be remedied by the integration of another attachment (Stroebe, Schut, & Stroebe, 2005). Sometimes the need to be touched is a correlate of loneliness. This is especially true in cases of conjugal bereavement (Van Baarsen, Van Duijn, Smit, Snijders, & Knipscheer, 2001).

Fatigue

Lindemann's patients reported fatigue, and we see this frequently in survivors. It may sometimes be experienced as apathy or listlessness. This high level of fatigue can be both surprising and distressing to the person who is usually very active. "I can't get out of bed in the morning," said one widow. "I am neglecting the house because I am tired all the time." Fatigue is usually self-limiting. If not, it may be a clinical sign of depression.

Helplessness

One factor that makes the event of death so stressful is the sense of helplessness it can engender. This close correlate of anxiety is frequently present in the early stage of a loss. Widows in particular often feel extremely helpless. A young widow left with a 7-week-old child said, "My family came and lived with me for the first 5 months. I was afraid I would freak out and not be able to care for my child."

Shock

Shock occurs most often in the case of a sudden death. Someone picks up the telephone and learns that a loved one or friend is dead. Even when the death is expected and follows a progressive deteriorating illness, when the phone call finally comes, it can still cause the survivor to experience shock.

Yearning

Yearning for the lost person is what the British call "pining." Parkes (2001) has noted that pining is a common experience of survivors, particularly among the widows he studied. Yearning is a normal response to loss. When it diminishes, it may be a sign that mourning is coming to an end. When it does not come to an end, it may be a clinical sign indicating traumatic grief (Jacobs, 1999). See chapter 5 for a discussion of traumatic grief as one of the complications of mourning, and the place of yearning in its diagnosis.

Emancipation

Emancipation can be a positive feeling after a death. I worked with a young woman whose father was a real potentate, a heavy-handed, unbending dictator over her existence. After his sudden death from a heart attack, she went through the normal grief feelings, but she also expressed a feeling of emancipation because she no longer had to live under his tyranny. At first she was uncomfortable with this feeling, but later she was able to accept it as the normal response to her changed status.

Relief

Many people feel relief after the death of a loved one, particularly if the loved one suffered a lengthy or particularly painful illness. "The knowing that his suffering, both physical and mental, is over helps me cope," said one elderly widow. It can also occur when the death involves a person with whom the mourner has had a particularly difficult relationship, often lifelong. Sometimes relief is the reaction following a completed suicide. However, a sense of guilt often accompanies this sense of relief.

Numbness

It's also important to mention that some people report a lack of feelings. After a loss, they feel numb. Again, this numbness is often experienced early in the grieving process, usually right after the person learns of the death. It probably occurs because there are so many feelings to deal with that to allow them all into consciousness would be overwhelming, so the person experiences numbness as a protection from this flood of feelings. Commenting on numbness, Parkes and Weiss (1983) have said, "We found *no* evidence that it is an unhealthy reaction. Blocking of sensation as a defense against what would otherwise be overwhelming pain would seem to be extremely 'normal'" (p. 55).

As you review this list, remember that each of these items represents normal grief feelings and there is nothing pathological about any one of them. However, feelings that exist for abnormally long periods of time and at excessive intensity may portend a complicated grief reaction. This will be discussed in chapter 5.

Physical Sensations

One of the interesting things about Lindemann's paper is that he describes not only the emotions that people experienced, but also the physical sensations associated with their acute grief reactions. These sensations are often overlooked, but they play a significant role in the grieving process. The following is a list of the most commonly reported sensations experienced by the people we see for grief counseling:

1. Hollowness in the stomach
2. Tightness in the chest
3. Tightness in the throat

4. Oversensitivity to noise
5. A sense of depersonalization: "I walk down the street and nothing seems real, including me."
6. Breathlessness, feeling short of breath
7. Weakness in the muscles
8. Lack of energy
9. Dry mouth

Many times these physical sensations are of concern to the survivor, and he or she will come to the physician for a checkup. Physicians need to inquire about deaths and losses.

Cognitions

There are many different thought patterns that mark the experience of grief. Certain thoughts are common in the early stages of grieving and usually disappear after a short time. But sometimes thoughts persist and trigger feelings that can lead to depression or anxiety.

Disbelief

"It didn't happen. There must be some mistake. I can't believe it happened. I don't want to believe it happened." These are often the first thoughts to occur after hearing of a death, especially if the death was sudden. One young widow said to me, "I keep waiting for someone to wake me and tell me I'm dreaming." Another said, "The passing of my husband came as a shock although he had been sick for some time. You are never quite ready for it."

Confusion

Many newly bereaved people say their thinking is very confused, they can't seem to order their thoughts, they have difficulty concentrating, or they forget things. I once went out for a social evening in Boston and took a cab home. I told the driver where I wanted to go and sat back while he proceeded down the road. A little later he asked me again where I wanted to go. I thought maybe he was a new driver and did not know the city, but he commented to me that he had a lot on his mind. A little later he asked again and then apologized and said that he was feeling very confused. This happened several more times, and finally I decided it would not hurt to ask him what was on his mind. He told me that his son had been killed the week before in a traffic accident.

Preoccupation

Preoccupations can be obsessive thoughts about the deceased. These often include obsessive thoughts about how to recover the lost person. Sometimes preoccupation takes the form of intrusive thoughts or images of the deceased suffering or dying. In our Harvard Child Bereavement Study, surviving parents with the highest levels of intrusive thoughts were those who unexpectedly lost a spouse with whom they had a highly conflicted relationship (Worden, 1996). Rumination is another form of preoccupation. People engaging in ruminative coping think persistently and repetitively about how bad they feel and about the circumstances that precipitated their feelings (Nolen-Hoeksema, 2001).

Sense of Presence

This is the cognitive counterpart to the experience of yearning. The grieving person may think that the deceased is somehow still in the current area of time and space. This can be especially true during the time shortly after the death. In our study of bereaved children, 81% of the children felt watched by their dead parent 4 months after the death, and this experience continued for many of the children (66%) 2 years after the death. Some found this sense of presence comforting, while others did not and were scared by it (Worden, 1996).

Hallucinations

Hallucinations of both the visual type and the auditory type are included in this list of normal behaviors because hallucinations are a frequent experience of the bereaved. They are usually transient illusory experiences, often occurring within a few weeks following the loss, and generally do not portend a more difficult or complicated mourning experience. Although disconcerting to some, many others find these experiences helpful. With all the recent interest in mysticism and spirituality, it is interesting to speculate whether these are really hallucinations or possibly some other kind of metaphysical phenomenon.

There is an obvious interface between thinking and feeling, and the current interest in cognitive psychology and cognitive therapy emphasizes this. Aaron Beck and his colleagues (1979) at the University of Pennsylvania found that the experience of depression frequently is triggered by depressive thought patterns. In the bereaved, certain thoughts will pass through the mind such as "I can't live without her" or "I'll never find love again." These thoughts can then trigger very intense, but normal, feelings of sadness and/or anxiety.

Behaviors

There are a number of specific behaviors frequently associated with normal grief reactions. These can range from sleep and appetite disturbances to absentmindedness and social withdrawal. The following behaviors are commonly reported after a loss and usually correct themselves over time.

Sleep Disturbances

It is not unusual for people who are in the early stages of loss to experience sleep disturbances. These may include difficulty going to sleep or early morning awakening. Sleep disturbances sometimes require medical intervention, but in normal grief they usually correct themselves. In the Harvard Child Bereavement Study, one-fifth of the children showed some sleep disturbance in the first 4 months after the death of one of their parents. Without any special intervention this figure dropped to a level not significantly different from that of their nonbereaved matched counterparts 1 and 2 years following the death (Worden, 1996).

After Bill lost his wife suddenly, he would wake up at five o'clock each morning filled with intense sadness and review over and over the circumstances surrounding the death and how it might have been prevented, including what he might have done differently. This happened morning after morning and soon caused problems because he could not function well at work. After about 6 weeks the disorder began to correct itself, and eventually it disappeared. This is not an unusual experience. However, if sleep disorder persists, it may indicate a more serious depressive disorder, which should be explored. Sleep disorders can sometimes symbolize various fears, including the fear of dreaming, the fear of being in bed alone, and the fear of not awakening. After her husband died, one woman solved the problem posed by her fear of being alone in bed by taking her dog to bed with her. The sound of the dog's breathing comforted her, and she continued to do this for almost a year until she was able to sleep alone.

Appetite Disturbances

Bereaved animals exhibit appetite disturbances, which are also very common in human mourning situations. Although appetite disturbances can manifest themselves in terms of both overeating and undereating, undereating is the more frequently described grief behavior. Significant changes in weight may result from changes in eating patterns.

Absentminded Behavior

The newly bereaved may find themselves acting in an absentminded way or doing things that may ultimately cause them inconvenience or harm. One client was concerned because on three separate occasions she had driven across the city in her car and, after completing her business, had forgotten that she had driven and returned home via public transportation. This behavior occurred following an important loss and eventually corrected itself.

Social Withdrawal

It is not unusual for people who have sustained a loss to want to withdraw from other people. Again, this is usually a short-lived phenomenon and corrects itself. I saw one young woman shortly after the death of her mother. This single woman was a very sociable person who loved to go to parties. For several months following her mother's death she declined all invitations because they seemed dissonant to the way she felt in the early stages of her grief. This may seem obvious and appropriate to the reader, but this woman saw her withdrawal as abnormal. Some people withdraw from friends perceived as over-solicitous. "My friends tried so hard that I wanted to avoid them. How many times can you hear, 'I'm sorry?'" Social withdrawal can also include a loss of interest in the outside world, such as not reading newspapers or watching television.

Dreams of the Deceased

It's very common to dream of the dead person, both normal kinds of dreams and distressing dreams or nightmares. Often these dreams serve a number of purposes and may give some diagnostic clues as to where the person is in the whole course of mourning.

For example, for several years after the death of her mother, Esther suffered from intense guilt over circumstances related to the death. This guilt was manifested in low self-esteem and personal recrimination and was associated with considerable anxiety. During one of her daily visits to her mother, Esther had left for coffee and a bite of food. While she was out, her mother died.

Esther was filled with remorse, and although we used the usual reality-testing techniques in therapy, the guilt still persisted. While in therapy, she had a dream about her mother. In this dream she saw herself trying to assist her mother to walk down a slippery pathway so she would not fall. But her mother fell, and nothing Esther could do in the dream would save her. It was impossible. This dream was a significant turning point in her therapy because she allowed herself to see that nothing she could have done would have kept her mother from dying. This important insight gave her permission to shed the guilt that she had been carrying for years. Some ways to utilize dreams in grief counseling and grief therapy are identified in chapter 6.

Avoiding Reminders of the Deceased

Some people will avoid places or things that trigger painful feelings of grief. They might avoid the place where the deceased died, the cemetery, or objects that remind them of their lost loved one. One middle-aged woman came for grief counseling when her husband died after a series of coronary attacks, leaving her with two children. For a period of time she put all pictures of her husband away in the closet, along with other things that reminded her of him. This obviously was only a short-term solution, and as she moved toward the end of her grief, she was able to bring out the items that she wanted to live with.

Quickly getting rid of all the things associated with the deceased—giving them away or disposing of them in any way possible even to the point of having a quick disposal of the body—can lead to a complicated grief reaction. This is usually not healthy behavior and is often indicative of a highly ambivalent relationship with the deceased. Ambivalent relationships are one of the mediators of mourning described in chapter 3.

Searching and Calling Out

Both Bowlby and Parkes have written much in their work about searching behavior. Calling out is related to this searching behavior. Frequently somebody may call out the name of the loved person: "John, John, John. Please come back to me!" When this is not done verbally, it can be going on internally.

Sighing

Sighing is a behavior frequently noted among the bereaved. It is a close correlate of the physical sensation of breathlessness. Colleagues at Massachusetts General Hospital tested respiration in a small group of bereaved parents and found that their oxygen and carbon dioxide levels were similar to those found in depressed patients (Jellinek, Goldenheim, & Jenike, 1985).

Restless Hyperactivity

A number of widows in our Harvard studies of bereavement entered into restless hyperactivity following the deaths of their husbands. The woman mentioned above whose husband left her with two teenage children could not stand to stay at home. She would get into her car and drive all over town trying to find some sense of relief from her restlessness. Another widow could stay in the house during the day because she was busy, but at night she fled.

Crying

There has been interesting speculation that tears may have potential healing value. Stress causes chemical imbalances in the body, and some researchers believe that tears remove toxic substances and help reestablish homeostasis. They hypothesize that the chemical content of tears caused by emotional stress is different from that of tears secreted as a function of eye irritation. Tests are being done to see what type of catecholamine (mood-altering chemicals produced by the brain) is present in tears of emotion (Frey, 1980). Tears do relieve emotional stress, but how they do this is still a question. Further research is needed on the deleterious effects, if any, of suppressed crying.

Visiting Places or Carrying Objects That Remind the Survivor of the Deceased

This is the opposite of the behavior that people engage in to avoid reminders of the lost person. Often underlying this behavior is the fear of losing memories of the deceased. "For 2 weeks I carried his picture with me constantly for fear I would forget his face," one widow told me.

Treasuring Objects That Belonged to the Deceased

One young woman went through her mother's closet shortly after her mother died and took many of her clothes home. They wore the same size, and although this might seem like an example of someone being thrifty, the fact was that the daughter did not feel comfortable unless she was wearing something that had belonged to her mother. She wore these clothes for several months. As her mourning progressed, she found it less and less necessary to wear clothing that had belonged to her mother. Finally, she gave most of it away to charity.

The reason for outlining these characteristics of normal grief in such detail is to show the wide variety of behaviors and experiences associated with loss. Obviously, not all these behaviors will be experienced by one person. However, it is important for bereavement counselors to understand the wide range of behaviors covered under normal grief so they do not pathologize behavior that should be recognized as normal. Having this understanding will also enable counselors to give reassurance to people who experience such behavior as disturbing, especially in the case of a first significant loss. However, if these experiences persist late in the bereavement process, they may be indicative of a more complicated grief (Demi & Miles, 1987).

GRIEF AND DEPRESSION

Many of the normal grief behaviors may seem like manifestations of depression. To shed some light on this, let's look at the debate about the similarities and differences between grief and depression.

Freud (1917/1957), in his early paper "Mourning and Melancholia," addressed this issue. He tried to point out that depression, or melancholia, as he called it, is a pathological form of grief and is very much like mourning (normal grief) except that it has a certain characteristic feature of its own—namely, angry impulses toward the ambivalently loved person turned inward. It is true that grief looks very much like depression, and it is also true that grieving may develop into a full-blown depression. Gerald Klerman (1977), who was a prominent depression researcher, believed that many depressions are precipitated by losses, either immediately following the loss or at some later time when the patient is reminded of the loss. Depression may also serve as a defense against mourning. If anger is directed against the self, it is deflected away from the deceased, and this keeps the survivor from dealing with ambivalent feelings toward the deceased (Dorpat, 1973).

The main distinctions between grief and depression are these: while in depression as well as grief, you may find the classic symptoms of sleep disturbance, appetite disturbance, and intense sadness, however, in a grief reaction, there is not the loss of self-esteem commonly found in most clinical depressions. That is, the people who have lost someone do not have less regard for themselves as a result of such a loss, or if they do, it tends to be for only a brief time. And if the survivors of the deceased experience guilt, it is usually guilt associated with some specific aspect of the loss rather than a general overall sense of culpability.

A section in the *Diagnostic and Statistical Manual IV-TR* of the American Psychiatric Association (2000) suggests:

> As part of their reaction to the loss, some grieving individuals present with symptoms characteristic of a Major Depressive Episode (e.g., feelings of sadness and associated symptoms such as insomnia, poor appetite, and weight loss). The bereaved individual typically regards the depressed mood as "normal," although the person may seek professional help for relief of associated symptoms such as insomnia or anorexia. (p. 299)

Even though grief and depression share similar objective and subjective features, they do seem to be different conditions. Depression overlaps with bereavement but is not the same (Robinson & Fleming, 1992; Wakefield, 2007; Worden & Silverman, 1993; Zisook & Kendler, 2007). Freud believed that in grief, the world looks poor and empty, while in depression, the person feels poor and empty. These differences in cognitive style have been identified by Beck and associates (1979) and other cognitive therapists who have suggested that the depressed have negative evaluations of themselves, the world, and the future. Although such negative evaluations can exist in the bereaved, they tend to be more transient.

However, there are some bereaved individuals who do develop major depressive episodes following a loss (Zisook & Shuchter, 1993). The APA *Diagnostic and Statistical Manual*, 4th Edition, allows for this distinction: symptoms associated with depression rather than grief are guilt about things other than actions taken or not taken by the survivors at the time of the death, the survivor's thoughts of death other than the feeling that he or she would be better off dead or should have died with the deceased person, morbid preoccupation with worthlessness, marked psychomotor retardation, prolonged and marked functional impairment, and hallucinatory experiences (this does not include experiences of hearing the voice of or transiently seeing the image of the deceased person). If a major depressive episode develops during bereavement, this should be considered a type of complicated mourning—exaggerated grief (see chapter 5).

At Yale, Jacobs and colleagues (1987, 1989, 1990) have been interested in depression within the context of bereavement and have said, "Although the majority of depressions of bereavement are transient and require no professional attention, there is growing appreciation that some depressions, especially those that persist throughout the first year of bereavement, are clinically significant" (1987, p. 501). They have used antidepressant medication to treat several patients whose depression persisted late in the course of bereavement and did not resolve spontaneously or respond to interpersonal interventions. These were usually people who had a history of depression or some other mental health disorder. They found improvement in sleep disorders and appetite disturbance as well as an improvement in mood and cognition. This response suggests a biological dimension to the depression.

One of the functions of the counselor who has contact with people during the time of acute grief is to assess which patients might be undergoing a major depression by using current standard diagnostic criteria. Patients so identified can then be given additional help such as a medical evaluation and possibly the use of antidepressant medications. Once depressions begin to lift through medication, then the focus of treatment changes to the underlying conflicts of the attachment. These conflicts cannot be addressed through medications alone (Miller et al., 1994).

If grief is defined as one's experiences after a loss, then mourning is the process one goes through leading to an adaptation to the loss. In the next two chapters we will look at the mourning process in detail.

NOTE

1. I am using the word *normal* in both a clinical and a statistical sense. *Clinical* defines what the clinician calls normal mourning behavior, while *statistical* refers to the frequency with which such behavior is found among a randomized bereaved population. The more frequent the behavior, the more it is defined as normal.

REFERENCES

Ainsworth, M., Blehar, M., Waters, E., & Wall, S. (1978). *Patterns of attachment.* Hilldale, NJ: Erlbaum.

American Psychiatric Association. (2000). *Diagnostic and statistical manual of mental disorders* (4th ed.). Washington, DC: Author.

Beck, A. T., et al. (1979). *Cognitive therapy of depression.* New York: Guilford Press.

Bowlby, J. (1977a). The making and breaking of affectional bonds: I. Aetiology and psychopathology in the light of attachment theory. *British Journal of Psychiatry, 130,* 201–210.

Bowlby, J. (1977b). The making and breaking of affectional bonds: II. Some principles of psychotherapy. *British Journal of Psychiatry, 130,* 421–431.

Bowlby, J. (1980). *Attachment and loss: Vol. 3. Loss, sadness, and depression.* New York: Basic Books.

Darwin, C. (1872). *The expression of emotions in man and animals.* London: Murray.

Demi, A. S., & Miles, M. S. (1987). Parameters of normal grief: A Delphi study. *Death Studies, 11,* 397–412.

Dorpat, T. L. (1973). Suicide, loss, and mourning. *Suicide & Life-Threatening Behavior, 3,* 213–224.

Engel, G. L. (1961). Is grief a disease? A challenge for medical research. *Psychosomatic Medicine, 23,* 18–22.

Erikson, E. H. (1950). *Childhood and society.* New York: Norton.

Freud, S. (1957). Mourning and melancholia. In J. Strachey (Ed. & Trans.), *The standard edition of the complete psychological works of Sigmund Freud* (Vol. 14, pp. 237–260). London: Hogarth. (Originally published 1917)

Frey, W. H. (1980). Not-so-idle-tears. *Psychology Today, 13,* 91–92.

Jacobs, S. (1999). *Traumatic grief: Diagnosis, treatment, and prevention.* Philadelphia: Brunner/Mazel.

Jacobs, S., Hansen, F., Berkman, L., Kasl, S., & Ostfeld, A. (1989). Depressions of bereavement. *Comprehensive Psychiatry, 30,* 218–224.

Jacobs, S., & Kim, K. (1990). Psychiatric complications of bereavement. *Psychiatric Annals, 20,* 314–317.

Jacobs, S., Nelson, J., & Zisook, S. (1987). Treating depression of bereavement with antidepressants: A pilot study. *Psychiatric Clinics of North America, 10,* 501–510.

Jellinek, M., Goldenheim, P., & Jenike, M. (1985). The impact of grief on ventilatory control. *American Journal of Psychiatry, 142,* 121–123.

Klein, M. (1940). Mourning and its relationship to manic-depressive states. *International Journal of Psychoanalysis, 21,* 125–153.

Klerman, G., & Weissman, M. (1986). The interpersonal approach to understanding depression. In T. Millon & G. Klerman (Eds.), *Contemporary directions in psychopathology: Toward the DSM IV.* New York: Guilford.

Lewis, C. S. (1961). *A grief observed.* London: Faber & Faber.

Lindemann, E. (1944). The Symptomatology and management of acute grief. *American Journal of Psychiatry, 101,* 141–148.

Lorenz, K. (1963). *On aggression.* London: Methuen.

Main, M., & Hesse, E. (1990). Parents' unresolved traumatic experiences are related to infant disorganized attachment status: Is frightened and/or frightening parental behavior the linking mechanism? In M. T. Greenberg, D. Cicchetti, & E. M. Cummings (Eds.), *Attachment in the preschool years: Theory, research, and intervention* (pp. 161–182). Chicago: University of Chicago Press.

Miller, M., Frank, E., Cornes, C., Imber, S., Anderson, B., Ehrenpreis, L., et al. (1994). Applying interpersonal psychotherapy to bereavement-related depression following loss of a spouse in late life. *Journal of Psychotherapy Practice and Research, 3,* 149–162.

Nolen-Hoeksema, S. (2001). Ruminative coping and adjustment to bereavement. In M. S. Stroebe, R. O. Hansson, W. Stroebe, & H. Schut (Eds.), *Handbook of bereavement research: Consequences, coping, and care* (pp. 545–562). Washington, DC: American Psychological Association.

Parkes, C. M. (1972). *Bereavement: Studies of grief in adult life.* New York: International Universities Press.

Parkes, C. M. (2001). A historical overview of the scientific study of bereavement. In M. S. Stroebe, R. O. Hansson, W. Stroebe, & H. Schut (Eds.), *Handbook of bereavement research: Consequences, coping, and care* (pp. 25–45). Washington, DC: American Psychological Press.

Parkes, C. M., Laungani, P., & Young, B. (1997). *Death and bereavement across cultures.* London: Routledge.

Parkes, C. M., & Stevenson-Hinde, J. (Eds.). (1982). *The place of attachment in human behavior.* New York: Basic Books.

Parkes, C. M., & Weiss, R. (1983). *Recovery from bereavement.* New York: Basic Books.

Robinson, P., & Fleming, S. (1992). Depressotypic cognitive patterns in major depression and conjugal bereavement. *Omega, 25,* 291–305.

Rosenblatt, P. C., Walsh, R. P., & Jackson, D. A. (1976). *Grief and mourning in cross-cultural perspective.* New Haven, CT: HRAF Press.

Stroebe, W., Schut, H., & Stroebe, M. S. (2005). Grief work, disclosure and counseling: Do they help the bereaved? *Clinical Psychology Review, 25,* 395–414.

Stroebe, W., Stroebe, M. S., Abakoumkin, G., & Schut, H. (1996). The role of loneliness and social support in adjustment to loss: A test of attachment versus stress theory. *Journal of Personality and Social Psychology, 70*, 1241–1249.

Taylor, S., & Rachman, S. J. (1991). Fear of sadness. *Journal of Anxiety Disorders, 5*, 375–381.

Van Baarsen, B., Van Duijn, M., Smit, J., Snijders, T., & Knipscheer, K. (2001). Patterns of adjustment to partner loss in old age: The widowhood adaptation longitudinal study. *Omega, 44*, 5–36.

Wakefield, J. C. (2007). Extending the bereavement exclusion for major depression to other losses: Evidence from the National Comorbidity Study. *Archives of General Psychiatry, 64*, 433–440.

Winnicott, D. (1953). Transitional objects and transitional phenomena. *International Journal of Psychoanalysis, 34*, 89–97.

Worden, J. W. (1976). *Personal death awareness.* Englewood Cliffs, NJ: Prentice-Hall.

Worden, J. W. (1996). *Children & grief: When a parent dies.* New York: Guilford Press.

Worden, J. W., & Silverman, P. R. (1993). Grief and depression in newly widowed parents with school-age children. *Omega, 27*, 251–260.

Zisook, S., & Kendler, K. S. (2007). Is bereavement-related depression different than non-bereavement-related depression? *Psychological Medicine, 37*, 779–794.

Zisook, S., & Shuchter, S. R. (1993). Uncomplicated bereavement. *Journal of Clinical Psychiatry, 54*, 365–372.

2

Understanding the Mourning Process

In this book I am using the term "mourning" to indicate the process that occurs after a loss, while "grief" refers to the personal experience of the loss. Since mourning is a process, it has been viewed by different theorists in various ways—primarily as stages, phases, and tasks.

Stages. One way to look at the mourning process is to view it in terms of stages. Many people writing on the subject of grief have listed up to 9 stages of mourning, and at least one person lists 12. One of the difficulties with using the stage approach is that people do not pass through stages in seriatim. Also, there's a tendency for the novice to take the stages too literally. An example of this literalism is the way that people responded to Elisabeth Kübler-Ross's stages of dying. After her first book, *On Death and Dying* (1969), many people expected dying patients to go through the stages she had listed in some neat order. And some were disappointed if a patient skipped a stage. Her stages of dying have also been used to describe the mourning process, with the same limitations (Maciejewski, Zhang, Block, & Prigerson, 2007).

Phases. An alternative approach to stages is the concept of phases used by Parkes, Bowlby, Sanders, and others. Parkes defines four phases of mourning. Phase I is the period of numbness that occurs close to the time of the loss. This numbness, which is experienced by most survivors, helps them to disregard the fact of the loss at least for a brief period of time. Then the person goes through phase II, the phase of yearning, in which he or she yearns for the lost one to return and tends to deny the permanence of the loss. Anger plays an important part in this phase. In phase III, the phase of disorganization and despair, the bereaved person finds it difficult to function in the environment. Finally, he or she is able to enter phase IV, the phase of reorganized behavior, and begin to pull his or her life back together (Parkes, 1972, 2001, 2006). Bowlby (1980), whose work and interest overlap with those of Parkes, reinforced the idea of phases and posits that the mourner must pass through a similar series of phases before mourning is finally resolved. As with stages, there are overlaps between the various phases, and they are seldom distinct.

Sanders (1989, 1999) has used the idea of phases to describe the mourning process, and she describes five of them: (1) shock, (2) awareness of loss, (3) conservation withdrawal, (4) healing, and (5) renewal.

Tasks. Although I have no quarrel with Bowlby, Parkes, and Sanders and their schemata of phasing, I think the tasks of mourning concept that I present in this book offers an equally valid understanding of the mourning process and is much more useful for the clinician. Phases imply a certain passivity, something that the mourner must pass through. The tasks concept, on the other hand, is much more consonant with Freud's concept of grief work and implies that the mourner needs to take action and can do something. Also, this approach implies that mourning can be influenced by intervention from the outside. In other words, the mourner may see the phases as something to be passed through, whereas the tasks approach can give the mourner some sense of leverage and hope that there is something that he or she can actively do to adapt to the death of a loved one.

There is obvious validity to both of these approaches. Grieving is something that takes time; the oft-repeated phrase "Time heals" holds true. There is also truth to the notion that mourning creates tasks that need to be accomplished, and although this may seem overwhelming to the person in the throes of acute grief, it can, with the facilitation of a counselor, offer hope that something can be done and that there is a way through it. This can be a powerful antidote to the feelings of helplessness that most mourners experience.

All human growth and development can be seen as influenced by various tasks. These are most obvious in child growth and development. According to Robert Havinghurst (1953), the renowned developmental psychologist, there are certain developmental tasks (physical, social, and emotional) that occur as the child grows. If the child does not complete a particular task on a lower level, then that child's adaptation will be impaired when trying to complete similar tasks on higher levels.

Likewise, mourning—the adaptation to loss—may be seen as involving the four basic tasks outlined below. It is essential that the grieving person address the issue of these tasks in order to adapt to the loss. Bereaved individuals make varied adaptations to the loss of a loved one. Some make a better adaptation, and some a less good one. Although the tasks do not need to be addressed in a specific order, there is some ordering suggested in their definitions. For example, you cannot handle the emotional impact of a loss until you first come to terms with the fact that the loss has happened and is irreversible at least in this lifetime. Since mourning is a process and not a state, the following tasks require effort, however, not every death loss we experience challenges these tasks in the same way. Grief is a cognitive process involving confrontation with and restructuring of thoughts about the deceased, the loss experience, and the changed world within which the bereaved must now live (Stroebe, 1992). Some would call this grief work.

TASKS OF MOURNING

Task I: To Accept the Reality of the Loss

When someone dies, even if the death is expected, there is always a sense that it hasn't happened. The first task of grieving is to come full face with the reality that the person is dead, that the person is gone and will not return. Part of the acceptance of this reality is coming to believe that reunion is impossible, at least in this life. The searching behavior, of which Bowlby and Parkes have written extensively, directly relates to the accomplishment of this task. Many people who have sustained a loss find themselves calling out for the lost person, and/or they sometimes tend to misidentify others in their environment. They may walk down the street, catch a glimpse of somebody who reminds them of the deceased, and then have to remind themselves, "No, that isn't my friend. My friend really is dead." Joan Didion (2005) experienced this after the death of her husband and wrote about it in her book *The Year of Magical Thinking.*

The opposite of accepting the reality of the loss is *not believing* through some type of denial. Some people refuse to believe that the death is real and get stuck in the mourning process at this first task. Denial can be practiced on several levels and can take various forms, but it most often involves either the facts of the loss, the meaning of the loss, or the irreversibility of the loss (Dorpat, 1973).

Denying the facts of the loss can vary in degree from a slight distortion to a full-blown delusion. Bizarre examples of denial through delusion are the rare cases in which the bereaved keeps the deceased's body in the house for a number of days before notifying anyone of the death. Gardiner and Pritchard (1977) describe six cases of this unusual behavior, and I have seen two cases. The people involved were either manifestly psychotic or eccentric and reclusive.

What is more likely to happen is that a person will go through what Geoffrey Gorer (1965) calls "mummification," that is, retaining possessions of the deceased's in a "mummified" condition ready for use when he or she returns. A classic example of this involved Queen Victoria, who after the death of her consort, Prince Albert, had his clothes and shaving gear laid out daily and often went around the palace speaking to him. Parents who lose a child often retain the child's room as it was before the death. This is not unusual in the short term but becomes denial if it goes on for years. An example of a distortion rather than a delusion would be the person who sees the deceased embodied in one of his or her children. This distorted thinking may buffer the intensity of the loss but is seldom satisfactory and hinders the acceptance of the reality of the death.

Another way that people protect themselves from reality is to deny the meaning of the loss. In this way the loss can be seen as less significant than it actually is. It is common to hear statements like "He wasn't a good father," "We weren't close," or "I don't miss him." Some people immediately jettison clothes and other personal items that remind them of the deceased. Removing all reminders of the deceased is the opposite of mummification and minimizes the loss. It is as though the survivors protect themselves through the absence of any artifacts that would bring them face to face with the reality of the loss. This phenomenon is not uncommon after a traumatic death. One woman I interviewed lost her husband suddenly after he was admitted to the hospital for a minor condition but arrested and died. She would not go home until everything of his was taken out of the house. She could barely wait until spring came and his footprints in the snow disappeared. This behavior is not common and frequently stems from a conflicted relationship with the deceased (see therapy interventions in chapter 6 for additional information on grieving conflicted relationships).

Still another way to deny the full meaning of the loss is to practice "selective forgetting." For example, Gary lost his father at the age of 12. Over the years, he had blocked all the reality of his father—even a visual image—from his mind. When he first came for psychotherapy as a college student, he could not even bring to mind the memory of his father's face. After he went through a course of therapy, not only was he able to remember what his father looked like, but he was also able to sense his father's presence when he received awards at his graduation ceremony.

Some people hinder the completion of task I by denying that death is irreversible. One good example of this was illustrated in a story aired by the TV show *60 Minutes* several years ago. It told of a middle-aged housewife who had lost her mother and her 12-year-old daughter in a house fire. For the first 2 years she went through her days saying aloud to herself, "I don't want you dead, I don't want you dead, I won't have you dead!" Part of her therapy required her to face the fact that they were dead and would never return.

Another strategy used to deny the finality of death involves the religion spiritualism. The hope for a reunion with the dead person is a normal feeling, particularly in the early days and weeks following the loss. However, the chronic hope for such a reunion is not normal. Parkes (2001) states:

> Spiritualism claims to help bereaved persons in their search for the dead, and seven of the bereaved people who were included in my

various studies described visits to séances or spiritualist churches. Their reactions were mixed—some felt that they had obtained some sort of contact with the dead and a few had been frightened by this. On the whole they did not feel satisfied by the experience and none had become a regular attendee at spiritualist meetings. (pp. 55–56)

An interesting paper was published recently on the history and current picture of spiritualism in the United States and Britain. The author interviewed a number of attendees at spiritualist meetings. Although many initially attended in an attempt to find out if their loved one was at peace or to hear words of advice from the other side, the majority of those interviewed continued attending spiritualist meetings because they liked the values and fellowship found in the group (Wallis, 2001).

Coming to an acceptance of the reality of the loss takes time since it involves not only an intellectual acceptance but also an emotional one. Many less experienced counselors do not recognize this and focus too much on mere intellectual acceptance of the loss, overlooking emotional acceptance. The bereaved person may be intellectually aware of the finality of the loss long before the emotions allow full acceptance of the information as true. A woman attending one of my bereavement groups would wake up every morning and reach over to her dead husband's side of the bed to see if he was there. She knew he wouldn't be there, but there was the hope that maybe he would be even though he had died 6 months earlier.

It is easy to believe that the loved one is still away on a trip or has gone to the hospital again. One nurse whose elderly mother had gone to the hospital for bypass surgery saw her mother incapacitated with tubes and other medical paraphernalia. After the mother died, she went on for several months believing that her mother was still in the hospital being prepped for the surgery and that was why her mother hadn't contacted her on her birthday. She would tell others this when they inquired about her mother. A mother whose son was killed in an accident refused to believe that he died, preferring to believe he was in Europe, where he had spent the previous year.

The reality hits hard when one wants to pick up the phone to share some experience only to remember that the loved one is not at the other end. It takes many a bereaved parent months to say, "My child is dead and I will never have him again." They may see children playing on the street or catch sight of a school bus and say to themselves, "How could I have forgotten that my child is dead?"

Belief and disbelief alternate while one is grappling with this task. Krupp, Genovese, and Krupp (1986) said it well when they wrote:

> At times mourners seem to be under the influence of reality and behave as though they fully accept that the deceased is gone; at other times they behave irrationally, under the sway of the fantasy of eventual reunion. Anger directed at the lost love object, the self, others believed to have caused the loss, and even at benevolent well-wishers who remind the mourner of the reality of the loss is a ubiquitous feature. (p. 345)

Another form of disbelief is what Avery Weisman (1972) calls "middle knowledge." A term borrowed from existential philosophy, middle knowledge is both knowing and not knowing at the same time. You can find this phenomenon in some terminally ill patients who both know and don't know that they are dying. Likewise, in bereavement the mourner may believe and disbelieve at the very same moment.

Although addressing this first task of mourning takes time, traditional rituals such as the funeral help many bereaved people move toward acceptance. Those who are not present at the burial may need external ways to validate the reality of the death. Unreality is particularly difficult in the case of sudden death, especially when the survivor does not see the body of the deceased. In our Harvard Child Bereavement Study, we found a strong relationship between the sudden loss of a spouse and the dreams of the surviving spouse in the early months after the death. It may be that dreaming the deceased is alive is not simply wish fulfillment but rather the mind's way of validating the reality of the death through the sharp contrast that occurs when one awakens from such a dream (Worden, 1996).

Task II: To Process the Pain of Grief

The German word *Schmerz* is appropriate to use in speaking of pain because its broad definition includes the literal physical pain that many people experience and the emotional and behavioral pain associated with loss. It is necessary to acknowledge and work through this pain or it can manifest itself through physical symptoms or some form of aberrant behavior. Parkes (1972) affirms this when he says, "If it is necessary for the bereaved person to go through the pain of grief in order to get the grief work done, then anything that continually allows the person to avoid or suppress this pain can be expected to prolong the course of mourning" (p. 173).

Not everyone experiences the same intensity of pain or feels it in the same way, but it is nearly impossible to lose someone to whom you have been deeply attached without experiencing some level of pain. The newly bereaved are often unprepared to deal with the sheer force and nature of the emotions that follow a loss (Rubin, 1990). The type of pain and its intensity are mediated by a number of factors identified in chapter 3. On the other hand, recent research on attachment styles indicates that there are some individuals who do not experience much, if any pain, after a death. One reason for this is that they do not let themselves become attached to anyone and display an avoidant-dismissing attachment style (Bonanno, 2004).

There may be a subtle interplay between society and the mourner that makes task II more difficult. Society may be uncomfortable with the mourner's feelings and hence may give the subtle message: "You don't need to grieve—you are only feeling sorry for yourself." Platitudes—"You are young and you can have another child," "Life is for the living and he wouldn't want you to feel this way"—are frequently dispensed by others in an attempt to be helpful. These comments collude with the mourner's own defenses, leading to the denial of the need to grieve, expressed as "I shouldn't be feeling this way" or "I don't need to grieve" (Pincus, 1974). Geoffrey Gorer (1965) recognizes this and says, "Giving way to grief is stigmatized as morbid, unhealthy, and demoralizing. The proper action of a friend and well wisher is felt to be distraction of a mourner from his or her grief" (p. 130).

The negation of this second task of processing the pain results in *not feeling*. People can short-circuit task II in any number of ways, the most obvious being to cut off their feelings and deny the pain that is present. Sometimes people hinder the process by avoiding painful thoughts. They use thought-stopping procedures to keep themselves from feeling the dysphoria associated with the loss. Some people handle it by stimulating only pleasant thoughts of the deceased, which protect them from the discomfort of unpleasant thoughts. Idealizing the dead, avoiding reminders of the dead, and using alcohol or drugs are still other ways in which people keep themselves from dealing with task II issues.

Some people who do not want to experience the pain of grief try to find a geographic cure. They travel from place to place and try to find some relief from their emotions, as opposed to allowing themselves to process the pain—to feel it and to know that one day it will pass.

One young woman minimized her loss by believing her brother was out of his dark place and in a better place after his suicide. This might have been true, but it kept her from feeling her intense anger at him for leaving her. In treatment, when she first allowed herself to feel anger, she said, "I'm angry with this behavior and not him!" Finally she was able to acknowledge this anger directly to him through the use of an empty chair.

There are a few cases in which the surviving person has a euphoric response to the death, but this is usually associated with an emphatic refusal to believe the death has occurred. It is often accompanied by a vivid sense of the dead person's continuing presence. Generally, these euphoric responses are extremely fragile and short lived (Parkes, 1972).

John Bowlby (1980) said, "Sooner or later, some of those who avoid all conscious grieving, break down—usually with some form of depression" (p. 158). One of the aims of grief counseling is to help people through this difficult second task so they don't carry the pain with them throughout their lives. If task II is not adequately addressed, therapy may be needed later on, at which point it can be more difficult for the person to go back and work through the pain he or she has been avoiding. This is very often a more complex and difficult experience than dealing with it at the time of the loss. Also, it can be complicated by the presence of a less supportive social system than would have been available at the time of the loss.

We tend to think of the pain of grief in terms of sadness and dysphoria. And indeed much pain of bereavement is of this sort.

There are, however, other affects associated with loss that need to be processed. Anxiety, anger, guilt, depression, and loneliness are also common feelings that mourners may experience. Ways of working with these feelings in counseling can be found in chapter 4.

Task III: To Adjust to a World Without the Deceased

There are three areas of adjustment that need to be addressed after the loss of a loved one to death. There are the external adjustments, or how the death affects one's everyday functioning in the world; internal adjustments, or how the death affects one's sense of self; and spiritual adjustments, or how the death affects one's beliefs, values, and assumptions about the world. Let's look at each of these separately.

External Adjustments

Adjusting to a new environment without the deceased means different things to different people, depending on what the relationship was with the deceased and the various roles the deceased played. It takes a considerable period of time for many widows to realize what it is like to live without their husbands. This realization often begins to emerge around 3 to 4 months after the loss and involves coming to terms with living alone, raising children alone, facing an empty house, and managing finances alone. Parkes (1972) makes an important point when he says:

> In any bereavement, it is seldom clear exactly what is lost. A loss of a husband, for instance, may or may not mean the loss of a sexual partner, companion, accountant, gardener, baby minder, audience, bed warmer, and so on, depending on the particular roles normally performed by this husband. (p. 7)

The survivor usually is not aware of all the roles played by the deceased until some time after the loss occurs.

Many survivors resent having to develop new skills and take on roles that were formerly performed by their partners. An example of this is Margot, a young mother whose husband died. He was the type of person who was very efficient, took charge of situations, and did most things for her. After his death, one of the children got into trouble in school, necessitating meetings with the guidance counselor. Previously, the husband would have made contact with the school and handled everything, but after his death Margot was forced to develop this skill. Although she developed it reluctantly and with resentment, she did come to the awareness that she liked having the skill to handle such a situation competently and that she would never have accomplished this had her husband still been alive. The coping strategy of redefining the loss in such a way that it can redound to the benefit of the survivor is often part of the successful completion of task III. Making sense of the loss and finding benefit in the loss are two dimensions of meaning making after a loss, and this certainly relates to the issue of finding a benefit from the death.

A current theory that has been championed by Neimeyer (1999) and many others is the need to make meaning after a loss. Meaning making is an important process for the grieving deaths that tend to challenge beliefs about oneself, others, and the world. Death can shatter the core of one's life purposes, and it is important to discover and invent new meaning in the face of loss (Attig, 1996).

Internal Adjustments

Not only do the bereaved have to adjust to the loss of roles previously played by the deceased, but death also presents them with the challenge of adjusting to their own sense of self. We are not merely talking about seeing themselves as widows or bereaved parents but, more fundamentally, how death affects self-definition, self-esteem, and sense of self-efficacy. Some studies posit that for women who define their identity through relationships and caring for others, bereavement means not only the loss of a significant other but also the sense of a loss of self (Zaiger, 1985–1986). One of the goals of bereavement for these women is to feel like a "self" rather than half of a dyad. For a year a widow I counseled would go around the house saying, "What would Jack do?" After the first anniversary, she told herself that he was no longer here and she could now say, "What do I want to do?"

There are some relationships in which the person's sense of esteem is dependent on the person to whom he or she is attached. Some like to think of these as secure attachments. Where there is such an attachment and the person dies, the bereaved person may suffer real damage to his or her self-esteem. This is particularly true if the deceased person was making up for serious developmental deficits in the mourner. Esther had one brief marriage and after that married Ernie. Esther had a family background that was full of emotional and physical abuse. She never felt that she belonged. Ernie provided a place where she felt wanted. After his sudden death, she went into a serious depression fueled by the thoughts that "No one will ever love me like Ernie did, and I will never find a place to belong again."

Bereavement can also affect a person's sense of *self-efficacy*—the degree to which people feel that they have some control over what happens to them. This can lead to intense regression, where the bereaved perceive themselves as helpless, inadequate, incapable, child-like, or personally bankrupt (Horowitz, Wilner, Marmar, & Krupnick, 1980). Attempts to fulfill the deceased's roles may fail, and this can lead to increasingly lowered self-esteem. When this happens, personal efficacy is challenged and people may attribute any change to chance or fate, not to their own strengths and abilities (Goalder, 1985).

Attig (1996) emphasizes the need to relearn the world after a death and focuses especially on the impact of a death on one's sense of self. The internal task for the mourner is to address the questions "Who am I now?" "How am I different from loving him/her?" Over time negative images usually give way to more positive ones, and the survivors are able to carry on with their tasks and learn new ways of dealing with the world (Shuchter & Zisook, 1986).

Spiritual Adjustments

The third area of adjustment is to one's sense of the world. Neimeyer (2000, 2001) writes that death can shake the foundations of one's assumptive world. Loss through death can challenge one's fundamental life values and philosophical beliefs—beliefs that are influenced by our families, peers, education, and religion as well as life experiences. It is not unusual for the bereaved to feel that they have lost direction in life. The bereaved person searches for meaning in the loss and its attendant life changes in order to make sense of it and to regain some control of his or her life. Janoff-Bulman (1992) has identified three basic assumptions that are often challenged by the death of a loved one: that the world is a benevolent place, that the world makes sense, and that the person him- or herself is worthy. The events of September 11, 2001, challenged these three basic assumptions and more.

Such challenges are also likely to occur when there are sudden and untimely deaths. Mothers whose very young children are the victims of drive-by shootings frequently struggle with why God allowed such a thing to happen. One told me, "I must be a bad person for this to happen."

Not all deaths, however, challenge one's basic beliefs. Some deaths fit our expectations and validate our assumptions. The appropriate death of an elderly person after a well-lived life would be an example of this.

For many there is no clear answer. A mother whose young son died in the 1988 crash of PanAm Flight 103 said, "It is not how to find an answer, but how to live without one." Over time, new beliefs may be adopted or old ones reasserted or modified to reflect the fragility of life and the limits of control (Shuchter & Zisook, 1986).

The arresting of task III results in a *failure to adapt to the loss.* People work against themselves by promoting their own helplessness, by not developing the skills they need to cope, or by withdrawing from the world and not facing up to environmental requirements. Most people do not take this negative course, however. They usually decide that they must fill the roles to which they are unaccustomed, develop skills they never had, and move forward with a reassessed sense of themselves and the world. Bowlby (1980) sums this up when he says:

> On how he achieves this [task III] turns the outcome of his mourning—either progress towards a recognition of his changed circumstances, a revision of his representational models, and a redefinition of his goals in life, or else a state of suspended growth in which he is held prisoner by a dilemma he cannot solve. (p. 139)

Task IV: To Find an Enduring Connection With the Deceased in the Midst of Embarking on a New Life

When I wrote the first edition of this book, I defined the fourth task of mourning as "withdrawing emotional energy from the deceased and reinvesting it in another relationship." This concept was posited by Freud (1917/1957) when he said, "Mourning has quite a precise psychical task to perform: its function is to detach the survivor's hopes and memories from the dead" (p. 268). We now know that people do not decathect from the dead but find ways to develop *continuing bonds* with the deceased (Klass, Silverman, & Nickman, 1996). In both the second and third editions of this book, I suggested that the fourth task of mourning is to find a place for the deceased that will enable the mourner to be connected with the deceased but in a way that will not preclude him or her from going on with life. We need to find ways to memorialize, that is, to remember dead loved ones—keeping them with us but still going on with life. In this edition, I have rewritten the fourth task as follows: to find an enduring connection with the deceased in the midst of embarking on a new life (Field, Gal-Oz, & Bonanno, 2003). This is a more precise way to articulate the definition of task IV than in the second and third editions of the book.

In the Harvard Child Bereavement Study we were surprised to find the large number of children who stayed connected with the parent who died by speaking to, thinking of, dreaming of, and feeling watched by that parent. Two years after the death, two-thirds of the children still felt watched by their dead parent (Silverman, Nickman, & Worden, 1992). Klass (1999), who has worked for many years with bereaved parents, also documents the need of these parents to stay connected with their dead children in some way.

Volkan (1985) has suggested:

A mourner never altogether forgets the dead person who was so highly valued in life and never totally withdraws his investment in his representation. We can never purge those who have been close to us from our own history except by psychic acts damaging to our own identity. (p. 326)

Volkan goes on to say that mourning ends when the mourner no longer has a need to reactivate the representation of the dead with exaggerated intensity in the course of daily living.

Shuchter and Zisook (1986) write:

> A survivor's readiness to enter new relationships depends not on "giving up" the dead spouse but on finding a suitable place for the spouse in the psychological life of the bereaved—a place that is important but that leaves room for others. (p. 117)

The counselor's task then becomes not to help the bereaved give up their relationship with the deceased, but to help them find an appropriate place for the dead in their emotional lives—a place that will enable them to go on living effectively in the world. Marris (1974) has captured this idea when he writes:

> At first, a widow cannot separate her purposes and understanding from the husband who figured so centrally in them: she has to revive the relationship, to continue it by symbols and make-believe, in order to feel alive. But as time goes by, she begins to reformulate life in terms which assimilate the fact of his death. She makes a gradual transformation from talking to him "as if he were sitting in the chair beside me," to thinking what he would have said and done, and from there to planning her own and her children's future in terms of what he would have wished. Until finally the wishes become her own, and she no longer consciously refers them to him. (pp. 37–38)

Bereaved parents often have difficulty understanding the notion of emotional withdrawal. If we think of relocation, then the task for bereaved parents is to evolve some ongoing relationship with the thoughts and memories that they associate with their child, but to do this in a way that allows them to continue with their lives after such a loss. One such parent eventually found an effective place for the thoughts and memories of her dead son so she could begin reinvesting in life. She wrote:

> Only recently have I begun to take notice of things in life that are still open to me. You know, things that can bring me pleasure. I know that

I will continue to grieve for Robbie for the rest of my life and that I will keep his loving memory alive. But life goes on, and like it or not, I am a part of it. Lately, there have been times when I notice how well I seem to be doing on some project at home or even taking part in some activity with friends. (Alexy, 1982, p. 503)

To me, this represents movement in the accomplishing of task IV. Attig (1996) affirms the following:

We can continue to "have" what we have "lost," that is, a continuing, albeit transformed, love for the deceased. We have not truly lost our years of living with the deceased or our memories. Nor have we lost their influences, the inspirations, the values, and the meanings embodied in their lives. We can actively incorporate these into new patterns of living that include the transformed but abiding relationships with those we have cared about and loved. (p. 189)

It is difficult to find a phrase that adequately defines the noncompletion of task IV, but I think the best description would perhaps be *not living.* One's life has stopped with the death and has not resumed. The fourth task is hindered when one holds on to the past attachment in a way that precludes one from forming new ones. Some people find loss so painful that they make a pact with themselves never to love again. Popular songs are replete with this theme, which gives it a validity it does not deserve.

For many people, task IV is the most difficult one to accomplish. They get stuck at this point in their grieving and later realize that their life in some way stopped at the point the loss occurred. But task IV can be accomplished. One teenage girl had an extremely difficult time adjusting to the death of her father. Two years later, as she began to move through the issues of task IV, she wrote a note to her mother from college that articulated what many people come to realize when they are grappling with emotional withdrawal and reinvestment: "There are other people to be loved," she wrote, "and it doesn't mean that I love Dad any less."

Many counselors have found these four tasks of mourning useful in understanding the bereavement process. My concern is that some novice counselors tend to see these tasks as a fixed progression and fall into the trap associated with fixed stages. Tasks can be revisited and worked through again and again over time. Various tasks can also be worked on *at the same time.* Grieving is a fluid process and is influenced by the mediators of mourning discussed in the next chapter.

DUAL-PROCESS MODEL OF GRIEVING

Stroebe and Schut (1999, 2001a, 2005) have developed the dual-process model of grieving. This was created to "better account for the diversity of stressful experiences in bereavement" (Stroebe & Schut, 1999, p. 197). They claim that it is different from the task model of mourning, but I don't find the differences that striking. They identify loss-oriented stressors and restoration-oriented stressors. Loss-oriented stressors focus on the deceased person and involve grief work on such issues as separation distress, appraisal of the meaning of the loss, and relocation of the deceased in a world without the deceased's presence. Restoration-oriented stressors involve skill mastery, identity change, and other psychosocial transitions and changes. This includes the rebuilding of shattered assumptions of the self and the world. Their loss orientation includes the very tasks that I have outlined in task I, task II, and task IV. Restoration orientation is almost identical to my task III.

Stroebe and Schut (1999) make the assumption that it is not possible to attend to both loss and restoration dimensions at the same time. People oscillate between these two dimensions, confronting one and avoiding the other, and going back and forth. They postulate that oscillation has an adaptive regulatory function. The reader should note that tasks are not linear and that people go back and forth dealing with them as needed. Tasks can be, and are, worked on simultaneously, and a layered approach may be a better descriptor. People can engage in tasks or they can back away from them. A good example of this is the "dosing" notion. Mourners frequently dose themselves as to the amount of pain that they will let themselves experience at any one time. Depending on their coping style, to be discussed in the next chapter, there are ways to deny the loss and distract from the pain

(Hogan & Schmidt, 2002). Coping style is an important mediator of the way people deal with the various tasks of mourning.

I think that when one maintains that "it is not possible to attend to both dimensions at the same time," this locks people into too fixed a pattern, and the penultimate of fixed patterns are the stage theories extant since the 1960s. A theory that posits flexibility is what is needed. People do not grieve the same way, and highlighting individual differences is most important. I believe that the task theory provides such flexibility. That people confront sometimes and avoid sometimes is not up for debate. The best model is one that does not lock people into one task at a time to the exclusion of other tasks.

REFERENCES

Alexy, W. D. (1982). Dimensions of psychological counseling that facilitate the growing process of bereaved parents. *Journal of Counseling Psychology, 29,* 498–507.

Attig, T. (1996). *How we grieve: Relearning the world.* New York: Oxford University Press.

Bonanno, G. A. (2004). Loss, trauma, and human resilience. *American Psychologist, 59,* 20–28.

Bowlby, J. (1980). *Attachment and loss: Vol. 3. Loss, sadness, and depression.* New York: Basic Books.

Didion, J. (2005). *The year of magical thinking.* New York: Knopf.

Dorpat, T. L. (1973). Suicide, loss, and mourning. *Suicide & Life-Threatening Behavior, 3,* 213–224.

Field, N. P., Gal-Oz, E., & Bonanno, G. A. (2003). Continuing bonds and adjustment at 5 years after the death of a spouse. *Journal of Consulting & Clinical Psychology, 71,* 110–117.

Freud, S. (1957). Mourning and melancholia. In J. Strachey (Ed. & Trans.), *The standard edition of the complete works of Sigmund Freud* (Vol. 14, pp. 237–260). New York: Basic Books. (Originally published in 1917)

Gardiner, A., & Pritchard, M. (1977). Mourning, mummification, and living with the dead. *British Journal of Psychiatry, 130,* 23–28.

Goalder, J. S. (1985). Morbid grief reaction: A social systems perspective. *Professional Psychology: Research & Practice, 16,* 833–842.

Gorer, G. D. (1965). *Death, grief, and mourning.* New York: Doubleday.

Havinghurst, R. J. (1953). *Developmental tasks and education.* New York: Longmans.

Hogan, N., & Schmidt, L. A. (2002). Testing the grief to personal growth model using structural equation modeling. *Death Studies, 26,* 615–634.

Horowitz, M. J., Wilner, N., Marmar, C., & Krupnick, J. (1980). Pathological grief and the activation of latent self images. *American Journal of Psychiatry, 137,* 1157–1162.

Janoff-Bulman, R. (1992). *Shattered assumptions: Towards a new psychology of trauma.* New York: Free Press.

Klass, D. (1999). *The spiritual lives of bereaved parents.* Philadelphia: Brunner/Mazel.

Klass, D., Silverman, P. R., & Nickman, S. (Eds.). (1996). *Continuing bonds: New understandings of grief.* Washington, DC: Taylor & Francis.

Krupp, G., Genovese, F., & Krupp, T. (1986). To have and have not: Multiple identifications in pathological bereavement. *Journal of the American Academy of Psychoanalysis, 14,* 337–348.

Kübler-Ross, E. (1969). *On death and dying.* New York: Macmillan.

Maciejewski, P. K., Zhang, B., Block, S. D., & Prigerson, H. G. (2007). An empirical examination of the stage theory of grief. *Journal of the American Medical Association, 297,* 716–723.

Marris, P. (1974). *Loss and change.* London: Routledge & Kegan Paul.

Neimeyer, R. (1999). Narrative strategies in grief therapy. *Journal of Constructive Psychology, 12,* 65–85.

Neimeyer, R. (2000). Searching for the meaning of meaning: Grief therapy and the process of reconstruction. *Death Studies, 24,* 541–558.

Neimeyer, R. (Ed.). (2001). *Meaning reconstruction and the experience of loss.* Washington, DC: American Psychological Association.

Parkes, C. M. (1972). *Bereavement: Studies of grief in adult life.* New York: International Universities Press.

Parkes, C. M. (2001). *Bereavement: Studies of grief in adult life* (3rd ed.). Philadelphia: Taylor & Francis.

Parkes, C. M. (2006). *Love and loss: The roots of grief and its complications.* New York: Routledge.

Pincus, L. (1974). *Death and the family: The importance of mourning.* New York: Pantheon.

Rubin, S. S. (1990). Treating the bereaved spouse: A focus on the loss process, the self and the other. *Psychotherapy Patient, 6,* 189–205.

Sanders, C. (1989). *Grief: The mourning after.* New York: Wiley.

Sanders, C. (1999). *Grief, the mourning after: Dealing with adult bereavement* (2nd ed.). New York: John Wiley.

Shuchter, S. R., & Zisook, S. (1986). Treatment of spousal bereavement: A multidimensional approach. *Psychiatric Annals, 16,* 295–305.

Silverman, P. R., Nickman, S., & Worden, J. W. (1992). Detachment revisited: The child's reconstruction of a dead parent. *American Journal of Orthopsychiatry, 62,* 494–503.

Stroebe, M. S. (1992). Coping with bereavement: A review of the grief work hypothesis. *Omega, 26,* 19–42.

Stroebe, M. S., & Schut, H. (1999). The dual process model of coping with bereavement: Rationale and description. *Death Studies, 23,* 197–224.

Stroebe, M. S., & Schut, H. (2001a). Meaning making in the dual process model of coping with bereavement. In R. A. Neimeyer (Ed.), *Meaning reconstruction and the experience of loss* (pp. 55–73). Washington, DC: American Psychological Association.

Stroebe, M. S., & Schut, H. (2001b). Models of coping with bereavement: A review. In M. Stroebe, R. Hansson, W. Stroebe, & H. Schut (Eds.), *Handbook of bereavement research* (pp. 375–403). Washington, DC: American Psychological Association.

Stroebe, M. S., & Schut, H. (2005). Complicated grief: A conceptual analysis of the field. *Omega, 52,* 53–70.

Volkan, V. D. (1985). Complicated mourning. *Annual of Psychoanalysis, 12,* 323–348.

Wallis, J. (2001). Continuing bonds: Relationship between the living and the dead within contemporary Spiritualism. *Mortality, 6,* 127–145.

Weisman, A. D. (1972). *On dying and denying.* New York: Aronson.

Worden, J. W. (1996). *Children & grief: When a parent dies.* New York: Guilford Press.

Zaiger, N. (1985–1986). Women and bereavement. *Women and Therapy, 4,* 33–43.

The Mourning Process: Mediators of Mourning

It is not sufficient to know only about the tasks of mourning. It is also important for the counselor to understand the second part of the mourning process—the *mediators of mourning.* If you assess a large number of grieving people, you will see a wide range of behaviors, and although these behaviors may reflect those on the list of normal grief reactions, there are major individual differences. For some, grief is a very intense experience, whereas for others it is rather mild. For some, grief begins at the time they hear of the loss, while for others it is a delayed experience. In some cases grief goes on for a relatively brief period of time, while in others it seems to go on forever. In order to understand why individuals handle the tasks of mourning in different ways, one must understand how these tasks are mediated by various factors. This is especially important when one is working with complicated mourning (described in chapter 5).

MEDIATOR 1: WHO THE PERSON WHO DIED WAS

To begin with the most obvious: if you want to understand how someone will respond to a loss, you need to know something about the deceased. Kinship identifies the dead person's relationship to the survivor. Such a relationship could be that of a spouse, child, parent, sibling, other relative, friend, or lover. A grandparent who dies of natural causes will probably be grieved differently than a sibling killed in a car accident. The loss of a distant cousin will be grieved differently than the loss of a child. The loss of a spouse may be grieved differently than the loss of a parent. In the case of two children whose father has died, there can be significant individual differences in grief responses. Who the father was to the 13-year-old daughter can be quite different from who the father was to the 9-year-old son. Each child lost a father, but each had a different relationship with him and different hopes and expectations about him.

MEDIATOR 2: THE NATURE OF THE ATTACHMENT

The tasks of mourning are mediated not only by who the deceased was, but also by the nature of the survivor's attachment to the person. You need to know something about:

1. *The strength of the attachment.* It is almost axiomatic that the intensity of grief is determined by the intensity of love. The grief reaction often increases in severity proportionately to the intensity of the love relationship.
2. *The security of the attachment.* How necessary was the deceased to the sense of well-being of the survivor? If the survivor needed the lost person for his or her own sense of self-esteem—to feel okay about him- or herself—this will portend a more difficult grief reaction. For many individuals, security and esteem needs are met by their spouse, and after their spouse dies, the needs remain the same, but the resources are missing.
3. *The ambivalence in the relationship.* In any close relationship there is always a certain degree of ambivalence. Basically, the person is loved, but there also coexist negative feelings. Usually the positive feelings far exceed the negative feelings, but in the case of a highly ambivalent relationship in which the negative feelings coexist in almost equal proportion to the positive ones, there is going to be a more difficult grief reaction. Often in a highly ambivalent relationship, the death leads to a tremendous

amount of guilt, often expressed as "Did I do enough for him?" along with intense anger at being left alone.

4. *Conflicts with the deceased.* This refers not just to conflicts around the time of death, but also to a history of conflicts. Of special note are conflicts stemming from earlier physical and/or sexual abuse (Krupp, Genovese, & Krupp, 1986). In conflicted relationships there is the possibility of unfinished business that never gets resolved before the death. This is especially true in the case of sudden death. Sarah, her husband, and her mother lived together in the same house. One morning Sarah and her mother had a big fight before the mother left for work. On her way to work, the mother's car was hit by an 18-wheeler truck and the mother was killed. Sarah carried a lot of guilt with regard to her interactions with her mother on the day of the death, as well as guilt about their long-standing conflicts with each other. She sought out counseling to help herself resolve this guilt and her unfinished business with her mother.

5. *Dependent relationships.* Such relationships can affect the person's adaptation to the death, especially task III issues. The external adjustments will be greater for a person who was dependent on the deceased for the fulfillment of various daily activities such as bill paying, driving, and meal preparation than for the person who had less dependency on the deceased for these activities of daily living.

MEDIATOR 3: HOW THE PERSON DIED

How the person died has an impact on how the survivor deals with the various tasks of mourning. Traditionally, deaths are cataloged under the NASH categories: natural, accidental, suicidal, and homicidal. The accidental death of a child may be grieved differently than the natural death of an older person, whose death would be seen as occurring at a more appropriate time. The suicidal death of a father may be grieved differently than the expected death of a young mother leaving small children. There is evidence that survivors of suicidal deaths have unique and very difficult problems handling their grief (see chapter 7). Other dimensions associated with the death that can affect bereavement are the following.

Proximity

Where did the death occur geographically—did it happen near the survivors or far away? Deaths occurring at a distance may give the loved one a sense of unreality regarding the death. One can assume that the person is still there, which affects task I of mourning. There have been different findings as to whether home deaths help or increase distress in bereavement. Addington-Hall and Karlsen (2000) studied home deaths in Britain and found that bereaved individuals who cared for a patient dying at home had more psychological distress, missed the deceased more, and had a more difficult time coming to terms with the death after it occurred. As part of Project Omega at Massachusetts General Hospital, Avery Weisman and I interviewed caregivers whose loved ones had died at home. We asked if they would do this again. The results were split 50/50. Half would do it again. They felt that they could give their dying loved one special attention and that their children could see death as a part of life. The other half said, "No way." They found it difficult to manage some of the medical procedures and always felt like they could be doing more for the dying person (Weisman & Worden, 1980). Hospice home care has developed since we did that study, so the latter attitude may be less of a problem now.

Suddenness or Unexpectedness

Was there some advance warning or was the death unexpected? A number of studies suggest that survivors of those who die sudden deaths, especially young survivors, have a more difficult time than people with advance warning a year or 2 years later (Parkes & Weiss, 1983). In the Harvard Child Bereavement Study, sudden death (40%) as opposed to expected death (60%) affected both the adjustment of the children as well as the adjustment of the family. This was most apparent during the first year of bereavement. As the family moved into the second year, other mediators were more prominent in affecting their adjustment. Although half of the children remained fearful of their surviving parent's safety 2 years after the death, it was not the suddenness of the death that created this fear but rather the poor functioning of the surviving parent. Sudden deaths overlap with violent deaths, and it may be the latter that is the most impactful. When it came to natural deaths, the longer the survivor had to anticipate the death, the better his or her adjustment. However, it was not necessarily objective time (i.e., weeks and months) but rather their perceptions of expectation that made the difference in adaptation in the Harvard study. However, Donnelly, Field, and Horowitz (2000) found that objective expectancy was a stronger predictor of symptoms than was subjective expectancy, so more investigation is needed.

Violent/Traumatic Deaths

The impact of violent and traumatic deaths can be long lasting and often leads to complicated mourning (the sequelae of homicides and suicides will be discussed in chapter 7). This type of death does several things to challenge the tasks of mourning. First, it challenges a person's sense of self-efficacy and the internal adjustments of task III—"What could I have done to have prevented this from happening?" is often a major preoccupation. Second, violent deaths are highly likely to shatter a person's worldview and pose a challenge to meaning making that is part of task III. Third, the circumstances surrounding the death may make it difficult for survivors to express their anger and blame (task II). This is particularly true in cases in which the survivor killed the person in an accident or a homicide; guilt will obviously be a key factor in coping with the loss. A fourth sequela following traumatic deaths is a possible posttraumatic stress disorder (PTSD).

Multiple Losses

Some people lose a number of loved ones in a single tragic event or in a relatively short period of time. One man I know saw his whole family killed in front of him when a construction crane collapsed on his car, killing his wife and two children. When such multiple losses occur there is the possibility of "bereavement overload" (Kastenbaum, 1969). There is too much grief and pain, and the person is unable to manage feelings associated with the second task of mourning. Intervention requires exploring each loss individually, beginning with the least complicated, looking at what has been lost, and gradually jump-starting the grieving process. For the man who lost both children in the accident exploring his relationship with each child separately was important, as his relationship with and expectations for each child were different.

Preventable Deaths

When the death is seen as preventable, issues of guilt, blame, and culpability come to the surface. These issues need to be worked through as a part of task II. Prolonged litigation is often a correlate of preventable deaths and can prolong the mourning process for those involved with it (Gamino, Sewell, & Easterling, 2000). Bugen (1977) brought this dimension to our attention and shows how it has an impact on the overall adaptation to a death, along with the dimension of emotional closeness. More recently, Guarnaccia, Hayslip, and Landry (1999) tested Bugen's model on a large group of adults and found that perceived preventability of the death was a very strong mediator affecting grief measures.

Ambiguous Deaths

There are some situations when the survivors are not sure whether their loved one is alive or dead. We saw this during the Vietnam War when military personnel were listed as missing in action. Families were not sure whether the person was dead or alive. This puts the mourner in an awkward position not knowing whether to hold out hope or to give into grief. Similar ambiguity can exist after an airplane crash into the ocean. I worked with some families after the KAL plane was shot out of the sky in 1983. No bodies from that flight were retrieved. Although these families knew their loved ones were dead, some held out hope. It was helpful to get closure when the South Korean government erected a monument with the names of the passengers on it. After the September 11, 2001, tragedy some bodies were not recovered leaving family members with the hope their loved one would show up at some point. We need more understanding of this type of loss, and this can be done by documenting the narratives of families who manage to change and move on in spite of an ambiguous loss (Tubbs & Boss, 2000).

Stigmatized Deaths

Doka and others have written about disenfranchised grief (Attig, 2004; Doka, 1989, 2002). Deaths such as suicide and death by AIDS are often seen as stigmatized deaths. When such stigma exists, social support for the mourner may be less than sufficient (Doka, 1989). Stigmatized deaths are related to socially unspeakable losses and socially negated losses, which are discussed in chapter 7.

MEDIATOR 4: HISTORICAL ANTECEDENTS

In order to understand how someone is going to grieve, you need to know if he or she has had previous losses and how these were grieved. Were they grieved adequately, or does the person bring to the new loss a lack of resolution from a previous one?

A person's mental health history may be important here. One historical focus has been on those who come to a loss with a history of depressive illness. Zisook, Paulus, Shuchter, and Judd (1997) believe that a major depression prior to the death can create an increased risk for major depression following spousal bereavement. On the other hand, Byrne and Raphael (1999) did not find that a major depressive episode was predicted by a past history of dysphoria in widowed older men. Such differences in findings can be explained, in part, by differences in populations, time frames, and measures used.

Another historical mediator has to do with family issues. Unresolved loss and grief can transcend several generations and affect the current mourning process (Paul & Grosser, 1965; Walsh & McGoldrick, 1991).

MEDIATOR 5: PERSONALITY VARIABLES

Bowlby (1980) makes a strong plea for therapists and other counselors to take the mourner's personality structure into account when trying to understand an individual's response to loss. Such personality variables include the following.

Age and Gender

There has been considerable recent interest in gender differences and the ability to grieve, especially men's ways of grieving (Martin & Doka, 1996). It is true that boys and girls are socialized differently, and many of the differences in how men and women approach the tasks of mourning may be more a part of this socialization than in some intrinsic genetic differences. One speculation has been that women may grieve differently and have different bereavement outcomes because they receive more social support than men. A well-done study by Stroebe, Stroebe, and Abakoumkin (1999) shows that such is not the case. Schut, Stroebe, de Keijser, and van den Bout (1997), however, found that there were strong gender differences in the type of intervention found to be efficacious. Men responded better to affect-stimulating interventions, and women to problem-solving interventions. The interventions appear to be the opposite of typical gender styles. Looking at men who had lost spouses, Lund (2001) found men in their 50s were the most effective in coping with their grief.

Coping Style

Distress is mediated by one's coping choices—how inhibited one is with feelings, how well one handles anxiety, and how one copes with stressful situations. Lazarus and Folkman (1984) define coping as the changing thoughts and acts that an individual uses to manage the external or internal demands of stressful situations. The death of a loved one certainly makes such demands. Coping styles vary from person to person. Coping research—whether coping with cancer, bereavement, or trauma—has been a major part of my professional life. There are different paradigms for understanding coping, but here is one that I find particularly useful both in research and clinical intervention. It is a problem-solving model in which coping can be seen as what one does with a problem to bring about relief and resolution. Both relief and resolution are interval measures and may vary as to the degree of relief and resolve. There are three main groups of coping functions.

Problem-Solving Coping

People vary in their ability to solve problems. Those with the poorest skills overuse ineffective strategies, or they try one thing to solve the problem and then give up when that doesn't work. There are ways to teach problem solving to people lacking these skills. One is a cognitive-behavioral intervention that Sobel and I developed (Sobel & Worden, 1982).

Active Emotional Coping

Active emotional coping is the most effective strategy for handling problems and managing stress. Redefinition is at the top of the list for effectiveness. This is the ability to find something positive or redemptive in a bad situation. The whole notion of growth through grief is predicated on the effective use of these strategies. In studies of both cancer patients and the bereaved, those with the lowest emotional distress were those who could reframe problems and find something positive in the difficult situation. Humor is another coping strategy that can be effective. To use humor requires a certain distancing from the problem that can be helpful in the short haul. Venting of emotions rather than bottling up feelings can be useful. However, venting is best when it involves positive as well as negative feelings and isn't the kind of affect display that blows others out the door. The ability to accept support is another dimension of an active emotional approach to coping. Accepting the support of others does not necessarily make one feel less efficacious. On the contrary, accepting support is a choice of the mourner that may enhance efficacy as well as esteem.

Avoidant Emotional Coping

Perhaps the least effective strategies are avoidant emotional coping. They may make the person feel better for the moment, but they are not particularly useful in solving a problem. Avoidant coping includes blame, both of self and others; distraction, which can be useful in the short haul, but not if it persists; denial, which like distraction can have short-term benefits as a buffer against difficult reality but is not effective over the long term; and social withdrawal, again helpful over the short term but not the most effective coping. Substance use and abuse may make the person feel better but do not solve the problems and may have their own iatrogenic effects.

In the Harvard Child Bereavement Study, the best outcomes both for the parents and for their children came from the use of active emotional coping strategies, especially the ability to redefine and reframe. Passive strategies (e.g., "There is nothing that I can do about it") are among the least effective (Worden, 1996). Schnider, Elhai, and Gray (2007) found that active coping was associated with best outcomes after a traumatic loss and that avoidant emotional coping was associated with the development of PTSD and/or complicated grief.

The question arises whether coping styles are stable in an individual or if they are modifiable. Folkman (2001) believes that some strategies like reframing and cognitive avoidance tend to be more stable types of coping, while others such as problem-solving skills and the use of social support are more modifiable. From my research I would agree with this. We had real success using a cognitive-behavioral approach to teach problem-solving skills to a group of poor problem solvers (Sobel & Worden, 1982). Also, through the use of bereavement groups, mourners can learn more effective ways to use social support.

Attachment Style

Another important mediator that affects how one handles the various tasks of mourning is one's attachment style. Attachment styles are set up early in life as the result of early parent-child bonding. The goal of these behaviors is to maintain or reestablish proximity to an attachment figure, usually the mother. The attachment figure's responsiveness to the child's emotional needs, especially under stress, determines these patterns. Attachment styles are seen by some as traits, traits that are somewhat malleable under situations like traumatic events and psychotherapy but basically firmly established (Fraley, 2002). The appraised availability or psychological proximity of the attachment figure is the important factor determining whether the person feels secure or distressed in the absence of the attachment figure. Generally attachment styles evolve as a result of experiences or relationships with important others early in life. Attachment bonds exist between adults but are considered to differ in important ways from the child-parent bond, because both partners can serve as an attachment figure to each other.

When the relationship to an attachment figure is severed through death, the survivor is under threat to maintain or reestablish proximity to the figure. Separation distress leads to searching behavior in order to reestablish the lost relationship, but gradually the bereaved comes to appreciate the permanence of the loss. A healthy adaptation to this new reality is for the mourner to internalize the deceased into him- or herself and his or her schema of life so that psychological proximity substitutes for the previous physical proximity. The bereaved can be emotionally sustained by the mental representation of the deceased, with less need for the physical presence no longer available. Internal models or representations have been described in terms of styles of attachment (Ainsworth, Blehar, Waters, & Wall, 1978; Main & Solomon, 1990; Mikulincer & Shaver, 2003).

Secure Attachment Style

Through good parenting and other healthy early relationships, many people develop what is called a secure attachment style. Those with secure attachments have positive mental models of being valued and of being worthy of support, concern, and affection. After experiencing the loss of an important attachment figure through death, individuals with a secure attachment style experience the pain of sorrow but are able to process this pain and move on to develop healthy continuing bonds with the lost loved one. Early intense grief (searching and pining) do not overwhelm their acceptance of the reality of the loss—task I.

Insecure Attachment Styles

There are four types of insecure attachment styles that people may have when parenting and early relationships have not gone well. These are anxious/preoccupied attachments, anxious/ambivalent attachments, avoidant/dismissing attachments, and avoidant/fearful attachments. (Some researchers may use other terms for the same phenomena.) These various attachment styles affect one's relationships throughout life and are important mediators for the grieving process when the attachment figure dies. These insecure attachment styles are particularly important mediators because they can make adaptation to the tasks difficult and contribute to the development of complicated mourning (Stroebe, Schut, & Stroebe, 2006). Let's look at these insecure attachment styles in some detail.

Anxious/Preoccupied Attachment. These are relationships that give a person a sense of uneasiness and in which the person is often supersensitive to slights and other perceived neglect in the relationship. These are individuals who keep extra boyfriends (or girlfriends) in the wings in case the current one does not work out. These people do not feel good about themselves and are likely to have their self-esteem needs determined by the significant other. When death takes the loved one, individuals with this attachment style often show high levels of distress that goes on for some time and may lead to the complication of chronic or prolonged grief. Their ability to regulate affect, as well as their ability to handle stress, may be deficient. Rumination over the loss may be high, and excessive pain may be handled by avoidant behavior—avoiding reminders of the loss to buffer the pain. Low self-efficacy is often apparent when the person sees him- or herself as helpless and unable to cope without the loved one. Clinging and help-seeking behavior are behavioral features of this style. The therapy goal for people with this style is to help them stop trying to regain physical proximity to the deceased and through internalization to feel secure through psychological proximity (Field, Gao, & Paderna, 2005).

Anxious/Ambivalent Attachment. In ambivalent relationships, love and hate coexist on almost equal levels. Individuals who form this kind of attachment see the other as undependable. Relationships can be stormy, and anger can be observed when the relationship is threatened. In my clinical work, I sometimes call these angry attachments. I have treated a number of couples over the years in which one partner has to leave for several days or weeks for legitimate business purposes and the other partner goes crazy with angry responses. On some level of awareness, the anger may be perceived as a way of keeping the person from leaving so that the anxiety that underlies this style does not have to be experienced. This is similar to the protest of the child to reestablish the physical proximity of the attachment figure. When the loved one dies, the intensity of anger and anxiety is excessive, so in order to keep stability, the mourner may focus on positive feelings—the polar opposite feelings from the anger. These are the mourners who make their loved ones bigger than life so as not to confront the depths of anger on the other side of their experience. When they talk about their loved one, the counselor gets the feeling that no one can be that great. Intervention should be directed toward the acknowledgment and expression of both types of feelings, positive and negative. If the anger cannot be expressed and integrated into the loving feelings, the person may experience high levels of depression or prolonged grief, along with extensive rumination.

Avoidant/Dismissing Attachment. Here the individual may have had an unresponsive parent and developed a pseudo self-sufficient style. Behavior is organized around the goal of self-reliance and independence. Some of these individuals are seen as unreliable. Autonomy and self-reliance are of paramount importance to them. After a death, these people may show few symptoms and minimal emotional reactions, basically because they are minimally attached. These individuals have an excessively positive view of themselves and often a negative opinion of others, to whom they are less likely to turn under stress. There is some controversy in the field as to whether individuals with this style, who initially show minimal emotional reactions to a loss, go on to develop a delayed grief reaction. Some, like Fraley and Bonanno (2004), do not think so. However, there is some likelihood that those with this style go on to experience somatic reactions after a loss, either immediately following the death or later, due to unconscious longings for detachment (Stroebe et al., 2006). Because of defensive exclusion, they cannot process the implications of the loss and task III issues may be a struggle.

Avoidant/Fearful Attachment. People with this style of attachment are very likely to make the poorest adaptation to the loss. Unlike the avoidant/dismissing person, who values self-sufficiency, they want relationships but have long histories of tentative attachments due to the fear that these attachments might be broken. When death takes away any attachments they have developed, they are very susceptible to developing high levels of depression. This depression often protects them against anger that they may be feeling. Social withdrawal is the behavior most frequently seen in bereavement situations and serves as a protection of the self.

Healthy attachments, when broken, lead to feelings of grief. Less healthy attachments lead to feelings of anger and guilt when the attachment is broken through death (Winnicott, 1953). Attachment problems are also of importance for the highly dependent person and the person who has difficulty forming relationships. Individuals diagnosed with certain personality disorders may also have a difficult time handling a loss. This is especially true of those classified with borderline personality disorders or narcissistic personality disorders (see American Psychiatric Association, 2000). Less healthy attachments can lead to separation disorders, which are the current focus of traumatic grief (Jacobs, 1999).

Cognitive Style

Different people have different cognitive styles. Some are more optimistic than others and are likely to report the glass half full rather than half empty. Associated with such an optimistic style is the ability to find something positive or redemptive in a bad situation. One cancer patient said, "I am not happy this happened to me, but it did give me the opportunity to reconcile with my mother." In the Harvard Child Bereavement Study we found that optimism and the ability to redefine were associated with lower levels of depression in the surviving parents during the first 2 years following the loss (Worden, 1996).

Likewise, Boelen and van den Bout (2002) found that positive thinking was inversely related to measures of anxiety and traumatic grief symptomatology but especially to depression. This should not be surprising since Beck et al. (1979) and other depression researchers find that depressed individuals have negative views of life, themselves, the world, and the future. This pessimistic attitude of the depressed often leads to a cognitive style that involves the use of overgeneralization. "I will never get over this" and "No one will ever love me again" are examples of this type of thinking.

Another important cognitive style is rumination. People who ruminate persistently and repetitively focus on their negative emotions without taking action to relieve these emotions. In the context of bereavement, this involves chronically and passively focusing on grief-related symptoms. This cognitive style lengthens the time that negative emotions are experienced, which does not lead to an effective handling of task II and may lead the depressed mood to become a depressive disorder (Nolen-Hoeksema, 2001; Nolen-Hoeksema, McBride, & Larson, 1997). Ruminators focus on their loss presumably to find meaning and understanding, but research shows that they are less likely to find it than are non-ruminators. One possible explanation for the perdurance of this cognitive style, despite the pain it brings, is that such pain represents the individual's last and perhaps final tie to the deceased. However, there are two main negative sequelae to this style: first, the mourner does not engage in good problem-solving behavior, and second, it can drive people away, people who might offer social support. There are several interventions that can be useful in work with bereaved people who ruminate a lot. Help them with their problem-solving focus and teach them skills for the same; help them to increase their social contacts in a way that doesn't drive people away; and help them find more appropriate ways to handle task IV issues, to stay connected without making the pain their point of connection, and to go on with their lives without the deceased.

Ego Strength: Self-Esteem and Self-Efficacy

All people come to a death event with attitudes about their own worth and attitudes about their ability to affect what happens to them in life. Some deaths can challenge a person's self-esteem and self-efficacy, thus making the internal adjustments of task III more of a challenge (Reich & Zautra, 1991). This is especially true when long-standing negative self-images have been compensated for by one's spouse. If the spouse dies, such a profound loss can reactivate previously held latent negative self-images (Horowitz, Wilner, Marmar, & Krupnick, 1980). Self-efficacy is another component of ego strength. It is similar to Rotter's locus of control and involves how much a person believes that he or she has control over what happens to him or her in life. The death mediator of preventability becomes a major focus for some when the death makes one feel impotent and out of control. Benight, Flores, and Tashiro (2001) found that older widows who had a stronger sense of coping self-efficacy had a better sense of emotional and spiritual well-being and were also in better physical health. In the Harvard Child Bereavement Study, self-esteem and self-efficacy were important strengths in the experience of children who made the best adjustments to the death of a parent (Worden, 1996). Haine's team (2003) also found locus of control and self-esteem to be important stress mediators in their study of bereaved children in Arizona (esteem more so than efficacy). Bauer and Bonanno (2001) found a strong link between self-efficacy and psychological health and found it predicted less grief over time in a group of midlife bereaved spouses. Efficacy was particularly useful in helping mourners with task III issues of finding meaning for the loss and establishing new identity constructions.

Assumptive World: Beliefs and Values

Each of us carries assumptions about the benevolence and the meaningfulness of the world (Schwartzberg & Janoff-Bulman, 1991). Some deaths can challenge a person's assumptive world more than others, causing a spiritual crisis for the individual who is uncertain of what is true and what is good. When this happens, the *spiritual adjustments* of task III are made more difficult. I have worked with several mothers whose young children were in the yard playing when they were shot and killed by drive-by shooters, often gang members. This senseless loss of their children presents a crisis of faith to these mothers, challenging their belief in the predictability of the world and God's place in it. However, certain worldviews can serve a protective function by allowing individuals to incorporate a major tragedy into their belief system. A person who holds a firm belief that all things are part of God's larger plan may show less distress following the loss of a spouse than a person who does not hold this view (Wortman & Silver, 2001). The belief that one will be reunited for all eternity with the deceased may also serve a protective function (Smith, Range, & Ulmer, 1991–1992).

MEDIATOR 6: SOCIAL VARIABLES

Grieving is a social phenomenon, and the need to grieve with others can be important. The degree of perceived emotional and social support from others, both inside and outside the family, is significant in the mourning process. Several studies have shown that perceived social support alleviates the adverse effects of stress, including the stress of bereavement (Schwartzberg & Janoff-Bulman, 1991; Sherkat & Reed, 1992; Stroebe et al., 1999). Even pet owners showed fewer symptoms than those without companion animals (Akiyama, Holtzman, & Britz, 1986). Most studies find that those who do less well with bereavement have inadequate or conflicted social support. One difficulty with social support is that although it may be present around the time of death and shortly thereafter, 6 months to a year later, when the mourner is realizing all that he or she lost when the loved one died, people who were there at the funeral may no longer be there, and if they are there, they are encouraging the person to get over it and move on with life.

Stroebe, Schut, and Stroebe (2005) looked at four longitudinal studies that examined the relationship between social support and depression over a 2-year period. These studies were the Tubingen Longitudinal Study of Bereavement (Stroebe, Stroebe, Abakoumkin, & Schut, 1996), the Changing Lives of Older Couples Study (Carr, House, Kessler, Nesse, Sonnega, & Wortman, 2000), a study of parents who had lost children to violence (Murphy, 2000), and a study of ruminative coping (Nolen-Hocksema & Morrow, 1991). In all four studies, those with more social support had lower depression scores at each assessed time point. However, in none of the studies did social support accelerate adjustment to the loss or make adjustment easier. Although knowing that one can call upon the support of friends and family members may help to soften the blow of loss, it does not necessarily accelerate the grief process. The following are important social mediators.

1. *Support satisfaction.* More important than the mere availability of support is the mourner's perception of social support and satisfaction with it. Research has shown numerous examples where support was available but the person defined it as less than satisfactory. Social integration—the time spent with others and utilization of social support (confiding in others)—are two dimensions that go into support satisfaction (Sherkat & Reed, 1992).

2. *Social role involvements.* Involvement in multiple roles has been found to affect adjustment to a loss by death. Persons who participate in more and varied social roles seem to adjust better to loss than those who don't. Some roles measured in the research include those of parent, employee, friend, and relative, as well as involvement in community, religions, and political groups (Hershberger & Walsh, 1990).

3. *Religious resources and ethnic expectations.* Each of us belongs to various social subcultures—including both ethnic and religious subcultures. They provide us with guidelines and rituals for behavior. The Irish, for example, grieve differently than the Italians, and the Old Yankees grieve still differently. In the Jewish faith, Shiva—a period of 7 days when the family stays home and friends and family come to help them and help facilitate their grief—is often observed. This is followed by other rituals such as going to the synagogue and unveiling the headstone a year later. Catholics have their own rituals, as do some Protestants. In order to adequately predict how a person is going to grieve, you have to know something about his or her social, ethnic, and religious background. The extent to which participation in ritual affects adjustment to bereavement is still

unknown. It stands to reason that it should be useful, but more research is needed here.

A final dimension that should be mentioned under social mediators is the secondary gain that the survivor may find in grieving. A survivor might get a lot of mileage in his or her social network out of grieving, and this would have an effect on how long it goes on. However, extended grieving can have the opposite effect and alienate the social network.

MEDIATOR 7: CONCURRENT STRESSES

Other factors that affect bereavement are the concurrent changes and crises that arise following a death. Some change is inevitable, but there are those individuals and families who experience high levels of disruption (secondary losses) following a death, including serious economic reversals. In the Harvard Child Bereavement Study, surviving parents who experienced the largest number of life-change events following the death of their spouse (as measured by the Family Inventory of Life Events) had the highest levels of depression, and their children were also functioning less well over the 2 years of follow-up (Worden, 1996).

CAUTION

Let me suggest a caution at this point. There is a tendency toward simplistic thinking about determinants of grief and mediators of mourning, especially in research. For example, one might look at the impact of sudden violent death on the survivor's depression and perhaps examine perceived and received social support as co-mediators. However, such research overlooks other important relationship mediators such as the subtleties of the attachment, a person's coping skills, the ability to make meaning out of a tragedy, and many other mediators of mourning. Mourning behavior is multi-determined, and the clinician *and* researcher would do well to keep this constantly in mind.

There has been recent interest in myths associated with coping and loss. Wortman and Silver (2001) challenge the assumption that loss leads to intense distress and depression. Any experienced clinician knows that it does for some people, while not for others. Levels of distress are clearly influenced by the various mediators of mourning. Wortman and Silver agree that mediators must be considered:

> It is important to identify the factors that may lead some people to express negative feelings after a death. First, people may be more likely to express negative feelings if they experience more negative feelings. People may suffer more following a loss for many reasons, including the closeness of attachment to the deceased, the manner of death, and the extent to which the death shatters previously held beliefs about themselves or their world. . . . Certain types of loss, such as the death of a child because of a drunk driver, may be more difficult to work through than the death of a beloved but elderly spouse. (p. 423)

WHEN IS MOURNING FINISHED?

Asking when mourning is finished is a little like asking, "How high is up?" There is no ready answer. Bowlby (1980) and Parkes (1972) both say that mourning is finished when a person completes the final mourning phase of restitution. In my view, mourning is finished when the tasks of mourning have been accomplished. It is impossible to set a definitive date for this. Yet in the bereavement literature, there are all sorts of attempts to set dates—4 months, 1 year, 2 years, never. In the loss of a close relationship, I would be suspicious of any full resolution that takes under a year, and for many, 2 years is not too long.

One benchmark of mourning moving to completion is when the person is able to think of the deceased without pain. There is always a sense of sadness when you think of someone you have loved and lost, but it is a different kind of sadness—it lacks the wrenching quality it previously had. One can think of the deceased without physical manifestations such as intense crying or feeling tightness in the chest.

Also, mourning is finished when a person can reinvest his or her emotions into life and in the living.

There are those, however, who never seem to complete their grieving. Bowlby (1980) quotes one widow in her mid-60s as saying, "Mourning never ends. Only, as time goes on, it erupts less frequently" (p. 101). Most studies show that of women who lose their husbands, fewer than half are themselves again at the end of the first year. Shuchter and Zisook (1986) found that the period around 2 years is the time when the great majority of widows and widowers have found a "modicum of stability . . . establishing a new identity and finding a direction in their lives" (p. 248). Parkes's (2001) studies show that widows may take 3 or 4 years to reach stability in their lives. One of the basic things that education through grief counseling can do is to alert people to the fact that mourning is a long-term process and that the culmination will not be a pre-grief state. The counselor can also let mourners know that even though mourning progresses, grieving does not proceed in a linear fashion; it may reappear to be reworked. One widow who also lost her young adult son said to me after a prolonged and painful mourning period, "Your expectations do you in! I now realize that the pain never goes completely away. The pain returns but I can remember the in-between times better." I have a friend who lost someone important to him and was feeling intense pain. He does not have a great tolerance for pain, particularly emotional pain, and shortly after the loss he said to me, "I'll be glad when 4 weeks is over and this will all be finished." Part of my job was to help him see that the pain would not go away in 4 weeks and probably would not go away in 4 months. Some people believe that it takes 4 full seasons of the year before grief begins to abate. Geoffrey Gorer (1965) believes that the way people respond to spoken condolences gives some indication of where they are in the mourning process. The grateful acceptance of condolences is one of the most reliable signs that the bereaved is working through mourning satisfactorily.

There is a sense in which mourning can be finished, when people regain an interest in life, feel more hopeful, experience gratification again, and adapt to new roles. There is also a sense in which mourning is never finished. You may find the following quote of Sigmund

Freud's to be helpful. He wrote to his friend Binswanger, whose son had died:

> We find a place for what we lose. Although we know that after such a loss the acute stage of mourning will subside, we also know that we shall remain inconsolable and will never find a substitute. No matter what may fill the gap, even if it be filled completely, it nevertheless remains something else. (Freud, 1961, p. 386)

REFERENCES

Addington-Hall, J., & Karlsen, S. (2000). Do home deaths increase distress in bereavement? *Palliative Medicine, 14,* 161–162.

Ainsworth, M., Blehar, M., Waters, E., & Wall, S. (1978). *Patterns of attachment: A psychological study of strange situations.* Hillsdale, NJ: Erlbaum.

Akiyama, H., Holtzman, J., & Britz, W. (1986). Pet ownership and health status during bereavement. *Omega, 17,* 187–193.

American Psychiatric Association. (2000). *Diagnostic and statistical manual of mental disorders* (4th ed.). Washington, DC: Author.

Attig, T. (2004). Disenfranchised grief revisited: Discounting hope and love. *Omega, 49,* 197–215.

Bauer, J., & Bonanno, G. A. (2001). I can, I do, I am: The narrative differentiation of self-efficacy and other self-evaluations while adapting to bereavement. *Journal of Research in Personality, 35,* 424–448.

Beck, A. T., Rush, J., Shaw, B., & Emery, G. et al. (1979). *Cognitive therapy of depression.* New York: Guilford Press.

Benight, C., Flores, J., & Tashiro, T. (2001). Bereavement coping self-efficacy in cancer widows. *Death Studies, 23,* 97–125.

Boelen, P. A., & van den Bout, J. (2002). Positive thinking in bereavement: Is it related to depression, anxiety, or grief symptomatology? *Psychological Reports, 91,* 857–863.

Bowlby, J. (1980). *Attachment and loss: Vol. 3. Loss, sadness, and depression.* New York: Basic Books.

Bugen, L. A. (1977). Human grief: A model for prediction and intervention. *American Journal of Orthopsychiatry, 47,* 196–206.

Byrne, G., & Raphael, B. (1999). Depressive symptoms and depressive episodes in recently widowed older men. *International Psychogeriatrics, 11,* 67–74.

Carr, D., House, J. S., Kessler, R., Nesse, R., Sonnega, J., & Wortman, C. (2000). Marital quality and psychological adjustment to widowhood among older adults: A longitudinal analysis. *Journals of Gerontology, 55B*, S197–S207.

Doka, K. (Ed.). (1989). *Disenfranchised grief: Recognizing hidden sorrow.* Lexington, MA: Lexington Books.

Doka, K. (2002). *Disenfranchised grief: New directions, challenges, and strategies for practice.* Champaign, IL: Research Press.

Donnelly, E. F., Field, N. P., & Horowitz, M. J. (2000). Expectancy of spousal death and adjustment of conjugal bereavement. *Omega, 42*, 195–208.

Field, N. P., Gao, B. I., & Paderna, L. (2005). Continuing bonds in bereavement: An attachment theory based perspective. *Death Studies, 29*, 277–299.

Folkman, S. (2001). Revised coping theory and the process of bereavement. In M. S. Stroebe, R. O. Hansson, W. Stroebe, & H. Schut (Eds.), *Handbook of bereavement research: Consequences, coping, and care* (pp. 563–584). Washington, DC: American Psychological Association.

Fraley, R. C. (2002). Attachment stability from infancy to adulthood: Meta-analysis and dynamic modeling of developmental mechanisms. *Personality and Social Psychology Review, 6*, 123–151.

Fraley, R. C., & Bonanno, G. A. (2004). Attachment and loss: A test of three competing models on the association between attachment-related avoidance and adaptation to bereavement. *Personality & Social Psychology Bulletin, 30*, 878–890.

Freud, S. (1961). *Letters of Sigmund Freud* (E. L. Freud, Ed.). New York: Basic Books.

Gamino, L. A., Sewell, K. W., & Easterling, L. (2000). Scott and White grief study— phase 2: Toward an adaptive model of grief. *Death Studies, 24*, 633–660.

Gorer, G. D. (1965). *Death, grief, and mourning.* New York: Doubleday.

Guarnaccia, C., Hayslip, B., & Landry, L. P. (1999). Influence of perceived preventability of the death and emotional closeness to the deceased: A test of Bugen's model. *Omega, 39*, 261–276.

Haine, R. A., Ayers, T. S., Sandler, I. N., Wolchik, S., & Weyer, J. (2003). Locus of control and self-esteem as stress-moderators or stress-mediators in parentally bereaved children. *Death Studies, 27*, 619–640.

Hershberger, P. J., & Walsh, W. B. (1990). Multiple role involvements and the adjustment to conjugal bereavement: An exploratory study. *Omega, 21*, 91–102.

Horowitz, M. J., Wilner, N., Marmar, C., & Krupnick, J. (1980). Pathological grief and the activation of latent self images. *American Journal of Psychiatry, 137*, 1157–1162.

Jacobs, S. (1999). *Traumatic grief: Diagnosis, treatment, and prevention.* Philadelphia: Brunner/Mazel.

Kastenbaum, R. (1969). Death and bereavement in later life. In A. H. Kutscher (Ed.), *Death and bereavement* (pp. 27–54). Springfield, IL: Thomas.

Krupp, G., Genovese, F., & Krupp, T. (1986). To have and have not: Multiple identifications in pathological bereavement. *Journal of the American Academy of Psychoanalysis, 14,* 337–348.

Lazarus, R., & Folkman, S. (1984). *Stress, appraisal, and coping.* New York: Springer Publishing.

Lund, D. A. (2001). *Men coping with grief.* Amityville, NY: Baywood.

Main, M., & Solomon, J. (1990). Procedures for identifying infants as disorganized/disoriented during the Ainesworth strange situation. In M. Greenberg, D. Cicchetti, & E. Cummins (Eds.), *Attachment in the preschool years* (pp. 121–160). Chicago: University of Chicago Press.

Martin, T., & Doka, K. (1996). Masculine grief. In K. Doka (Ed.), *Living with grief: After sudden loss* (pp. 161–171). Washington, DC: Taylor & Francis.

Mikulincer, M., & Shaver, P. (2003). The attachment behavioral system in adulthood. In M. Zanna (Ed.), *Advances in experimental social psychology* (pp. 53–152). Washington, DC: American Psychological Association.

Murphy, S. (2000). The use of research findings in bereavement programs: A case study. *Death Studies, 24,* 585–602.

Nolen-Hoeksema, S. (2001). Ruminative coping and adjustment to bereavement. In M. S. Stroebe, R. O. Hansson, W. Stroebe, & H. Schut (Eds.), *Handbook of bereavement research: Consequences, coping, and care* (pp. 545–562). Washington, DC: American Psychological Association.

Nolen-Hoeksema, S., McBride, A., & Larson, J. (1997). Rumination and psychological distress among bereaved partners. *Journal of Personality and Social Psychology, 72,* 855–862.

Nolen-Hoeksema, S., & Morrow, J. (1991). A prospective study of depression and posttraumatic stress symptoms after a natural disaster: The 1989 Loma Prieta earthquake. *Journal of Personality and Social Psychology, 61,* 115–121.

Parkes, C. M. (1972). *Bereavement: Studies of grief in adult life.* New York: International Universities Press.

Parkes, C. M. (2001). A historical overview of the scientific study of bereavement. In M. S. Stroebe, R. O. Hansson, W. Stroebe, & H. Schut (Eds.), *Handbook of bereavement research: Consequences, coping, and care* (pp. 25–45). Washington, DC: American Psychological Press.

Parkes, C. M., & Weiss, R. (1983). *Recovery from bereavement.* New York: Basic Books.

Paul, N. L., & Grosser, G. H. (1965). Operational mourning and its role in conjoint family therapy. *Community Mental Health Journal, 1,* 339–345.

Reich, J., & Zautra, A. (1991). Experimental and measurement approaches to internal control in at-risk older adults. *Journal of Social Issues, 447,* 143–158.

Schnider, K. R., Elhai, J. D., & Gray, M. J. (2007). Coping style use predicts posttraumatic stress and complicated grief symptom severity among college students reporting a traumatic loss. *Journal of Counseling Psychology, 54,* 344–350.

Schut, H., Stroebe, M. S., de Keijser, J., & van den Bout, J. (1997). Intervention for the bereaved: Gender differences in the efficacy of grief counseling. *British Journal of Clinical Psychology, 36,* 63–72.

Schwartzberg, S. S., & Janoff-Bulman, R. (1991). Grief and the search for meaning: Exploring the assumptive worlds of bereaved college students. *Journal of Social and Clinical Psychology, 10,* 270–288.

Sherkat, D. E., & Reed, M. D. (1992). The effects of religion and social support on self-esteem and depression among the suddenly bereaved. *Social Indicators Research, 26,* 259–275.

Shuchter, S. R., & Zisook, S. (1986). Treatment of spousal bereavement: A multidimensional approach. *Psychiatric Annals, 16,* 295–305.

Smith, P. C., Range, L. M., & Ulmer, A. (1991–1992). Belief in afterlife as a buffer in suicidal and other bereavement. *Omega, 24,* 217–225.

Sobel, H., & Worden, J. W. (1982). *Helping cancer patients cope.* New York: Guilford Press.

Stroebe, M. S., Schut, H., & Stroebe, W. (2005). Attachment in coping with bereavement: A theoretical integration. *Review of General Psychology, 9,* 48–66.

Stroebe, M. S., Schut, H., & Stroebe, W. (2006). Who benefits from disclosure? Exploration of attachment style differences in the effects of expressing emotions. *Clinical Psychology Review, 26,* 133–139.

Stroebe, W., Stroebe, M. S., & Abakoumkin, G. (1999). Does differential social support cause sex differences in bereavement outcome? *Journal of Community & Applied Social Psychology, 9,* 1–12.

Stroebe, W., Stroebe, M. S., Abakoumkin, G., & Schut, H. (1996). The role of loneliness and social support in adjustment to loss: A test of attachment versus stress theory. *Journal of Personality & Social Psychology, 70,* 1241–1249.

Tubbs, C., & Boss, P. (2000). An essay for practitioners: Dealing with ambiguous loss. *Family Relations, 49,* 285–286.

Walsh, F., & McGoldrick, M. (1991). *Living beyond loss: Death in the family.* New York: Norton.

Weisman, A. D., & Worden, J. W. (1980). *Psychological screening and intervention with cancer patients.* Boston: Massachusetts General Hospital.

Winnicott, D. (1953). Transitional objects and transitional phenomena. *International Journal of Psychoanalysis, 34,* 89–97.

Worden, J. W. (1996). *Children & grief: When a parent dies.* New York: Guilford Press.

Wortman, C. B., & Silver, R. C. (2001). The myths of coping with loss revisited. In M. S. Stroebe, R. O. Hansson, W. Stroebe, & H. Schut (Eds.), *Handbook of bereavement research: Consequences, coping, and care* (pp. 405–429). Washington, DC: American Psychological Association.

Zisook, S., Paulus, M., Shuchter, S. R., & Judd, L. L. (1997). The many faces of depression following spousal bereavement. *Journal of Affective Disorders, 45,* 85–94.

4

Grief Counseling: Facilitating Uncomplicated Grief

The loss of a significant other causes a broad range of grief reactions, which we have seen are normal after such an experience. Most people are able to cope with these reactions and address the four tasks of mourning on their own, thereby making some kind of an adaptation to the loss. However, some people experience high levels of distress that bring them to counseling. Since an initial high level of distress is one of the best predictors of later distress, it can indicate that the person is at risk for a poor bereavement outcome. In such cases, counseling can often help bring about a more effective adaptation to the loss (Stroebe, Schut, & Stroebe, 2005).

I make a distinction between grief counseling and grief therapy. Counseling involves helping people facilitate uncomplicated, or normal, grief to a healthy adaptation to the tasks of mourning within a reasonable time frame. I reserve the term *grief therapy* for those specialized techniques, described in chapter 6, that are used to help people with abnormal or complicated grief reactions.

To some it may seem presumptuous to suggest that any counseling is needed to help people manage acute grief. Indeed, Freud (1917/1957) saw grieving as a natural process and in "Mourning and Melancholia" wrote that it should not be tampered with. However, grieving has historically been facilitated through the family, religious organizations, funeral rituals, and other social customs. But times change. Today we observe that some people who struggle with the tasks of mourning may seek professional counseling for help with thoughts, feelings, and behaviors with which they are finding it difficult to cope. Others who have not sought out counseling directly often accept an offer of help, especially when they are having difficulty resolving the loss on their own. I see grief counseling as a valid supplement to more traditional facilitations, which may not be as effective with or available to some people. There is always the risk that the formal intervention of a mental health worker may make grief seem pathological, but with skilled counseling this need not be the case.

GOALS OF GRIEF COUNSELING

The overall goal of grief counseling is to help the survivor adapt to the loss of a loved one and be able to adjust to a new reality without him or her. There are specific goals that correspond to the four tasks of mourning: (1) increasing the reality of the loss, (2) helping the counselee deal with both the emotional and behavioral pain, (3) helping the counselee overcome various impediments to readjustment after the loss, and (4) helping the counselee find a way to maintain a bond with the deceased while feeling comfortable reinvesting in life.

Who Does Grief Counseling?

Different types of counselors can be used to facilitate these goals. Parkes, in his 1980 paper "Bereavement Counseling: Does It Work?" outlines three basic types of grief counseling. The first involves professional services provided by trained doctors, nurses, psychologists, or social workers who support a person who has sustained a significant loss. This can be done on an individual basis or in a group setting. The second type of bereavement counseling involves those services in which volunteers are selected and trained, and supported by professionals. Good examples of this are the widow-to-widow programs, one of the earliest of which was established through the Harvard Laboratory for Community Psychiatry (Silverman, 1986). A third type of service involves self-help groups in which bereaved people offer help to other bereaved people, with or without the support of professionals.

Compassionate Friends is such an example. Again, these services can be provided on an individual basis, or in a group counseling setting.

An interesting phenomenon that has occurred with the onset of the hospice movement in the United States is the renewed attention on the area of bereavement. If you look at the guidelines that are set up for hospice care, you will find that one important requirement for a comprehensive hospice program is that it provide counseling and support for all families whose loved ones are dying in the hospice setting, and to other bereaved individuals in the community as well (Beresford, 1993). Although hospices range from palliative care units and free-standing institutions to home care programs, whatever the setting of the care, there is general agreement that comprehensive end-of-life care includes work with the family both before and after the death. Most hospice programs use some combination of professionals and volunteers to do the counseling.

When To Do Grief Counseling

In most instances grief counseling begins, at the earliest, a week or so following the funeral. In general, the first 24 hours is too soon for a counselor to call unless there has been contact prior to the death. The bereaved person is still in a state of numbness or shock and is not ready to come to grips with his or her confusion. In some situations, where there is awareness of an impending death, the counselor can make contact with the family members in advance of the death, reconnect with them briefly at the time of the loss, and offer more extended contact a week or so after the funeral service. Again, there is no set rule, and this time schedule should not be taken as a hard-and-fast rule. This really depends on the circumstances of the death and the role and setting of the grief counseling.

Where Should Grief Counseling Be Done?

Grief counseling does not necessarily have to take place in a professional office, although it might. I have done grief counseling in various parts of the hospital, including the hospital garden and various other informal settings. One setting that can be utilized effectively is the home setting; counselors who make home visits may find that it is the most suitable context for their interventions. Parkes (1980) supports this and says, "Telephone contacts and office consultations are no substitutes for home visits" (p. 5). Even though the counselor will want to make clear the contract with the client and the goals and objectives of their interactions, this does not necessitate that the contacts take place in a more formal office setting. Grief therapy, on the other hand, would be more appropriate in a professional setting rather than in a home environment or in an informal setting.

Who Receives Grief Counseling?

There are basically three approaches to bereavement counseling—one might call them philosophies. The first suggests that bereavement counseling be offered to all individuals who have experienced a death-related loss, particularly to families in which the death has taken a parent or child. The assumption behind this philosophy is that death is a very traumatic event for the people involved and counseling should be offered to them all. While this philosophy is understandable, cost and other factors may make it impossible to offer help on such a universal basis. Furthermore, our research shows that it is not needed by everyone (Worden, 1996). Most do well without our help. Parkes (1998) makes a poignant comment when he says, "There is no evidence that all bereaved people will benefit from counseling; and research has shown *no* benefit to arise from the routine referral of people to counseling for no other reason than that they have suffered bereavement" (p. 18).

The second philosophy assumes that some people need help with their bereavement but wait until they experience difficulty, recognize their need for help, and reach out for assistance. This philosophy is more cost effective than the first, but it requires individuals to experience a degree of distress before help is sought. There is, however, some evidence that people who seek out counseling do better than those to whom counseling is unsolicitedly offered (Stroebe, Hansson, Stroebe, & Schut, 2001).

The third philosophy is based on a preventive mental health model. If we can predict in advance who is likely to have difficulty a year or two following the loss, then we can do something by way of early intervention to preclude a poor adaptation to the loss. This approach was used by Parkes and Weiss (1983) and colleagues in the Harvard Bereavement Study, in which significant predictors identified high-risk widows and widowers less than 45 years of age.

In this project, bereaved widows and widowers were studied descriptively at regular intervals for a period of up to 3 years following the death of the spouse. A group of them who were not doing well 13 and 24 months later was identified, and data collected early in the bereavement were used to define significant predictors of the high-risk population. Below is a description of the high-risk widow, as defined in this seminal study. The focus here is on widows rather than widowers because there are significantly more widows, the ratio being 5:1 in the United States. No one woman in the study met all the at-risk criteria. This is a composite picture, but it gives an idea of the kind of woman who is at risk, and who can be identified early and offered counseling, which may help her bring her grief to a more adequate resolution.

IDENTIFYING THE AT-RISK BEREAVED

The woman who will not handle bereavement well tends to be young, with children living at home and no close relatives living nearby to help form a support network. She is timid and clinging and was overly dependent on her husband or had ambivalent feelings about their relationship, and her cultural and familial background prevents her from expressing her feelings. In the past she reacted badly to separation, and she may have a previous history of depressive illness. Her husband's death causes additional stress in her life—loss of income, a possible move, and difficulties with the children, who are also trying to adjust to the loss. At first she seems to be coping well, but that slowly gives way to intensive pining and feelings of self-reproach and/or anger. Instead of declining, these feelings persist as time goes on (Parkes & Weiss, 1983).

Identification of the high-risk widow or widower was also attempted by Beverley Raphael in another landmark study. While observing widows and widowers in Australia, Raphael (1977) discovered that the following characteristics were significant predictors of the person who would not do well 1 and 2 years later:

1. A high level of perceived non-supportiveness in the bereaved's social network response during the crisis
2. A moderate level of perceived non-supportiveness in social network response to the bereavement crisis occurring together with particularly "traumatic" circumstances of the death
3. A previously highly ambivalent marital relationship with the deceased, traumatic circumstances of the death, and any unmet needs
4. The presence of a concurrent life crisis

At the Clark Institute in Toronto, Sheldon, Cochrane, Vachon, Lyall, Rogers, and Freeman (1981) found that four main groups of predictors were important in explaining adjustment to bereavement in 80 widows. These four groups were sociodemographic variables, personality factors, social support variables, and the meaning of the death event. Of all of these, the sociodemographic factors—being younger and coming from a low socioeconomic background—were among the strongest predictors of later distress.

In the Harvard Child Bereavement Study we looked at predictors of high distress in men and women whose spouses had died, leaving them with school-age children. Those experiencing the highest levels of distress around the first anniversary of the loss were women who had not anticipated the death and who had also experienced high levels of stress and distress 4 months after the death. These were women who had more children under the age of 12 living at home, and who also were experiencing a larger number of life-change events and stressors in the early months following the loss (Worden, 1996).

A predictive approach can also be applied to *family members* other than spouses. Parkes and his colleagues (1983) at St. Christopher's Hospice in England use an eight-variable bereavement risk index to identify family members in special need of support. If several of these dimensions are present in the 4-week post-death assessment, the person is identified as in need of intervention. The dimensions are:

1. More young children at home
2. Lower social class
3. Employment little, if any
4. Anger high
5. Pining high
6. Self-reproach high
7. Lacking current relationships
8. Coping assessment by rater requiring help

Beckwith, Beckwith, Gray, Micsko, Holm, Plummer, and Flaa (1990) used these same predictors in their North Dakota hospice and found those at risk over the first year after spousal loss were younger, with younger children at home, of low socioeconomic status, had fewer close relationships, and had experienced a drop in income.

It would be good if we had one set of predictors that applied to all bereaved populations. Such, however, is not the case. Although there may be overlap, what predicts difficult bereavement in one population may differ from that which predicts difficulty in another group. Clinicians wanting to use a predictive approach need to do careful descriptive studies, gathering measures early in the bereavement, and then do systematic follow-ups with subjects not receiving intervention at selected time intervals in order to see which of the early measures are the best predictors of later difficulty. Predictors should be selected with reference to the important mediators of mourning listed in chapter 3. We used such an approach in our study of parentally bereaved school-age children. In this longitudinal study we identified children who were not doing well 2 years after the death. Using information gathered on these children and their family shortly after the death, we created a highly accurate instrument for early identification of these children, thus enabling early intervention. This instrument and its development can be found in Worden (1996).

COUNSELING PRINCIPLES AND PROCEDURES

Whatever one's philosophy of grief counseling and whatever the setting, there are certain principles and procedures that help make grief counseling effective. The following will serve as guidelines for the counselor so that he or she can help the client work through an acute grief situation and come to a good adaptation.

Principle 1: Help the Survivor Actualize the Loss

When one loses a significant other, even though there may have been some advance warning of the death, there is always a certain sense of unreality, a sense that it did not really happen. Therefore, the first grief task is to come to a more complete awareness that the loss actually has occurred and that the person is dead and will not return. Survivors must accept this reality before they can deal with the emotional impact of the loss.

How do you help someone actualize the loss? One of the best ways is to help survivors talk about the loss. This can be encouraged by the counselor. Where did the death occur? How did it happen? Who told you about it? Where were you when you heard? What was the funeral like? What was said at the service? All these questions are geared to help the person talk specifically about the circumstances surrounding the death. Many people need to go over and over it in their minds, reviewing the events of the loss, before they can actually come to the full awareness that it has happened. This may take some time. Many of the widows we have studied said that it took up to 3 months before they could really begin to believe and understand that their spouse was dead and not going to return. The importance of talking about a loss was recognized by Shakespeare, who, through Macbeth, admonished, "Give Sorrow words; the grief that does not speak knits up the o'erwrought heart and bids it break."

Visiting the gravesite, or the place where the remains reside or are scattered, can also bring home the reality of the loss. Explore with clients whether they ever visit the grave and what it is like for them. If they don't visit the grave, ask what their fantasy about going is. Gravesite visits have their roots in cultural expectations and practices, but they can also give some clue as to where a person is with regard to task I issues. Some people need to be encouraged to visit the grave as part of their grief work. This can be done with care, sensitivity, and an eye to the timing of the suggestion.

The counselor can be a patient listener and can continue encouraging the person to talk about the loss. In many families, when the widow talks about the death, the response is "Don't tell me what happened. I know what happened. Why are you torturing yourself by talking about it?" The family members do not realize that she needs to talk about it, that talking helps her to come to grips with the reality of the death. The counselor is not subject to the same impatience shown by the family and can facilitate the growing awareness of the loss and its impact by encouraging the patient to verbalize memories of the deceased, both current and past.

Principle 2: Help the Survivor to Identify and Experience Feelings

In chapter 1, I outlined a number of feelings that people experience during grief, many of which could be labeled dysphoric. Because of their pain and unpleasantness, many feelings may not be recognized by the survivor or they might not be felt to the degree they need to be in order for an effective resolution to be brought about. Many clients come to see us because they want immediate relief from their pain. They want a pill that will help them attenuate the pain. Helping them to accept and work through their pain is a major part of our intervention. Some feelings that are most problematic to survivors are anger, guilt, anxiety, helplessness, and loneliness.

Anger

When someone you love dies, it's very common to feel angry. "What helped me was people who cared and who listened to me rant and rave," said one man in his 20s whose wife had died. I've suggested that anger probably comes from two sources: from frustration and from a sense of regressive helplessness. Whatever the source, it is true that many people experience intense anger, but they don't always see it as anger toward the deceased. This anger is real, and it must go somewhere, so if it is not directed toward the deceased (the real target), it may be deflected onto other people such as the physician, the hospital staff, the funeral director, the clergy person, or a family member.

If the anger is not directed toward the deceased or displaced onto someone else, it may be retroflected, turned inward, and experienced as depression, guilt, or lowered self-esteem. In extreme cases, retroflected anger may result in suicidal behavior, either in thought or in action. The competent grief counselor will always inquire about suicidal ideation. A simple question like "Has it been so bad that you've thought of hurting yourself?" is more apt to have positive results than to prompt someone to take self-destructive action. Suicidal thoughts do not always represent retroflected anger. They can also come from a desire to rejoin the deceased.

Some of the angry feelings stem from the intense pain experienced during bereavement, and the counselor can help the client get in touch with this. Most of the time, however, it is not productive to attack the anger issue directly. For example, in many cases if you ask, "Are you angry that he died?" the person will say, "How can I be angry he died? He didn't want to die. He had a heart attack." Or people will respond as a widow I once worked did, with: "How can I be angry? He was an active Christian layman. He had a strong belief in an afterlife and he's much better off." The fact is that she was much worse off. He left her with many worries, cares, and concerns, and we did not have to scratch very far beneath the surface to find an intense well of anger at him for dying and leaving her with all these problems.

Some people will not admit to angry feelings if you inquire directly about anger. Either they are not consciously aware of the feeling or they are adhering to the cultural admonition not to speak ill of the dead. One indirect technique that I have found beneficial is to use the low-key word "miss." I sometimes ask a survivor, "What do you miss about him?" and the person will respond with a list that often brings on sadness and tears. After a short while, I will ask, "What don't you miss about him?" There is usually a pause and a startled look, and then the person says something like, "Well, I never thought about it that way, but now that you mention it, I don't miss his drinking too much, not coming home for dinner on time," and many more things. Then the person begins to acknowledge some of his or her more negative feelings. It is important not to leave clients with these negative feelings, but to help them find a better balance between the negative and positive feelings they have for the deceased so that they see that the negative feelings do not preclude the positive feelings, and vice versa. The counselor plays an active role in achieving this. Another useful word is the word "disappointment." I ask, "How did she disappoint you?" It is rare that any close relationship does not have its share of disappointments. The word "unfair" can also be useful here.

In some cases, all the person has is negative feelings, and it is important to help him or her get in contact with the corresponding positive feelings that exist, even though these may be few in number. Holding only negative feelings may be a way of avoiding sadness that would become conscious upon admission of any significant loss. Admitting positive feelings is a necessary part of the process of achieving an adequate and healthy resolution to one's grief. Here the problem is not the suppression of a dysphoric feeling such as anger, but suppressed feelings of affection.

Mike was 23 when his alcoholic father died. Over the years Mike had felt mistreated by him. "He created in me a dependency and I kept coming back to him for something I never got. After he died I wanted to resent him." Three years after the death, Mike was befriended by an older man. One evening as he was preparing to retire, the man touched him in a way that his father had years earlier when putting him to bed. This touch triggered off a very vivid image of his father's funeral and of his father lying in the casket. Accompanying this image was an intense feeling of sadness, and an awareness of how much he missed his father's love. He tried to counter this feeling by telling himself that it was not his father lying in the casket in his mind's eye, but this didn't work. The sadness prevailed. "How can I explain that I miss my father's love," he asked me when he came for therapy, "when I never had it?" Through our work he was able to get a more balanced sense of his feelings. Gradually he found resolution and relief in the thought "I loved him, but he was unable, because of his own upbringing, to express his love to me."

Focusing strongly on negativity may put mourners at greater risk for complications in the bereavement adjustment and make them suitable for therapeutic intervention (Neimeyer, 2000). There is no question that a balanced outlook is the healthiest, and a skilled clinician is necessary to help achieve this. We learn in therapy training that timing is paramount in making interpretations. Asking a mourner who is focusing on negativity to consider possible positive affects or growth-related meaning from the loss must be done carefully. Bringing this up too soon may make mourners feel that they have been disrespected and that their loss experience has been invalidated (Gamino & Sewell, 2004).

Guilt

There are a number of things that can cause feelings of guilt after a loss. For example, survivors can feel guilt because they did not provide better medical care, they should not have allowed an operation, they did not consult a doctor sooner, or they did not choose the right hospital. Parents whose children die are highly vulnerable to feelings of guilt that are focused on the fact that they could not help the child stop hurting or prevent the child from dying. Some feel guilty that they are not experiencing what they believe to be the appropriate amount of sadness. Whatever the reasons, most of this guilt is irrational and centers around the circumstances of the death. The counselor can help here because irrational guilt yields to reality testing. If someone says, "I didn't do enough," I'll ask, "What did you do?" and the person will answer, "I did that." And then I'll say, "What else did you do?" "Well, I did this." "What else?" "Well, I did that." And then more things will occur to the person, and he or she will say, "I did this, and this, and this." After awhile the person will come to the conclusion, "Maybe I did all I could do under the circumstances."

However, there is such a thing as real guilt, real culpability, and this is much more difficult to work with. On some occasions I have used psychodrama techniques in a group therapy situation in order to help the person work through this kind of guilt. In one of these groups, Vicki, a young woman, confessed that on the night her father died, she had decided to stay with her boyfriend and was not at home with her family. She felt she had wronged her father, her mother, her brother, and herself. In the psychodrama, I had her choose different group members to be the individual family members, including herself. Then I had her interact with each of these people, confessing her sense of wrongdoing and, in turn, hearing the response from each of the principals in the drama. The session was very moving, but perhaps the most moving moment came at the end when Vicki embraced the person who portrayed her. At that point she experienced a kind of reconciliation and healing within her own being.

Anxiety and Helplessness

People left behind after a death often feel very anxious and fearful. Much of this anxiety stems from feelings of helplessness, the feeling that they cannot get along by themselves or survive alone. This is a regressive experience that usually eases with time and the realization that, even though it is difficult, they can manage. The counselor's role is to help them recognize, through cognitive restructuring, the ways they managed on their own before the loss, and this helps to throw these feelings of anxiety and helplessness into some sort of perspective.

A second source of anxiety is increased personal death awareness (Worden, 1976). Personal death awareness is the awareness not of death in general, or of someone else's death, but of one's own death. This is something all of us have, something that lingers in the back of our consciousness. From time to time it comes forward, for example when we lose a contemporary or have a near accident on the highway.

For most of us, our own personal death awareness exists at a very low level. However, with the loss of a significant other, whether it is a close friend or a family member, there is usually a heightened awareness of our own mortality, which results in existential anxiety. The counselor can take several directions, depending on the client. For some, it is better not to address this issue directly but to let it go and assume that the death awareness will mitigate and fade. With others, it is helpful to address the issue directly and get them to talk about their fears and apprehensions regarding their own death. Articulating this to the counselor may give clients a sense of relief as they unburden their concerns and explore options. In any case, the counselor should use his or her best judgment to decide which choice is most appropriate.

Sadness

There are some occasions when sadness and crying need to be encouraged by the counselor. Frequently people refuse to cry in front of friends for fear of taxing the friendship, or losing the friendship and sustaining yet another loss. Some suppress their tears in social situations in order to avoid criticism from others. One widow overheard an acquaintance say, "It's been 3 months. Surely she should be pulling herself together and get out of that self-pitying mood." Needless to say, this did not help her with her sadness, nor did it give her the support she needed.

Some people fear that crying openly will not look dignified or that it will embarrass others. Stella lost her 4-year-old daughter suddenly, and the funeral was held in the home of her Old Yankee in-laws some distance from where the death occurred. Stella was used to open expressions of grief, but her mother-in-law so intimidated her with her stoic presence at the funeral that Stella not only suppressed her own sadness but also ordered her aged mother to do the same, lest she embarrass her husband's family. Counseling helped her put this into perspective and gave her permission to cry, which she needed and was denying herself.

Crying alone may be useful, but it may not be as efficacious as crying with someone and receiving support. "Merely crying, however, is not enough. The bereaved need help in identifying the meaning of the tears, and this meaning will change . . . as the grief work progresses" (Simos, 1979, p. 89).

It is important that the counselor not be satisfied simply with the expression of vehement emotions. *Experiencing* the affect is the focus of this task, not just *expressing* the affect. In fact, some who are the most emotionally vehement in the early months after a loss are likely to be the most expressively vehement a year later (Parkes, 2001; Wortman & Silver, 1989). Focus is essential. Sadness must be accompanied by an awareness of what one has lost, anger needs to be properly and effectively targeted, guilt needs to be evaluated and resolved, and anxiety needs to be identified and managed. Without this focus, the counselor is not being effective, regardless of the amount or degree of feeling that is being evoked (van der Hart, 1988).

Along with the need for focus comes the need for balance. The be-reaved must achieve some balance that allows them to experience their pain, sense of loss, loneliness, fear, anger, guilt, and sadness; to let in their anguish and let out their expressions of such anguish; to know and feel in the very core of their souls what has happened to them; and yet to do all this in doses, so they will not be overwhelmed by such feelings. (Schwartz-Borden, 1986, p. 500)

Principle 3: Assist Living Without the Deceased

This principle involves helping people adapt to a loss by facilitat-ing their ability to live without the deceased and to make decisions independently. To do this the counselor may use a problem-solving approach that asks, What are the problems the survivor faces and how can they be solved? Problem solving is one of the coping skills mentioned in chapter 3. Some individuals have better-developed problem-solving skills than others. The deceased played varying roles in the survivor's life, and the ability to adjust to the loss is in part determined by these various roles. One role that is important in families is the decision-making role, and this role often causes prob-lems after the loss of a spouse. In many relationships one spouse, often the man, is the primary decision maker. When he dies, the wife may feel "at sixes and sevens" when it comes to making de-cisions independently. The counselor can help her learn effective coping and decision-making skills so she will be able to take over the role formerly filled by her husband and, in doing so, reduce her emotional distress.

Another important role that needs to be addressed when one is dealing with loss of a partner is that of the loss of a sexual partner. Some counselors are hesitant to address this important issue, or it can be overemphasized to the point that the survivor experiences dis-comfort. Rita, a 60-year-old housewife, was asked to join a widows' group after the sudden death of her husband. A well-meaning but inept counselor told her the group would help her find new relation-ships and would help her with her sexual needs. This was not what this rather repressed middle-aged woman wanted to hear, and she turned down what could have been a supportive group experience had the issue been presented in a different way. Being able to discuss emerging sexual feelings, including the need to be touched and to be held, is important. The counselor can suggest ways to meet these needs that are commensurate with the client's personality and value system. There are those whose only sexual experiences have been with their deceased spouse, so the counselor may need to address any anxiety concerning new sexual experiences.

As a general principle, the recently bereaved should be discouraged from making major life-changing decisions, such as selling property, changing jobs or careers, or adopting children, too soon after a death. Good judgment is difficult to exercise during acute grief, when there is increased risk of a maladaptive response. "Don't move or sell things, for you may be running away. Work through grief where things are familiar," advised one widow in our widows' group.

Another widow moved to Boston from New York right after her husband's suicide. "I thought it would make me miss him less," she told me. After a year in Boston she found it did not work and she sought out therapy. One area she had not adequately assessed was her support system, which was large in New York but very meager in Boston. In discouraging the bereaved from making major life-changing decisions too soon, be careful that you are not promoting a sense of helplessness. Rather, communicate that they will be quite capable of making decisions and taking actions when they are ready and that they should not make decisions just to reduce the pain.

Principle 4: Help Find Meaning in the Loss

One of the goals of grief counseling is to help clients find meaning in the death of a loved one. Counselors can facilitate this. The process may be as important as the meaning they find. Schwartzberg and Halgin (1991) write:

> The specific ways in which people find meaning—strategies such as, "there's a spiritual order to the universe," "she drank too much," or "I needed to learn something"—may be less salient than the process itself. In other words, the ability to reascribe meaning to a changed world

may be more significant than the specific content by which that need is fulfilled. (p. 245)

Some who cannot find the answer to why the death occurred become involved in philanthropic, political, or caretaking activities related to the manner of death that took the loved one. Parents whose young adult child was killed in an off-campus house fire have set up a Web site memorial in his honor, have established a scholarship in his name, and have lobbied for a change in smoke alarm inspection procedures in the community in which he was killed. In the context of what seems to them a senseless and unnecessary death, these activities help them to believe and say that their son's death was not in vain.

Finding meaning stemming from the loss involves grappling not only with the question why this happened, but also why did this happen to me? How am I different because of this loss? Some losses challenge a person's sense of him- or herself by challenging the notion that he or she is worthy. This can seem an illusion caused by the impact of loss, particularly traumatic loss. Loss of self-esteem often goes hand in hand with loss of self-efficacy and the best intervention is to help the person reestablish a sense of control by heightening awareness of areas in which his or her attempts to exercise control have been successful.

Principle 5: Facilitate Emotional Relocation of the Deceased

By facilitating emotional relocation, the counselor can help the survivor find a new place in his or her life for the lost loved one, a place that will allow the survivor to move forward with life and form new relationships. Reminiscing is one way to gradually divest the emotional energy tied up with the deceased. Some people do not need any encouragement, but there are many who do, and this is particularly true with the loss of a spouse. Some people are hesitant to form these new relationships because they believe this will dishonor the memory of their departed spouse. Others hesitate because they feel that no one can ever fill the place of the lost person. To a certain extent this is true, but the counselor can help them realize that although the lost person can never be replaced, it is all right to fill the void with a new relationship.

There are those who, rather than hesitating, quickly jump into new relationships, and the counselor can help interpret how appropriate this is. "If I can just get remarried everything will be okay," said one widow shortly after the death. Many times this action is not appropriate because it can hinder adequate resolution of grief and possibly lead to a divorce, which would be an additional loss. I once met a man who picked out his next wife at his wife's funeral. He successfully pursued this person and very soon had replaced his wife. It was my sense that this was a bit bizarre and inappropriate. Rushing in for a quick replacement may make people feel better for a time, but it may also prevent them experiencing the intensity and the depth of the loss. This intensity needs to be experienced before the grieving can be completed. Also, for the relationship to work, the new person must be recognized and appreciated for him- or herself.

Principle 6: Provide Time to Grieve

Grieving requires time. It is the process of adjusting to a world without the deceased and such a process is gradual. One impediment can come in the form of family members who are eager to get over the loss and its pain and to move back into a normal routine. Children sometimes say to their mothers, "Come on, you've got to get back to living. Dad wouldn't want you to mope around all the time." They don't realize that it takes time to accommodate to the loss and all its ramifications. In grief counseling, the counselor can help interpret this to the family; this is something that may seem obvious but, surprisingly, is not always obvious to family members.

I have found that certain points in time are particularly difficult, and I encourage those who are doing grief counseling to recognize these critical time periods and get in touch with the person if there is no regular ongoing contact. Three months after the death is one such time point. I worked with one family for a number of months during the father's struggle with cancer. After his death I attended the funeral. The father was a minister, and there could not have been any more support for the widow and her three children than there was at the funeral and afterward. However, when I contacted the widow at the 3-month period, she was incredibly angry because no one was calling anymore and people were avoiding her, and she was displacing her anger onto her husband's successor, the new minister of the church.

Another critical time is around the first anniversary of the death. If the counselor does not have regular contact with the survivor, I would encourage contacting her or him around that first anniversary. All kinds of thoughts and feelings come to the fore during that time, and often a person will need extra support. Counselors are encouraged to make a note on their calendar as to when the death occurred and then to make arrangements to contact by looking ahead to these critical points. For many, the holidays are toughest. One effective intervention is to help the client anticipate this and prepare in advance. "Thinking through Christmas before it occurred definitely helped me," said one young widowed mother.

Again, how often you contact the survivor depends on the relationship you have with him and on the counseling contract, be it formal or informal. However, the point I am making is that grieving takes time and the counselor needs to see the intervention role as one that may, of necessity, stretch over some time, though the actual contacts may not be frequent.

Principle 7: Interpret "Normal" Behavior

The seventh principle is understanding and interpreting normal grief behaviors. After a significant loss many people have the sense that they are going crazy. This can be heightened because they often are distracted and experience things that are not normally part of their lives. If the counselor has a clear understanding of what normal grief behavior is, then he or she can give the bereaved some reassurance about the normality of these new experiences. It is rare for a person to decompensate and become psychotic as the result of a loss, but there are exceptions. They sometimes occur when a person has had previous psychotic episodes and among those who have a diagnosis of borderline personality disorder. However, it is quite common for people to *feel* they are going crazy, particularly people who have not sustained a major loss before. And if a counselor understands, for example, that hallucinations, heightened distractibility, and a preoccupation with the deceased are normal behaviors, then the person can be quite re-assured by the counselor. A listing of commonly found grief behaviors can be found in chapter 1.

Principle 8: Allow for Individual Differences

There is a wide range of behavioral responses to grieving. Just as it is important not to expect everyone who is dying to die in a similar man-ner, likewise it is important not to expect all people who are grieving to grieve in the same way. Grieving is a phenomenon with tremen-dous interpersonal variability, and with strong individual differences in the intensity of affective reactions, the degree of impairment, and the length of time a person experiences the painful affect of the loss (Schwartzberg & Halgin, 1991). However, this is sometimes difficult for families to understand. They are uncomfortable when one fam-ily member deviates from the behavior of the rest, or an individual who is experiencing something different from the rest of the family may be uneasy about his or her own behavior. Counselors can help interpret this variability to the family who expects everyone to grieve the same way.

Once, when lecturing in the Midwest, I was approached after the meeting by a young woman wanting to talk about her family. Her par-ents had recently lost an infant, and she and her mother were grieving this loss, but she was afraid that her father was not grieving. She was concerned that he might not adequately grieve and as a result have an arrested grief reaction. As I spoke with her, I learned that the father had asked to carry the tiny casket on his shoulders, all the way from the church through the town out to the cemetery. His daughter said that ever since the death, her father, a farmer, had spent long hours out on his tractor alone in the fields. It was my sense that her father was doing his grieving, but he was doing it in his own way, and my hunch was later confirmed in a letter from her.

Principle 9: Examine Defenses and Coping Styles

The ninth principle involves helping clients examine their particu-lar defenses and coping styles, because they will be heightened by a significant loss. (A paradigm for understanding coping styles can be found in chapter 3.) This is most easily accomplished after a trust develops between the client and the counselor, when clients are more willing to discuss their behavior. Some of these defenses and coping styles portend competent behavior; others do not. For example, a person who copes by using alcohol or drugs excessively is probably not making an effective adjustment to the loss:

> The utility of small amounts of alcohol for sleep, diminishing anxiety, and obliterating ruminative thinking predispose the grieving survivor to find comfort in drinking, at times leading to gradual escalation and eventually to degrees of uncontrolled or obligatory consumption. At greatest risk are those bereaved who are recovering alcoholics or who have strong family histories of alcoholism. (Shuchter & Zisook, 1987, p. 184)

The counselor needs to be alert to this and to inquire about alcohol or other drug use and/or abuse. Heavy use of drugs or alcohol can intensify the experience of grief and depression and impair the bereavement process. If a problem exists or is suspected, the counselor would do well to pursue aggressive treatment, which might involve the resources of groups like Alcoholics Anonymous or Narcotics Anonymous.

Overall, active emotional coping tends to be the most effective way to deal with problems, including the problems of bereavement. This includes the use of humor, the ability to reframe or redefine a difficult situation, adequate emotional regulation skills, and the ability to accept social support. Avoidant emotional coping tends to be the least effective, especially when it comes to resolving a problem. Blame, distraction, denial, social withdrawal, and substance abuse may make the person feel better in the short haul, but these are not effective strategies for problem resolution.

Someone who withdraws and refuses to look at pictures of the deceased or keep anything around that is a reminder of the deceased may have a coping style that is not healthy. The counselor can highlight these coping styles and help the client evaluate their effectiveness. Then, together, client and counselor can explore other possible coping avenues that may be more effective in lowering distress and resolving problems.

Principle 10: Identify Pathology and Refer

The tenth and final principle on this list is identifying those in serious trouble and knowing when to refer. A person doing grief counseling may be able to identify the existence of pathology that has been triggered by the loss and the subsequent grieving and, having spotted such difficulty, may find it necessary to make a professional referral. This particular role is often called the gatekeeper role. For some people, grief counseling or the facilitation of grief is not sufficient, and the loss (or the way that they are handling the loss) may give rise to more difficult problems. A small subset (10%–15%) of bereaved people will continue to struggle and develop some type of complicated mourning such as chronic or prolonged grief reactions. Some of these problems may require special interventions discussed in chapter 5. Because these difficulties require special techniques and interventions plus an understanding of psychodynamics, dealing with them may not be within the purview and skill of the grief counselor. And even if it is, the strategies, techniques, and goals of intervention may change. It is important for grief counselors to recognize their limitations and to know when to refer a person for grief therapy or other psychotherapy.

Before we leave the principles and practices of grief counseling, platitudes should be mentioned. These are often dispensed by well-meaning friends and occasionally by a counselor. Platitudes, for the most part, are not helpful. Many of the women in our studies said, "When somebody came up to me and said, 'I know how you feel,' this comment made me want to scream and shout back at them, 'You don't know how I feel, you couldn't possibly know how I feel, you've never lost a husband.'" Comments like "Be a brave little boy," "Life is for the living," "This will soon end," "You're standing up well," "It will be over in a year," "You'll be fine," and "Keep a stiff upper lip" are generally not at all helpful. Even "I'm sorry" can close off further discussion. And there are those who, in an attempt to make somebody feel better, start speaking about the losses and tragedies they have had in their own lives, perhaps unaware that comparing tragedies is not helpful. People in pain make us feel helpless. This helplessness can be acknowledged in a simple statement like "I don't know what to say to you."

USEFUL TECHNIQUES

Any counseling or therapy should be based on a solid theoretical understanding of human personality and behavior, not be merely a set of techniques. However, there are several techniques I have found useful in doing grief counseling, and I want to mention them here.

A. Evocative Language

The counselor can use tough words that evoke feelings, for example, "Your son died" versus "You lost your son." This language helps people with reality issues surrounding the loss and can stimulate some of the painful feelings that need to be felt. Also, speaking of the deceased in the past tense ("Your husband was. . . . ") can be helpful.

B. Use of Symbols

Have the mourner bring photos of the deceased to the counseling sessions. This not only helps the counselor get a clearer sense of who the person was but also creates a sense of immediacy of the deceased and provides a concrete focus for talking to the deceased rather than talking about him or her. Other symbols I have found helpful are letters written by the deceased, audio- or videotapes of the deceased, and articles of clothing and jewelry that belonged to the deceased.

C. Writing

Have the survivor write a letter or letters expressing thoughts and feelings to the deceased. This can help survivors take care of unfinished business by expressing the things that they need to say to the deceased. I encourage extensive letter writing, including writing a farewell letter to the deceased. Translating experiences into language and constructing a coherent narrative of the event enables thoughts and feelings to be integrated, sometimes leading to a sense of resolution and fewer negative feelings associated with the experience (O'Connor, Nikoletti, Kristjanson, Loh, & Willcock, 2003). Keeping a journal of one's grief experience or writing poetry can also facilitate the expression of feelings and lend personal meaning to the experience of loss. Lattanzi and Hale (1984) have written a good article on the various uses of writing with the bereaved.

D. Drawing

Like writing, drawing pictures that reflect one's feelings as well as experiences with the deceased can also be helpful. This is a very good technique to use with bereaved children, but it works with adults as well. Drawings are less susceptible to defensive distortions than talking. Irwin (1991) has identified four advantages to using art in bereavement counseling. It helps facilitate feelings, identify conflicts that the mourner may be unaware of, heighten awareness of what the person lost, and identify where the person is in the mourning process.

Schut, de Keijser, van den Bout, and Stroebe (1996) have used drawings for grief therapy with inpatient groups in the Netherlands and found it to be effective. They employ music-guided visualizations of fantasies to stimulate feelings and then have patients paint what they are feeling. This activity is a part of multiple modalities used with these patients.

Turetsky and Hays (2003) have developed an art therapy model for the prevention and treatment of unresolved grief during midlife. Although this is basically a psychotherapeutic intervention, it has been found useful in helping people identify unresolved losses from earlier life that are impinging on their present functioning and move toward a better resolution.

E. Role-Playing

Helping the bereaved to role-play various situations that they fear or feel awkward about is one way to build skills—something that is very useful in working with task III issues. The counselor can enter into the role-playing, either as a facilitator or to model possible new behaviors for the client.

F. Cognitive Restructuring

Cognitive restructuring may be necessary because our thoughts influence our feelings, particularly the covert thoughts and self-talk that constantly go on in our minds. By helping the client identify these thoughts and reality test them for accuracy or overgeneralization, the counselor can help to lessen the dysphoric feelings triggered by certain irrational thoughts such as "No one will ever love me again," a thought that is certainly not provable in the present. For a further discussion of this approach, see *Mind Over Mood* by Greenberger and Padesky (1995).

G. Memory Books

One activity a bereaved family can do together is make a memory book of the lost family member. This book can include stories about family events, memorabilia such as snapshots and other photographs, and poems and drawings made by various family members, including the children. This activity can help the family reminisce and eventually mourn a more realistic image of the dead person. In addition, children can go back and revisit this memory book in order to reintegrate the loss into their growing and changing lives.

H. Directed Imagery

Helping people imagine the deceased, either with eyes closed or visualizing their presence in an empty chair, and then encouraging them to say what they need to say to the deceased can be a very powerful technique. The power comes not from the imagery, but from being in the present and talking to the person rather than talking about the person. Brown (1990) provides a good overview and techniques for using guided imagery with bereaved individuals.

I. Metaphors

Another technique that can be useful in grief counseling is the use of metaphor as a visual aid. Schwartz-Borden (1992) talks about metaphor as a useful tool for lowering resistance to the pain of bereavement when patients cannot directly confront feelings surrounding the death. Metaphors offer a more acceptable symbolic representation through which the mourner may express feelings and work through the second task of mourning. The use of metaphor allows the grieving person to focus on a graphic image that may symbolize his or her experience in a more acceptable and less painful way. One particularly helpful image Schwartz-Borden uses is that of amputation and the phantom pain associated with that image of loss.

The purpose of all these techniques is to encourage the fullest expression of thoughts and feelings regarding the loss, including regrets and disappointments. Additional techniques and grief rituals can be found in the article by Castle and Phillips (2003), which also discusses which ones mourners found the most useful.

THE USE OF MEDICATION

There has been considerable discussion about the use of medication in the management of acute normal grief. The consensus is that medication ought to be used sparingly and focused on giving relief from anxiety or from insomnia as opposed to providing relief from depressive symptoms. The late Thomas P. Hackett, chief of psychiatry at Massachusetts General Hospital, had considerable experience treating bereaved people. He used anti-anxiety agents to treat both anxiety and insomnia (Hackett, 1974). However, in administering any pharmaceuticals to patients undergoing an acute grief reaction, it is particularly important to keep any potentially lethal quantities of such drugs out of their hands.

It is usually inadvisable to give antidepressant medications to people undergoing an acute grief reaction. These antidepressants take a long time to work, they rarely relieve normal grief symptoms, and they could pave the way for an abnormal grief response, though this has yet to be proved through controlled studies. The exception would be in cases of major depressive episodes.

Raphael, Minkov, and Dobson (2001) affirm that although our psychological understanding of bereavement has increased, there is not yet a good basis for biological intervention. Pharmacological approaches should, for the most part, only be provided where there is an established disorder for which they are indicated. I would concur with this. Psychiatric disorders precipitated by a death often require psychopharmacological intervention, and these are discussed in chapter 5 under "Exaggerated Grief Reactions."

GRIEF COUNSELING IN GROUPS

Bereavement counseling can be done within the context of a group. This not only is very efficient but can also be an effective way to offer the emotional support the bereaved person is seeking. The following are guidelines for setting up a group and for making the group work effectively.

Choose a Group Format

There are several decisions that need to be made about purpose and structure when one is establishing a group. What is the group's purpose? Bereavement groups usually exist for one or more of the following: emotional support, education, or social purposes. Sometimes groups begin for one purpose, which then evolves into another. Groups that begin for emotional support may continue with the same people for a period of time and become more social in their purpose, even though emotional support is still offered. Although each of these purposes can be valuable, I am a strong advocate of groups that are set up for emotional support.

How will the group be structured? Some groups are closed ended, meaning they exist for a limited time period and people enter and leave the group at the same time. Other groups are open ended with no definite ending. People come and go as the group fulfills their individual needs. There are pros and cons for each type of group structure. In open-ended groups it is more difficult to bring new members up to speed since they do not know the history of important actions and breakthroughs that have occurred prior to their arrival. Also, as people are added, a sense of trust must be developed anew among the members.

What will the logistics of the group be? The number of meetings, length of meetings, size of the group, and location and cost of meetings are all important decisions that need to be made before the sessions begin. The Hospice of Pasadena has closed-ended groups of 8 to 10 people who meet for purposes of education and emotional support. The groups are facilitated by co-leaders, and they meet weekly for eight 90-minute sessions. Members are asked to contribute financially in the belief that this will encourage attendance and motivate people to get more out of the group.

Prescreen Participants

A key factor in making a group work is the selection of its members. There is much to say for homogeneity—putting together people who have had similar losses, for example, a group for bereaved spouses or one for bereaved parents. However, some bereavement programs are not large enough or do not serve areas where there is a sufficient number of people sharing similar losses to have a homogeneous group. If so, try to have at least two people with similar types of losses in a group. If there will be one widower in a group of widows, it is helpful to have a second widower so that the first doesn't feel like the group deviant or the odd person out. The same holds true for including at least two people with other types of losses.

Another factor in selection is how recent the loss is. It is important not to include people whose loss was 6 or fewer weeks earlier. Most people this early in bereavement are not ready for a group experience. Some bereavement groups have potential members wait until 6 months after the loss to join. However, some time spread can be useful. A newly widowed woman can learn something from one who is further along in her bereavement, and who can model how one might move forward in terms of adaptation to loss.

It is essential to rule out serious pathology when people are being selected for membership in bereavement groups. Those who have serious pathological and emotional problems are much better served by individual counseling or therapy.

In selection there are two kinds of losses that may present particular problems, and these potential group members ought to be carefully considered before they are selected for inclusion. One type is multiple losses. People who have lost a number of loved ones over a short period of time often are so overwhelmed by their grief that they can't participate effectively in a bereavement group. These might be people who have lost many family members suddenly in an accident or a house fire, or they could be people who have sustained a number of losses in a short period of time.

Losses that are difficult to talk about, such as suicide, may also present problems in bereavement groups. Including one person whose loved one died by suicide can make other people in the group very anxious, and this should be taken into account during the selection process. It would be better to include at least two people who are survivors of a person who died by suicide. The same consideration applies to losses from AIDS. Specific groups for the survivors of those who have taken their own lives and victims of AIDS can be very effective.

Define Expectations

People come to the group with various expectations, and if the group does not meet these expectations, people will be disappointed and may not return. This is not only unfortunate for the individual, but also demoralizing to the group when someone doesn't return. Before the first group meeting, the intake worker who is interviewing people for group selection can shape people's expectations and deal with any misconceptions or unrealistic fears about group membership. Recently a woman approached us about joining our hospice bereavement group, and we referred her to another group because she clearly wanted anonymity. In our group everyone is encouraged to share as much as they want, and the non-sharing person would clearly not fit into the group. We referred her to a larger group that had more of an educational focus than a support focus, and where she could find the anonymity she wanted. When selecting people for a bereavement group, be sure to deal with their expectations up front.

Establish Ground Rules

Ground rules are rules that are laid out by the group leader right at the start, and they serve several purposes. They provide structure, which can help members feel safe. Knowing that there are certain rules regarding behavior and deportment can add to a sense of support. Ground rules also help leaders with control. For example, if a ground rule states that everybody gets a fair share of time to talk about his or her personal experience and one group member is taking up an inordinate amount of time, the leader can cite the ground rule to make the sharing more equitable. Or if someone in the group has broken the ground rule of confidentiality, the leader can address that issue openly. Always explain the ground rules in the first session and reiterate them in the first couple of group sessions.

Examples of ground rules we use in our bereavement support groups are:

1. Members are expected to attend each of the sessions and to be on time.
2. Information shared in the group stays in the group. When outside the group, members are not free to talk about another group member's experience.
3. People are free to share as much or as little about their loss as they choose.
4. Everybody gets equal time to share his or her experience. This rule helps avoid the problem of one person monopolizing the group's attention.
5. We do not give advice unless it's asked for. It's very easy in group situations, particularly in bereavement groups, for people to give advice. Generally, the advice is not solicited and is not appreciated.

When ground rules are established and expectations are shaped during the screening interview, people arrive at the group knowing that it will be a safe environment, that no one's experience is more or less important or valuable than someone else's, that each person will have time to share as much or as little as he or she chooses, and that they will not be told what they should be feeling or given unwanted advice.

Determine Leadership Approach

A fifth factor that makes groups work is effective leadership, and there are different formats to choose from. Some groups are run only by bereaved individuals. For example, in Compassionate Friends, bereaved parents lead groups for other bereaved parents. Other groups are led by mental health care professionals, and a third model of leadership encompasses groups led by laypeople, but with professional backup. Professional backup gives the lay leader someone to consult with if questions arise about individuals or group interactions. At the Hospice of Pasadena, groups are led by trained mental health professionals with co-leaders who are students in training for one of the mental health professions.

Among the various styles of leadership, some may be more effective than others, depending on the purpose of the group. Some leaders are more active, while others are more passive. I believe that it is most effective for an emotional support bereavement group leader to be active early in the life of the group, and then, as the group bonds and indigenous leadership emerges from within the group, the stated leader can retreat and become less active. Early on, a passive leader can provoke feelings of anxiety on the part of group members, especially when the group is new. The style of leadership depends, of course, on the goals of the group. If the goal is educational, then the designated leader may serve as more of a lecturer or informant. If the purpose is emotional support, the leader's role is to facilitate its development by making sure that people share their stories and find support and encouragement from the other group members. A group set up for the purpose of social interaction would again require a different kind of leader.

The issue of co-leadership is important in any discussion of leadership. Should there be one leader or more than one? When groups are large, co-leadership is essential. If a group uses the co-leadership model, it's important for the leaders to maintain clear and open communication with each other. I suggest they meet shortly after the group sessions and debrief. Tensions that may be subtle and disruptive to the group can arise between leaders. This is one way to prevent this from happening.

It is important that the leader avoid choosing favorites in a group. A group replicates family dynamics, and people bring whatever experiences they've had with their own siblings and parents. These feelings and experiences emerge in group life. It's not unusual for someone to want to be the special person in the leader's life, and this can create difficulties in a group if it's allowed to happen. The leader needs to be aware of this and to turn down special invitations or favors offered by individual members of the group. The leader also needs to be aware of his or her own issues that would make special deals personally desirable. It's also important for any private meetings between the leader and individuals in the group to be discussed openly at the next group meeting.

Understand Interpersonal Dynamics

What do people want when they come together in any kind of a group, whether it is a bereavement, political, or therapy group? Following Schutz (1967), I believe there are three needs that, at some level of awareness, are on the minds of people when they participate in groups.

1. *Inclusion.* Most people coming in new to a group will look around and ask themselves, "Do I fit?" and "Are these my kind of people?" Unless they can answer in the affirmative, they probably won't come back for a second session. Even if they do come back, this concern will still be present in the early sessions in any group experience.

2. *Control.* A second concern has to do with control. "Am I important?" "Do I matter in this group?" "Does what I say make a difference?" "To what degree can I influence this group?" or "To what degree will I be influenced by other members in this group?" are questions members may ask themselves. Just as it is important for people to feel that they fit into a group situation, it's important for people to feel that they have some degree of influence over other members of the group. If they don't, they're likely not to complete the course of group counseling.

3. *Affection.* The third thing people are looking for in group participation is affection. I'm using the word "affection" broadly. "Am I cared for?" "Do people really care what happens to me?" Affection needs tend to be met only as a group develops a sense of identity and cohesiveness. The degree of caring varies. In some groups a strong sense of affection develops among

the various members. People really do care and feel cared for. In other groups this sense of affection is much less.

To summarize, people want to feel safe, and people want to feel important. If problem behaviors arise that are disruptive, it is important to raise the question "Is this person not feeling safe? Is this person not feeling important?" Addressing these issues may help to attenuate problem behavior.

Handle Disruptive Behaviors Effectively

There are several behaviors that are disruptive to groups and that give leaders difficulty. I have summarized them here, along with suggestions for handling them.

The Attitude That "My Loss Is Bigger Than Your Loss"

This attitude occurs from time to time in bereavement groups. I recently led a group in which two women had lost young adult daughters. One of the women still had a husband, while the other didn't. The woman without the husband told the group that her loss was bigger than the other woman's because the other woman had a husband and she didn't. One way to handle this is for the leader to say, "Everyone's loss is important in this group," and "We're not here to compare losses."

The Advice Giver

Lehman, Ellard, and Wortman (1986) interviewed bereaved people as to what was helpful and what was not helpful to them in their bereavement. Among the least helpful things reported by these people was receiving advice. Managing the advice giver is rather easy if there is a ground rule in your group that "We do not give advice unless it's asked for."

The Moralist

Another kind of difficult person is the moralist. This is the person who is giving moralistic advice couched as "musts," "shoulds," and "have-tos." We recently had a member in our bereavement group who had come out of the twelve-step tradition and, though well-meaning, was quite preachy to other people in the group. Several members of the group resented this. We encouraged him to say, "This is what I would do," rather than "This is what you should do."

The Nonparticipant

Another difficulty comes from the nonparticipating person. People who participate very little or not at all are often mistaken by others in the group as being critical. The easiest way to avoid nonparticipation is for the leader to help everyone share something about his or her loss at the very first session. Allowing someone to remain silent at the first session will only encourage that person to continue this behavior during later sessions.

The Person Who Brings Up Something Important at the End of the Group

Two minutes before the end of the group, this person says, "By the way, my son was in an accident last week." Group leaders should encourage people who do this to bring the issue up first thing at the next session, rather than allowing the group to go overtime and get into various control struggles.

The Person Who Shares With the Therapist After the Group

This person doesn't share with the group but shares something important with the leader after the meeting. It's easy for the leader to say to the person, "I think it's important for everyone to hear this; let's begin the next session by talking about it. Could you?"

The Interrupter

Frequently in groups somebody will interrupt another person. A strong leader can fend off the interrupter and then, at a more appropriate time, allow the interrupter to speak about the issue that's on his or her mind.

The Person Who Shows Inappropriate Affect

An example of this is a person who laughs when everyone else is sad. An appropriate intervention is for the leader to say, "I wonder what you are experiencing when these things are happening in our group. I see you laughing and I wonder what you're feeling inside." People are often experiencing anxiety that finds its expression in laughter.

The Person Who Makes Irrelevant Comments

If this happens, the leader can inquire, "I don't understand how this relates to the issues we are discussing. Could you tell me how this is relevant to what we're doing right now?"

The Person Who Shares Too Much

Sometimes a group member shares too much early in the life of the group and then backs off and doesn't share later on or doesn't return to the group. A leader can sometimes see this coming and gently caution the person who might share too much too soon.

The Group Member Who Challenges or Criticizes the Leader

This is perhaps more of a problem for the leader than for the group itself, but it can make group members feel uncomfortable. In one of our meetings, a member accused a colleague of mine of being homophobic. Rather than being defensive, the challenged leader inquired, "What have I just done that you perceive as being homophobic?" Rather than jumping on the defensive and escalating the problem, the leader was able to use this question to facilitate discussion.

Although bereavement groups are an important vehicle for grief counseling, some people will choose not to participate in a group. In other cases, people may not be willing at one point in time but will want to participate later. A woman I know was approached by a member of Compassionate Friends shortly after the sudden death of her 19-year-old son. She attended one meeting and left, saying that she didn't ever want to attend another group. However, over a year later she reconsidered and told me she was ready to attend a group and to find some benefit in that experience.

In many psychotherapy groups a ground rule states that group members will not see each other socially between sessions. This stipulation is, in my judgment, not needed in bereavement groups. One would hope that friendships would develop among the members and that these friendships might continue beyond the life of the group. One of the tasks of mourning is being able to allow new people into one's life and to allow oneself to form new relationships. Friendships that form among members of bereavement support groups and that continue beyond the life of the group are small but important steps forward in the overall healing process that we're trying to facilitate through our counseling efforts. Additional information on establishing bereavement groups can be found in Hoy (2007).

FACILITATING GRIEF THROUGH FUNERAL RITUAL

The funeral service has come in for considerable criticism, especially after the 1984 report of the Federal Trade Commission. But the funeral service, if it is done well, can be an important adjunct in aiding and abetting the healthy resolution of grief. Let me outline some of the things I think a funeral can do.

It can help make real the fact of the loss. Seeing the body of the deceased person helps to bring home the reality and finality of death. Whether one has a wake, an open casket, or a closed casket is subject to regional, ethnic, and religious differences. However, there is a strong advantage to having the family members see the body of the deceased loved one, whether at the funeral home or at the hospital. Even in the case of cremation (and there seems to be growing interest in cremation as an option for disposal), the body can still be present at the funeral service in either an open or closed casket, and then the cremation done after the service. In this way, the funeral service can be a strong asset in helping the survivors work through the first task of grief.

The funeral service can give people an opportunity to express thoughts and feelings about the deceased. Earlier we saw how important it is to verbalize thoughts and feelings about the dead person. In its best tradition, the funeral can provide this opportunity. However, there is a great tendency to over-idealize and over-eulogize a person at a funeral. The best situation is one in which people can express both the things that they are going to miss about the lost loved one and things that they are not going to miss, even though some may consider this inappropriate. The funeral service can help the grief process, as it allows people to talk about the deceased.

The funeral service has the effect of drawing a social support network close to the bereaved family shortly after the loss has occurred, and this kind of social support can be extremely helpful in the facilitation of grief. The service can also be a reflection of the life of the person who is gone. It is possible to have some accoutrements of the deceased woven into the overall service so this can affirm what was important to the deceased. In one funeral service of a minister, people stood up from various parts of the congregation and read brief statements that had been extracted from his various writings.

One fact that dilutes the effect of funerals is that they happen too soon. Often the immediate family members are in a dazed or numb condition and the service does not have the positive psychological impact that it might have.

Funerals have changed over the past 25 years to reflect a more comprehensive understanding of ritual, a community as well as an individual focus, the importance of facing death, a better understanding of mourning, and a more pluralistic society (Irion, 1991).

Funeral directors might consider their own role in grief counseling. In addition to their role of advising people and helping them cope with the arrangements that need to be made around the time of death, some type of ongoing contact with these families might be considered for the purpose of grief counseling. Although some might feel awkward about continuing contact with the funeral director after the funeral, other families would not be offended and would appreciate such continued interest. Some larger funeral homes have counselors on their paid staff. Others have counselors in the community to whom they can refer.

Funeral directors might also consider sponsoring widow-to-widow groups and other such bereavement support groups in the community (Steele, 1975).[1] This is already being done in many areas. Here is an ideal opportunity for the funeral director to be involved in an important aspect of grief counseling. Funeral directors can also provide the service of teaching people about grief and healthy grieving by sponsoring educational programs in the community.

DOES GRIEF COUNSELING WORK?

Since the publication of the last edition of *Grief Counseling & Grief Therapy*, there has been a heated discussion about the efficacy of grief counseling. There are those who say that it is no more effective than doing nothing, while others postulate that it may even be harmful for some people. This discussion has been led by John Jordan and Robert Neimeyer (2003) and joined by others (Allumbaugh & Hoyt, 1999; Bonanno, 2001; Kato & Mann, 1999; Larson & Hoyt, 2007; Stroebe et al., 2001). Their conclusions have been based on research findings and then meta-analytic analysis finding *effect sizes* across these studies. The rather low effect sizes call into question the efficacy of grief counseling. The reality is that most of the research they are looking at is bad research for one methodological reason or another—no controls, the use of recruited versus self-referred participants, lack of screening, inadequate or simplistic outcome measures, small sample sizes, initial participation numbers, large attrition, single-item outcome measures, unclear treatment plan, not accounting for time from death, and the like.

The negative effects of grief counseling (i.e., treatment-induced deterioration) discussed by Neimeyer and colleagues (Currier, Holland, & Neimeyer, 2007; Jordan & Neimeyer, 2003; Neimeyer, 2000) have been strongly challenged by Larson and Hoyt (2007) as not valid due to erroneous statistical analysis.

Although most bereavement is self-limiting without formal intervention, those who seem most helped by counseling intervention are those who are younger; women; and people who have experienced some passage of time since the death, experienced sudden/violent death, or showed evidence of chronic grief. People who were screened for high levels of distress (e.g., traumatic/complicated grief)

(Prigerson & Jacobs, 2001), who belong to a subgroup of mourners at elevated risk for dysfunction (older widowers, bereaved parents), and who sought help for self-identified bereavement-related distress (exaggerated grief, discussed in chapter 5) tend to find intervention more effective.

Here are some suggestions for clinicians that may help to make their interventions more efficacious:

1. Don't assume that all mourners need grief counseling. Parkes (1998) concurs when he says, "There is no evidence that all bereaved people will benefit from counseling, and research has shown no benefit to arise from the routine referral of people to counseling for no other reason than they have suffered bereavement" (p. 18).

2. Remember that one type of grief counseling does not fit all mourners. Grief is unique to each individual (Neimeyer, 2000).

3. Customize your interventions for the perceived needs of individual mourners based on the seven groups of mediators that moderate the grieving process (found in chapter 3).

4. Base your grief counseling intervention on a unified theory such as the tasks of mourning.

5. Do an extensive pre-intervention intake. We do this in psychotherapy before we accept a patient into treatment. This can be done for grief counseling whether one is doing individual, family, or group treatment.

6. Take a "customer service" approach. Ask clients what they need and what they are looking for, and assess throughout the treatment whether they are getting what they want/need and, if not, how you can help them get it.

7. Use a screening instrument, when available, such as the one we developed in the Harvard Child Bereavement Study to identify children at risk for poor adaptation to the death of a parent, and then offer early intervention to preclude a negative sequelae at 2 years post-loss (Worden, 1996).

8. If a screening instrument is not available, identify high-risk groups in your population and target your intervention toward

them. Among these would be older and isolated widowers; mothers who lose children; survivors of those who die sudden/ violent deaths (including homicide); and those with abuse/ trauma histories, high dependency on the deceased, and poor coping styles, along with low self-efficacy and self-esteem (Jordan & Neimeyer, 2003).

If the mourner presents with high levels of depression, anger, rumination, or anxiety, then complicated mourning should be considered and grief therapy instituted (see chapter 6).

In attempting to evaluate whether grief counseling can be effective, Parkes reviewed a number of research studies. He looked at professional services offering support to the bereaved as well as volunteer peer-group support. At the end of his examination of these studies, Parkes (1980) concluded:

> The evidence presented here suggests that professional services and professionally supported voluntary and self-help services are capable of reducing the risk of psychiatric and psychosomatic disorder resulting from bereavement. Services are most beneficial among bereaved people who perceive their families as unsupportive or who, for other reasons, are thought to be at special risk. (p. 6)

Margaret and Wolfgang Stroebe (1987) along with Beverly Raphael (1977) concur with Parkes's observation that the risk of psychological or physical debility following bereavement can be reduced with intervention. They too affirm that those at risk tend to benefit most from intervention. My own clinical experience validates this conclusion.

NOTE

1. A directory of services for the widowed in the United States and Canada is available through the Grief and Loss Program of the AARP, 601 E Street, NW, Washington, DC 20049.

REFERENCES

Allumbaugh, D., & Hoyt, W. (1999). Effectiveness of grief therapy: A meta-analysis. *Journal of Counseling Psychology, 46*, 370–380.

Beckwith, B. E., Beckwith, S. K., Gray, T., Micsko, M. M., Holm, J. H., Plummer, V. H., & Flaa, S. L. (1990). Identification of spouses at high risk during bereavement: A preliminary assessment of Parkes and Weiss' Risk Index. *Hospice Journal, 6,* 35–46.

Beresford, L. (1993). *The hospice handbook.* Boston: Little, Brown.

Bonanno, G. (2001). Introduction: New directions in bereavement research and theory. *American Behavioral Scientist, 44,* 718–725.

Brown, J. C. (1990). Loss and grief: An overview and guided imagery intervention model. *Journal of Mental Health Counseling, 12*(4), 434–445.

Castle, J., & Phillips, W. L. (2003). Grief rituals: Aspects that facilitate adjustment to bereavement. *Journal of Loss & Trauma, 8,* 41–71.

Currier, J., Holland, J., & Neimeyer, R. (2007). The effectiveness of bereavement interventions with children: A meta-analytic review of controlled outcome research. *Journal of Clinical Child & Adolescent Psychology, 36,* 253–259.

Freud, S. (1957). Mourning and melancholia. In J. Strachey (Ed. & Trans.), *The standard edition of the complete psychological works of Sigmund Freud* (Vol. 14, pp. 237–260). London: Hogarth. (Originally published 1917)

Gamino, L. A., & Sewell, K. W. (2004). Meaning constructs as predictors of bereavement adjustment: A report from the Scott & White grief study. *Death Studies, 28,* 397–421.

Greenberger, D., & Padesky, C. (1995). *Mind over mood: Change how you feel by changing the way you think.* New York: Guilford.

Hackett, T. P. (1974). Recognizing and treating abnormal grief. *Hospital Physician, 10,* 49–50, 56.

Hoy, W. (2007). *Guiding people through grief: How to start and lead bereavement support groups.* Dallas, TX: Compass Press.

Irion, P. (1991). Changing patterns of ritual responses to death. *Omega, 22,* 159–172.

Irwin, H. J. (1991). The depiction of loss: Uses of clients' drawings in bereavement counseling. *Death Studies, 15,* 481–497.

Jordan, J., & Neimeyer, R. A. (2003). Does grief counseling work? *Death Studies, 27,* 765–786.

Kato, P., & Mann, T. (1999). A synthesis of psychological interventions for the bereaved. *Clinical Psychology Review, 19,* 275–296.

Larson, D., & Hoyt, W. (2007). What has become of grief counseling? An evaluation of the empirical foundations of the new pessimism. *Professional Psychology: Research & Practice, 38,* 347–355.

Lattanzi, M., & Hale, M. E. (1984). Giving grief words: Writing during bereavement. *Omega, 15,* 45–52.

Lehman, D. R., Ellard, J. H., & Wortman, C. B. (1986). Social support for the bereaved: Recipients' and providers' perspectives on what is helpful. *Journal of Consulting & Clinical Psychology, 54,* 438–446.

Neimeyer, R. (2000). Searching for the meaning of meaning: Grief therapy and the process of reconstruction. *Death Studies, 24,* 541–558.

O'Connor, M., Nikoletti, S., Kristjanson, L. J., Loh, R., & Willcock, B. (2003). Writing therapy for the bereaved: Evaluation of an intervention. *Journal of Palliative Medicine, 6,* 195–204.

Parkes, C. M. (1980). Bereavement counselling: Does it work? *British Medical Journal, 281,* 3–6.

Parkes, C. M. (1998). Editorial. *Bereavement Care, 17,* 18.

Parkes, C. M. (2001). *Bereavement: Studies of grief in adult life* (3rd ed.). Philadelphia: Taylor & Francis.

Parkes, C. M., & Weiss, R. (1983). *Recovery from bereavement.* New York: Basic Books.

Prigerson, H. G., & Jacobs, S. (2001). Traumatic grief as a distinct disorder. In M. S. Stroebe, R. O. Hansson, W. Stroebe, & H. Schut (Eds.), *Handbook of bereavement research: Consequences, coping, and care* (pp. 613–645). Washington, DC: American Psychological Association.

Raphael, B. (1977). Preventive intervention with the recently bereaved. *Archives of General Psychiatry, 34,* 1450–1454.

Raphael, B., Minkov, C., & Dobson, M. (2001). Psychotherapeutic and pharmacological intervention for bereaved persons. In M. S. Stroebe, R. O. Hansson, W. Stroebe, & H. Schut (Eds.), *Handbook of bereavement research: Consequences, coping, and care* (pp. 587–612). Washington, DC: American Psychological Association.

Schut, H., de Keijser, J., van den Bout, J., & Stroebe, M. S. (1996). Cross-modality group therapy: Description and assessment of a new program. *Journal of Clinical Psychology, 52,* 357–365.

Schutz, W. (1967). *Joy: Expanding human awareness.* New York: Grove.

Schwartzberg, S., & Halgin, R. (1991). Treating grieving clients: The importance of cognitive change. *Professional Psychology, 22,* 240–246.

Schwartz-Borden, G. (1986). Grief work: Prevention and intervention. *Social Casework,* 499–505.

Schwartz-Borden, G. (1992). Metaphor: Visual aid in grief work. *Omega, 25,* 239–248.

Sheldon, A., Cochrane, J., Vachon, M., Lyall, W., Rogers, J., & Freeman, S. (1981). A psychosocial analysis of risk of psychological impairment following bereavement. *Journal of Nervous & Mental Disease, 169,* 253–255.

Shuchter, S. R., & Zisook, S. (1987). The therapeutic tasks of grief. In S. Zisook (Ed.), *Biopsychosocial aspects of bereavement.* Washington, DC: American Psychiatric Association.

Silverman, P. R. (1986). *Widow to widow.* New York: Springer Publishing.

Simos, B. G. (1979). *A time to grieve.* New York: Family Service Association.

Steele, D. W. (1975). *The funeral director's guide to designing and implementing programs for the widowed.* Milwaukee, WI: National Funeral Directors Association.

Stroebe, M. S., Hansson, R. O., Stroebe, W., & Schut, H. (Eds.). (2001). *Handbook of bereavement research: Consequences, coping and care.* Washington, DC: American Psychological Association.

Stroebe, W., Schut, H., & Stroebe, M. S. (2005). Grief work, disclosure and counseling: Do they help the bereaved? *Clinical Psychology Review, 25,* 395–414.

Stroebe, W., & Stroebe, M. S. (1987). *Bereavement and health: The psychological and physical consequences of partner loss.* Cambridge: Cambridge University Press.

Turetsky, C. J., & Hays, R. (2003). Development of an art psychotherapy model for the prevention and treatment of unresolved grief during midlife. *Art Therapy, 20,* 148–156.

Van der Hart, O. (1988). An imaginary leave-taking ritual in mourning therapy: A brief communication. *International Journal of Clinical and Experimental Hypnosis, 36,* 63–69.

Worden, J. W. (1976). *Personal death awareness.* Englewood Cliffs, NJ: Prentice-Hall.

Worden, J. W. (1996). *Children & grief: When a parent dies.* New York: Guilford Press.

Wortman, C. B., & Silver, R. C. (1989). The myths of coping with loss. *Journal of Consulting & Clinical Psychology, 57,* 349–357.

5

Abnormal Grief Reactions: Complicated Mourning

Before we consider specific abnormal grief reactions that would require grief therapy, it is important to understand why people fail to grieve. Later we will examine types of abnormal or complicated grief and see how the clinician can diagnose and determine these cases.

WHY PEOPLE FAIL TO GRIEVE

When we looked at the mourning process in chapters 2 and 3, we identified seven major mediators that can influence the type, intensity, and duration of grief. Most of these areas are important when we consider why people fail to grieve.

Relational Factors

Relational variables define the type of relationship the person had with the deceased. The type of relationship that most frequently hinders people from adequately grieving is the highly ambivalent one with unexpressed hostility. Here an inability to face up to and deal with a high titre of ambivalence in one's relationship with the deceased inhibits grief and usually portends excessive amounts of anger and guilt that cause the survivor difficulty. Another type of relationship that causes difficulty is a highly narcissistic one, whereby the deceased represents an extension of oneself. To admit to the loss would necessitate confronting a loss of part of oneself, so the loss is denied.

In some cases, the death may reopen old wounds. The death of a parent, stepparent, or other person who has been sexually abusive to the mourner may reopen residual feelings from this situation. Research on abuse has shown that victims often suffer from low self-esteem and self-blaming attributional styles. This self-blame can rearise around and after a death and can move a person into more complicated forms of grief. This is less likely to happen if the feelings surrounding the abuse have been worked out prior to the death event. However, even in cases where one has dealt with the abuse issues earlier, the death can bring up thoughts and feelings that stem from this type of complicated and conflicted relationship with the abuser.

In some relationships we grieve for what we wished for and never had or will never have. I once worked with a woman whose mother suffered from Alzheimer's disease and needed nursing home care. As she watched her mother's progressive deterioration, she became acutely aware that she was losing the opportunity for her abusive mother to ever love her and care for her. After her mother died, she came for treatment of her depression. Grief work involved helping her grieve her mother and grieve the dissolution of her dream of ever receiving the kind of love and acceptance she craved from her mother.

Highly dependent relationships are also difficult to grieve. Mardi Horowitz, Nancy Wilner, Charles Marmar, and Janice Krupnick (1980) at the University of California, San Francisco Medical School believe that dependency and orality play an important part in predisposing a person to a pathological grief reaction. A person who has a highly dependent relationship and then loses the source of that dependency experiences a change in self-image from that of a strong person, well sustained by the relationship with a strong other, to the preexistent structure of a weak, helpless waif supplicating in vain for rescue by a lost or abandoning person.

Most people who lose a significant other will feel somewhat helpless and see themselves in a helpless position, but this sense of helplessness does not have the desperate quality that it does in the life of a person coming from an overly dependent relationship, and in a healthier person this sense of helplessness precludes other more positive self-images. In a normal, healthy personality there is a balance of positive and negative in one's self-image. For the person who loses an excessively dependent relationship, feelings of helplessness and the self-concept of oneself as a helpless person tend to overwhelm any other feelings or any ability to modulate this negative self-concept with a more positive one.

Circumstantial Factors

Earlier, we saw that the circumstances surrounding a loss are important mediators of the strength and the outcome of the grief reaction. There are certain specific circumstances that may preclude a person from grieving or make it difficult for him or her to bring grief to a satisfactory conclusion. The first of these is when the loss is uncertain (Lazare, 1979). One example of this would be a soldier missing in action. His wife does not know whether he is alive or dead and consequently is unable to go through an adequate grieving process. After the Vietnam War some women finally came to believe that their missing husbands were actually dead. They went through the grieving process and dealt with their loss only to have their husbands, who had been prisoners of war, released and returned to them. This may sound like a good plot for a Hollywood romance, but in reality this situation caused great difficulties for these couples, and some of the marriages ended in divorce.

The opposite situation also causes inconclusive grieving. There are women who still believe that their husbands are alive somewhere in Vietnam, and they will hold onto this belief and be unable to resolve their grief until they know for sure their husbands are dead. One woman's son disappeared over the North Atlantic while returning to the States on a military plane. For years she believed that her son was picked up by the Russians and was living in Russia. The rest of the family believed that he was dead and grieved this loss. When Russia opened to outside visitors, she was one of the first to obtain a visa and go there. She searched, but obviously he was not there and for the first time, she was able to get into her grief.

Another circumstantial difficulty arises when there are multiple losses, such as those occurring in earthquakes, fires, and airplane crashes, or when an accident kills many members of a family. Multiple deaths occurred in the tragic events of September 11, 2001. Many lost several friends and family members in the same event. Another example of multiple losses was the mass suicide in Jonestown, Guyana, in which several hundred people died. The circumstances and extent of this loss made it very difficult for the surviving families to go through an adequate grieving period. The sheer volume of people to be grieved was overwhelming, and in a case like this, it can seem easier to close down the mourning process altogether. Multiple losses also occur in less dramatic ways. I treated a woman who lost four close family members in 3 years. She was so overwhelmed that she did not openly grieve but experienced her grief as disabling anxiety, the symptom that brought her in for treatment. This could be seen as *bereavement overload* (Kastenbaum, 1969).

Historical Factors

People who have had abnormal grief reactions in the past have a higher probability of having an abnormal reaction in the present. "Past losses and separations have an impact on current losses and separations and attachments and all these factors bear on fear of future loss and separations and capacity to make future attachments" (Simos, 1979, p. 27). People who have had a history of depressive illness also run a higher risk of developing a complicated reaction.

One area that is of particular interest is the influence of early parental loss on the development of subsequent complicated grief reactions to other losses. There have been a number of studies of this as it relates to the development of later mental health problems, but to date the evidence is not conclusive. Early parental loss may be important, but so is early parenting. In his longitudinal studies of men, Vaillant (1985) found orality and dependence that made grieving difficult stemmed more from a person's experiencee living with inconsistent, immature, and incompatible parents than from having lost good parents. There is some evidence that people experiencing complicated grief reactions felt insecure in their childhood attachments and were ambivalent toward their mothers—their first love objects (Pincus, 1974).

Personality Factors

Personality factors are related to the person's character and how it affects his or her ability to cope with emotional distress. There are some people who are unable to tolerate extremes of emotional distress, so they withdraw in order to defend themselves against such strong feelings. Because of this inability to tolerate emotional distress, they short-circuit the process and often develop a complicated grief reaction.

Those whose personalities do not tolerate dependency feelings well have difficulty grieving:

> Because the resolution of grief demands the experiencing of universal feelings of helplessness in the face of existential loss, those individuals whose major defenses are built around avoidance of feelings of helplessness may be among those likely to have dysfunctional reactions of grief. Thus the individuals who normally function most competently on the surface may be the very ones thrown more heavily by a major loss as it strikes at the core of their defensive system. (Simos, 1979, p. 170)

Another personality dimension that may hinder grief is one's self-concept. Each of us has ideas about who we are, and generally we try to live within our definition of ourselves. If part of a person's self-concept is that he or she is the strong one in the family, he or she may need to play that role to his or her own detriment. Such people (and usually this self-concept is socially reinforced) often do not allow themselves to experience the feelings required for an adequate resolution of a loss (Lazare, 1979).

June was a middle-aged woman whose father died when she was very young. Her mother assumed the role of the strong one in the family. Circumstances necessitated that she put June in a religious orphanage where they spoke only French. Although June found it difficult to cope, she identified with her mother's strength, took on the role of the strong person, and survived. Years later when she had married and her husband died, leaving her with young children, she needed to draw on that same strength. But 2 years after the loss she found she was unable to resolve it and came for treatment. One of the things that was standing in her way was her need to be strong for her children, even though that strength had served her well in other difficult situations. In therapy she was able to set this need aside and explore her deeper feelings about the loss.

Social Factors

Another mediator of mourning that can play an extremely important part in the development of complicated grief reactions involves social factors. Grief is really a social process and is best dealt with in a social setting in which people can support and reinforce each other in their reactions to the loss. Lazare (1979) outlines three social conditions that may portend or give rise to complicated grief reactions. The first is when the loss is *socially unspeakable,* as often happens in instances of suicidal death. When someone dies in this manner, particularly if the circumstances are somewhat ambiguous and no one wants to say whether it was suicide or an accident, there is a tendency for the family and friends to keep quiet about the circumstances surrounding the death. This conspiracy of silence causes great harm to the surviving person, who may need to communicate with others to resolve his or her own grief.

Rusty, an only child, lost his mother when he was 5 years old. She went into the garage, hooked up a hose to the car, and killed herself. His father was so distraught that he immediately left for the West Coast, leaving Rusty in the care of relatives some distance from his hometown in the Midwest. No one ever spoke to him about his mother's death and particularly about how it happened. But the problems caused by this early loss, and his father's subsequent abandonment, resurfaced when he reached his late 20s. He was having problems in his marriage and his wife was threatening to leave him. In therapy Rusty was finally allowed to examine his childhood and the effects his loss and unresolved grief had on his adult life.

In reaction to the silence surrounding suicide, there are support groups set up specifically for the families and friends of those who kill themselves. This kind of support group plays a particularly important role for those people who are not allowed the comfort derived from open communication among their family and friends.

A second social factor that complicates a grief reaction happens when the loss is *socially negated*; in other words, when the person and those around him or her act as if the loss did not happen. I think a good example of this is the way some people deal with abortion. Many single young women who get pregnant choose to terminate the pregnancy. One problem here is that the decision is often made in isolation—the man often is not told about the pregnancy and the woman's family is not involved, often because of her fear. So the woman has the abortion and then buries the incident deep in her mind, as if it did not happen. But the loss still needs to be grieved, and if it is not, it may surface later in some other situation. (Grieving an abortion will be discussed in more detail in chapter 7.) Socially negated losses lead to what Doka (1989) calls disenfranched grief, in which the mourner's grief is not recognized or sanctioned by society.

A third social dimension that may cause complications is the *absence of a social support network* consisting of people who had known the deceased and can give each other support. In our society, people frequently move far away from friends and family members. When someone living in Boston experiences the death of a significant loved one in California, that person may receive some support from his or her peer group in the Boston area, but it does not have the impact that it would have if people in the peer group knew the deceased. This particular absence of a social support network is due to geography, but social support can be missing for other reasons. It may be absent because of social isolation.

In Parkes's (1972) study of London widows, he found that those who were the angriest following the loss of their husbands also experienced the highest degree of social isolation. This relationship between anger and social isolation has been noted in our research. A woman who loses her husband and who is very angry may also experience isolation, even though there are family and friends around her. This not only makes her grieving more difficult but probably serves to increase the amount of anger she is feeling. One young widow was left with three children. She received much support from her friends. However, 6 months later, she was very, very angry because no one was approaching or calling her anymore. My sense was that her anger only served to push people away and to isolate her further.

HOW GRIEF GOES WRONG

Complicated mourning manifests in several forms and has been given different labels. It is sometimes called pathological grief, unresolved grief, complicated grief, chronic grief, delayed grief, or exaggerated grief. In early versions of the *Diagnostic and Statistical Manual* of the American Psychiatric Association, abnormal grief reactions were referred to as "complicated bereavement." But whatever you choose to call it, whether it is abnormal grief or pathological grief, it is

> the intensification of grief to the level where the person is overwhelmed, resorts to maladaptive behavior, or remains interminably in the state of grief without progression of the mourning process towards completion. . . . [It] involves processes that do not move progressively toward assimilation or accommodation but, instead, lead to stereotyped repetitions or extensive interruptions of healing. (Horowitz et al., 1980, p. 1157)

Early in the century, Freud (1917/1957) and Abraham (1927) wrote papers that differentiated normal from pathological grief. However, their approach was basically to describe certain characteristics as common to normal grief, and others as common to pathological grief reactions. This descriptive approach is generally not sufficient or satisfactory. Subsequent field studies indicate that some of the characteristics that Freud and Abraham described as characteristics of pathological grief are found in typical normal grief reactions found in random populations. An example of this would be episodes of pain following a loss. Freud and Abraham thought that these episodes were indicative of a pathological reaction, whereas now we see it as a fairly common experience. Today we find that there is more of a continuous relationship between normal and abnormal grief reactions, between the complicated and uncomplicated, and that pathology is more related to the intensity of a reaction or the duration of a reaction than to the simple presence or absence of a specific symptom or behavior (Horowitz et al., 1980).

AN EMERGING DIAGNOSIS OF COMPLICATED GRIEF

Over the past decade there has been an attempt to define complicated grief in a way in which it could be reliably measured and introduced into the next edition of the *Diagnostic and Statistical Manual*. Acceptance of complicated grief as a bona fide disorder would open the door for more research funding and for third-party payment to those treating individuals with this diagnosis. Much of the work during the past 10 years has been definitional—proposing and refining the criteria for the disorder. There have been two major groups spearheading this effort: the first at Pittsburgh (later Yale and now at Harvard) under the leadership of Holly Prigerson, and the other spearheaded by Mardi Horowitz in San Francisco.

The idea for the currently developing diagnosis was spawned by Prigerson and colleagues (1995) when she was at the University of Pittsburgh. Data already collected in a study of the elderly were used to factor analyze measures of grief and depression; not surprisingly, most of the grief items loaded on one factor and the depression items loaded on a second factor. The group concluded that grief and depression were two separate entities. The big leap came when the grief items were identified as complicated grief even though they came from an inventory used to measure bereaved individuals in general, and some items clearly defined experiences of normal mourners. Specific grief items were extracted based on their sensitivity and specificity as predictors of adverse mental and physical health outcomes.

Two ideas emerged early in their work. The first is that there were two factors at work in complicated grief; one was *traumatic distress* and the other *separation distress*. Although this is interesting theoretically, these two types of distress tended to overlap and correlated highly so this idea received less attention along the way. The other idea that emerged is that this phenomenon of complicated grief was distinctly separate from anxiety and depression. They posited that there are three distinct entities: complicated grief, anxiety, and depression with minimal overlap (Prigerson, Bierhals, Kasl, & Reynolds, 1996). Some later research validates this notion (Boelen & van den Bout, 2005; Boelen, van den Bout, & de Keijser, 2003). Other research raises questions about this distinctiveness (Hogan, Worden, & Schmidt, 2004, 2005).

Along the way the name for this diagnosis was changed several times. It began as "complicated grief" and then was changed to "traumatic grief," even though it had nothing to do with bereavement arising from a traumatic death (Prigerson & Jacobs, 2001). Later the name was changed back to "complicated grief," and more recently "prolonged grief" disorder is the name being used (Goldsmith et al., 2008).

In 1999 a consensus conference bringing together major grief researchers was called and a more specific set of criteria was hammered out until a consensus was reached as to which behaviors and symptoms should be included in the diagnosis (Prigerson et al., 1999). These items were outlined according to the standard format for *DSM* disorders and placed in formal groups (Criterion A through Criterion D), as used in the *DSM-IV*. These criteria encompass difficulties in acknowledging the death on cognitive, emotional, and social levels and underscore the marked and persistent disruption in function associated with this symptomatology (Boelen, van den Hout, & van den Bout, 2006).

The question of time has been one of the struggles that researchers have faced in defining this diagnosis. First, how long must the symptoms last before the diagnosis is made? And secondly, how much time should elapse after the death before the diagnosis is made? Current criteria states that the symptom must last for 6 months. Earlier versions of the definition looked at symptoms lasting for 2 months. The amount of time that must elapse since the death before a diagnosis is made has also been debated. Those promoting an *early* diagnostic time frame, within 6 months of the death, argue that such grief behaviors occurring soon after the loss portend later difficulty for the mourner in terms of health and mental health problems. Those promoting a *later* diagnosis argue that many of the items found in Criterion B such as numbness, detachment from others, and difficulty accepting the death are common experiences of normal mourners and pass with time without any special intervention. Horowitz has suggested that assessments for complicated grief should not be made until after the first anniversary of the death, and this has always made a lot of sense to me.

A call went out in 2005 for researchers to do sound empirical testing and evaluation of the criteria for complicated grief proposed for
the *DSM-V,* scheduled to be released in 2010. Such research may lead
to changes and modifications of the existing criteria, but I doubt this
research will conclude that such a diagnosis is not a good idea. There is
already too much energy and ego invested in this diagnosis to scratch
the effort. Horowitz (2005) has come up with an alternate proposal
outlined in an article titled "Meditating on Complicated Grief Disorder as a Diagnosis." He would prefer that complicated grief be included as a trauma disorder and that all the *DSM* categories related
to trauma be reorganized and redefined. He knows, however, that
the political forces at work are not going to let this happen. He then
concludes this interesting think piece by affirming that some diagnosis for complicated grief is necessary if for no other reason than
that those whose grief is not heading for mending can be helped by
a diagnosis, formulation, and treatment that would be covered by
third-party payers. It is not which specific behaviors are included in
the formal *DSM* diagnosis that is important, but rather the clinical
judgment of the experienced professional who can assess coping and
defenses and identify those mourners who are doing well versus those
whose grief is sufficiently derailed to be complicated, thus calling for
diagnosis and treatment. To this end Horowitz would like to see a
formal diagnosis in the *DSM-V* that would help everyone: the patient
to be treated, the doctor to be paid, and the research on grief and loss
to move forward.

AN EXISTING MODEL OF COMPLICATED MOURNING

While the struggle to define an acceptable diagnosis for the 2010 *DSM*
continues, there are people dealing with complicated mourning who
need our help and intervention. Incidentally, I prefer the term "complicated mourning" to the term "abnormal grief." It is not the grief
that people experience that is abnormal. Their experience of grief *is*
their experience of grief. I can't overemphasize the importance of individual differences in the experience of grief. Each man's grief is like
no other man's grief (Allport, 1957, class lecture notes). The difficulty

lies in the mourning process. There is something that is impeding the mourning process and not allowing it to move forward toward a good adaptation to the loss. The mourning tasks and mourning mediators can give the therapist and patient a clue as to what is going on and provide a framework for effective interventions.

There are several ways to outline complicated mourning reactions. I would like to suggest a paradigm that I find useful in my clinical work and one that you may also find useful. This paradigm describes complicated mourning under four headings: (1) chronic grief reactions, (2) delayed grief reactions, (3) exaggerated grief reactions, and (4) masked grief reactions. Let's examine each one of these individually.

Chronic Grief Reactions

A chronic or prolonged grief reaction is one that is excessive in duration and never comes to a satisfactory conclusion. Anniversary reactions are common for 10 years or longer, but these in themselves do not indicate chronic grief. This type of grief reaction is fairly easy to diagnose because the person experiencing it is very much aware that he or she is not getting through the period of mourning. This awareness is particularly strong when the grieving has gone on for several years and the person is feeling unfinished. It is common for people to come 2 to 5 years after the death and say things like, "I'm not getting back to living," "This thing is not ending for me," or "I need help to be myself again." Even though the person is aware of the condition, chronic grief does not necessarily resolve on its own. However, self-referral makes the diagnosis of this phenomenon easy.

The emerging diagnosis of complicated grief (now called prolonged grief) discussed above relates well here because it suggests that chronic grief may be identified early through the criteria found in the diagnosis (either assessed by a clinician or by a self-report inventory), and early intervention with these people may keep grief from developing into a chronic condition. Prediction and early intervention are part of the preventive mental health philosophy at Harvard, and I have developed screening instruments for the early identification of at-risk cancer patients (Weisman & Worden, 1980) and at-risk bereaved children (Worden, 1996).

For some, treatment will require facing the fact that the person is gone and will never return, no matter how much they wish otherwise (task I). Not wanting the person dead is understandable, particularly when a child dies. The counselor should explore the special meanings the child had for the parent besides the obvious. Rita struggled for more than 2 years with the death of her 12-year-old daughter. When she lost her daughter she not only lost a child but the only person in her world who could rub her neck for relief from migraine headaches.

For others, it may be of assistance to sort out and deal with confusing and ambivalent feelings toward the deceased (task II). The suicidal death of her son 3 years earlier not only left a woman struggling with difficult feelings concerning his taking his own life but also resurrected feelings about his conception when she was an unmarried teenager, and the rejection she felt from family and friends (Cerney & Buskirk, 1991). Some with chronic grief reactions may yearn for a relationship that never was but might have been (Paterson, 1987). I have seen this in some individuals who had alcoholism as well as physical and sexual abuse in their backgrounds.

For those who had a highly dependent relationship with the deceased, helping to adapt to the absence of the loved one and skill building may be a part of the intervention. For still others with insecure attachment needs, loss leaves them feeling unsafe and unable to make it on their own. They may need help and encouragement in forming new relationships that can help fill some of that need (task III).

Five years after the sudden death of his wife, a young man came for therapy because he was unable to establish a relationship with a woman even though he dated several. Having him interact with the dead wife in an "empty chair" experience allowed him to hear the wife encouraging him to move on with his life, find a new wife, and be happy. After our work he went to visit her grave and returned to tell me, "When I want to remember her, I can always go to the cemetery to do this." He had moved her from his heart to a place he could appropriately memorialize her, and that freed him up to move on with his life and find a new wife. He has since done this and established a new family. This was clearly an effective adaptation to the fourth task of mourning, something he had been unable to do in the previous 5 years of chronic grief.

A chronic or prolonged grief reaction requires that the therapist and client assess which of the mourning tasks are not being resolved and which mediators of mourning may be influencing this. Then intervention is focused on the resolution of these tasks.

Delayed Grief Reactions

Delayed grief reactions are sometimes called inhibited, suppressed, or postponed grief reactions. In this case the person may have had an emotional reaction at the time of the loss, but it is not sufficient to the loss. At a future date the person may experience the symptoms of grief over some subsequent and immediate loss, and the intensity of his or her grieving will seem excessive. What is happening here is that some of the grieving, particularly as it is related to mourning task II, which was not adequately done at the time of the original loss, is carried forward and is being experienced at the time of the current loss. The person generally has the distinct impression that the response he or she is experiencing to the current situation is excessive. One mediator that frequently is associated with delayed grief reactions is the lack of social support at the time of the loss.

An interesting example of delayed grief occurred in the case of a woman who lost several of her children in an accident. She was pregnant at the time and was advised not to get too upset because intense feelings could jeopardize her pregnancy. She heeded this advice, only to have intense grief appear when her last child left home (Geller, 1985).

Overwhelming feelings at the time of the loss may cause the person to delay his or her grief. This is often true in the case of a death by suicide. Although some grieving is done at the time, it is not sufficient for the loss, and grief may surface later. Delayed grief can also be stimulated by other types of losses. I have seen several people whose grief for an earlier loss from death has been triggered by an impending or recent divorce. Delayed grief can also arise years after a spontaneous abortion.

Multiple losses can also cause grieving to be postponed due to the magnitude of the loss and bereavement overload (Kastenbaum, 1969). A client of mine lost a number of buddies during the Vietnam War in an ambush but, due to the circumstances, was not able to grieve. After the war he married and became physically abusive to his new wife. In counseling he was more in touch with the anger than the deep sorrow that eventually surfaced. Doing grief work in the office and at the Vietnam Memorial in Washington, D.C., gave him a sense of closure on his losses, and the angry behavior abated.

Such delayed reactions can occur not only after a subsequent loss, but also when one is watching someone else go through a loss, or watching a film, television program, or other media event in which loss is the main theme. When you see a sad play, it is normal to have sad feelings. But what characterizes a delayed grief reaction is the *intensity* of these feelings, which, on further examination, often turn out to be unresolved grief for a former loss. Bowlby (1980) suggests a probable explanation of the tendency for a recent loss to activate or reactivate grieving for a loss sustained earlier. When a person loses the figure to whom he or she is currently attached, it is natural for him or her to turn for comfort to an earlier attachment figure. If, however, the latter, for example a parent, is dead, the pain of the earlier loss will be felt afresh or possibly for the first time.

My colleague George Bonanno argues that there is no such phenomenon as delayed grief (Bonanno et al., 2002). He has never seen a case of it, and his research does not support its validity. I respectfully have to disagree. I along with my colleagues, such as Therese Rando, have treated a number of cases that fit the above description. One of the problems is tying delayed grief into the phenomenon of absent grief described by Helena Deutsch (1937) in her classic paper. In most of those I have treated, grief was *not absent* around the time of the loss, but for some reason, usually the absence of social support, the person didn't process it adequately, and it reappeared much later, often in the form of deep sorrow and excessive crying related to a lesser loss. Investigators trying to validate or invalidate this diagnosis may need to extend their research farther out in time and also remember that this is a *low-frequency phenomenon*. Bonanno and colleagues (2002) found a low frequency of 4% delayed grief in 205 individuals assessed for 18 months following the death of a spouse. Using the same instruments, we found a low frequency of 8% in 70 individuals followed for 2 years after spousal death.

Exaggerated Grief Reactions

The third diagnostic category has to do with exaggerated grief responses in which the person experiencing the intensification of a normal grief reaction either feels overwhelmed or resorts to maladaptive behavior. Unlike masked grief, where the person is unaware that his or her symptoms are related to a loss, people with an exaggerated grief response are aware that the symptoms and behaviors they are experiencing are related to the loss, and they seek therapy because their experience is excessive and disabling. Exaggerated grief responses include major psychiatric disorders that develop following a loss and often receive a *DSM* diagnosis.

Clinical depression that develops following a loss is one example. Feeling depressed and hopeless after the loss of a significant other is a common and usually transient experience for many bereaved individuals. But most are not clinically depressed. However, if these feelings of hopelessness blossom into irrational despair and are accompanied by other depressive features, a diagnosis of clinical depression may result, along with the need for pharmacological intervention. Maureen went into a deep retarded depression after the death of her father. After the depression began to lift through antidepressant medications, we were able to look at the conflicts she had with her father. She had long-standing anger at her father, who was absent for most of her childhood, and this anger was feeding the depression. She was able to identify these feelings and confront her father by using the empty chair technique. Finally she was able to go to the gravesite and read a letter to him that reflected both her negative and positive feelings. Of interest is the fact that she had no history of depression prior to this event, and long-term follow-up has indicated no further depressive episodes.

Anxiety is another common response following loss. If the anxiety is experienced as panic attacks, phobic behavior, or some other type of anxiety disorder, then I would include these disorders under the category of exaggerated grief. Jacobs, Hansen, Kasl, Ostfeld, Berkman, and Kim (1990) found that anxiety disorders during acute bereavement were frequent. More than 40% of bereaved participants in their study of bereaved spouses reported an episode of anxiety disorder at some time during the first year of bereavement. A large group of those experiencing anxiety disorders also reported a depressive syndrome.

Phobias that arise in the context of loss are often centered around death. One patient who had a previous history of psychiatric care lost her father and then, within a 3-month period, began to develop a serious fear of death and returned for treatment to get relief from the symptoms. Often underlying this type of phobia are unconscious guilt and the thought "I deserve to die too," usually stemming from an ambivalent relationship with the deceased.

One 29-year-old woman developed a social phobia after the sudden death of her mother. Six months later she found herself pervasively anxious in social situations, including situations that she had to engage in for her livelihood. She had a longtime ambivalent relationship with her depressed and psychotic mother, who saw the world as a dangerous place. This required her to tiptoe around the mother's fragility. After the death she pathologically identified with some of her mother's symptomatology, and the symptom protected her from her aggressive impulses (Zerbe, 1994).

Agoraphobia is another anxiety disorder than can emerge after a death, and often there is a previous history of this disorder (Sahakian & Charlesworth, 1994).

Serious *alcoholism and other substance abuse* that develop or are exacerbated by a death would be included here under exaggerated grief reactions. Those who treat alcoholism should explore the possibility of unresolved grief as part of the recovery process. Some can trace their alcohol abuse directly to their grief experience. One man whose wife died said, "Before her death I was a social drinker. Afterwards I used the booze to try to forget. Then I'd feel guilty and depressed for being drunk all the time, and I'd drink some more" (Hughes & Fleming, 1991, p. 112).

There are some who suffer loss, usually of a catastrophic nature, who develop signs and symptoms of *posttraumatic stress disorder* (PTSD). I have worked with Vietnam veterans as well as survivors of serious automobile accidents who exhibited the classic symptoms of PTSD. One interesting case was the 72-year-old veteran of World War II who had never experienced PTSD symptoms from his battlefield experiences. Fifty years later, following the death of his wife, these symptoms appeared for the first time (Herrmann & Eryavec, 1994). Similar trauma reactions could be found in some veterans following the screening of *Saving Private Ryan,* which brought back repressed memories. There are specific approaches to working with PTSD, which are beyond the scope of our discussion of grief therapy. However, this trauma disorder precipitated by a death would fall under exaggerated grief.

Several cases of mania occurring after loss have been reported in the literature. Usually this occurs in a person with a history of affective disorder. I would consider such occurrences a form of complicated grief (Rosenman & Tayler, 1986).

Masked Grief Reactions

Masked grief reactions are interesting. Here patients experience symptoms and behaviors that cause them difficulty, but they do not recognize the fact that these symptoms or behaviors are related to the loss. They develop non-affective symptoms or, as Parkes (1972, 2006) says, symptoms that are seen as affective equivalents of grief. Helene Deutsch (1937), in her paper on the absence of grief, comments on this phenomenon. She says that the death of a beloved person must produce some kind of reactive expression of feeling and that the omission of such is just as much a variation of normal grief as grief that is excessive in its duration and intensity. She further states that if a person does not express feelings in an overt manner, this unmanifested grief will be expressed completely in some other way. Her suggestion is that people may have absent grief reactions because their egos are not sufficiently developed to bear the strain of this work of mourning and that they use some mechanisms of narcissistic self-protection to circumvent the process.

Masked or repressed grief generally turns up in one of two ways: either it is masked as a *physical symptom* or it is masked by some type of aberrant or *maladaptive behavior.* Individuals who do not allow themselves to experience grief directly may develop medical symptoms similar to those that the deceased displayed, or they may develop some other kind of psychosomatic complaint. For example, pain can often be a symbol for suppressed grief, or patients being treated for various somatoform disorders may have an underlying grief issue.

Zisook and DeVaul (1977) report on several cases where the physical symptoms experienced by the survivor were similar to those suffered by the deceased during his or her last illness. They call these "facsimile illnesses." One case involved a woman who presented with chest pains identical to those suffered by her husband before he died of a heart attack. The symptoms first appeared around the anniversary of his death. In another case a woman presented with stomach pain. Her mother had died 7 years earlier, and the first episode of pain occurred on the first anniversary of the loss. In both cases there was no organic pathology, and the symptoms abated after the grief issues were dealt with in therapy.

On the other hand, physical symptoms may not be the only manifestation of repressed grief—it may also be masked as a psychiatric symptom, such as unexplained depression, or as some type of acting-out or other maladaptive behavior. There have been some studies that suggest that delinquent behavior can be seen as an adaptive equivalent in the case of a masked grief reaction (Shoor & Speed, 1963). Randall (1993) describes the case of a woman who developed anorexia nervosa 4 months after the accidental death of her son, with whom she had an overly dependent attachment. Since the age of 12 this son had had an eating disorder, for which he was hospitalized. Her introjection of her son's pathology was identified, and through the skilled use of linking objects, the therapist was able to help her appropriately disengage from him and master the eating disorder.

It is necessary to note the important distinction between *exaggerated grief* and *masked grief*. Both may give rise to a formal psychiatric and/or medical diagnosis. In exaggerated grief, the patient knows that the symptoms began around the time of the death and are the result of the experience of the loss. The severity of the symptoms gives the patient a formal *DSM* diagnosis, and treatment for that condition, frequently involving medication, is begun. When the symptoms lift as the result of the initial treatment, the conflicts of separation then become the focus of the treatment. On the other hand, those with masked grief do not associate their symptoms with a death, but once the therapist helps the patient make this connection and works with him or her to identify and resolve the underlying separation conflicts, there is a decided improvement in the physical and/or mental symptoms.

DIAGNOSING COMPLICATED MOURNING

How does a therapist go about diagnosing a complicated grief reaction? There are generally two ways. Either a patient will come with a self-diagnosis, as in the case of chronic grief, or the patient will come for some kind of medical or psychiatric problem, quite unaware that attachment issues and unresolved grief are at the heart of the distress. The latter case requires the skill of the clinician to determine that unresolved grief is the underlying problem, while in the first case, diagnosis is a rather easy matter. I have yet to see a case in which a person came for therapy because he or she believed that the condition related to a loss where this has not been true. May is a good example. When she was in her early 50s, her son was killed in a midair collision over Florida. There were a number of factors that made it difficult for her to grieve her son: it was a sudden death; it happened far away from their home; and because of the circumstances surrounding the death, there was no body at the funeral. Approximately 2 years later, May approached her minister and said that she was not getting through her grief. She was not back doing the kinds of things that she had done prior to the loss. She had a definite feeling of being stuck in the grieving process and requested his help. This type of self-diagnosis is very typical.

However, many times people come for medical or psychiatric care unaware of the dynamics of grief, and this requires that the clinician help make the diagnosis. Most intake procedures require a fairly detailed history from the patient, but deaths and losses can be overlooked, and these can have a direct relationship to the current problems. It is very important to take a loss history when one is doing a formal intake procedure.

There are a number of clues to an unresolved grief reaction. Lazare (1979) has given us an excellent taxonomy of these. Any one of these clues in and of itself may not be sufficient for a diagnostic conclusion. However, any of these clues should be taken seriously, and the diagnosis of complicated grief should be considered when they appear.

Clue 1

The person being interviewed cannot speak of the deceased without experiencing intense and fresh grief. A man in his early 30s came to my office, not for grief therapy, but with a sexual dysfunction problem. In doing the intake, I inquired about deaths and losses, and he told me his father had died. As he spoke of the loss, there was a great freshness to his sadness, which made me think that the loss might have been quite recent. However, on inquiry, he told me that his father had died some 13 years earlier. Later on in therapy we explored the lack of resolution to his loss and its relationship to his sexual dysfunction. So when a person is unable to speak about a previous loss without losing equanimity, one should consider the possibility of unresolved grief. Again, what you look for here is a fresh, intense sadness that occurs many years after the loss.

Clue 2

Some relatively minor event triggers an intense grief reaction. This is usually a clue to delayed grief. In chapter 6, I present the case of a young woman whose friend lost a baby in utero and her continuous overreaction to her friend's trouble, which led us to discover an un-mourned abortion of her own some years earlier.

Clue 3

Themes of loss come up in a clinical interview. In any good counseling or therapy, it is important to listen for themes and, when they concern loss, watch for the possibility of unresolved grief.

Clue 4

The person who has sustained the loss is unwilling to move material possessions belonging to the deceased. Someone who preserves the environment of the deceased just as it was when the death occurred may be harboring an unresolved grief reaction. One must factor in cultural and religious differences before making a judgment here. Tossing everything that belonged to the deceased right after the death can also be a clue to disordered mourning.

Clue 5

An examination of a person's medical record reveals that he or she has developed physical symptoms like those the deceased experienced before death. Often these physical symptoms occur annually, either around the time of the anniversary of the death or around holiday seasons. These symptoms can also surface when the client reaches the age the deceased was at the time of death. This particular phenomenon can happen when the client reaches the age at which the parent of the same sex died. One young woman began an affair on the anniversary of her mother's death. In group therapy she confessed this, only to experience cardiovascular symptoms. Later we discovered the symptoms were similar to those her mother had had before her death.

Physicians who see patients presenting with vague somatic complaints, increased susceptibility to illness, or chronic illness behavior may want to consider the possibility of grief-related issues. A simple inquiry into recent or past losses, how they feel they have adjusted to the loss, and if they still cry or feel the need to cry can give the doctor important clues as to whether there is a possible grief component.

Clue 6

Those who make radical changes to their lifestyle following a death or who exclude from their life friends, family members, and/or activities associated with the deceased may be revealing unresolved grief.

Clue 7

A patient presents a long history of subclinical depression, often marked by persistent guilt and lowered self-esteem. The opposite of this can also be a clue. The person who experiences a false euphoria subsequent to a death may be experiencing unresolved grief.

Clue 8

A compulsion to imitate the dead person, particularly if the client has no conscious desire or competence for the same behavior, comes from the individual's need to compensate for the loss by identifying with the deceased. "Just as the frightened child has to set up a permanent mother inside himself, the adult mourner has to internalize, take into himself, his loved object so he will never lose it" (Pincus, 1974, p. 128). The person might even take on personality characteristics of the deceased that previously were rejected by the survivor. Through imitation, the survivor may attempt to repair the rejection and gain restitution.

Clue 9

Although self-destructive impulses can be stimulated by a number of situations, unresolved grief can be one of these and should be considered.

Clue 10

Unaccountable sadness occurring at a certain time each year can also be a clue to unresolved grief. This feeling may occur around times that were shared with the deceased such as holidays and anniversaries.

Clue 11

A phobia about illness or about death is often related to the specific illness that took the deceased. For example, if the death was a result of cancer, the person may develop a cancer phobia, or if the person died of heart disease, the client may have an abnormal fear of heart attacks.

Clue 12

A knowledge of the circumstances surrounding the death can help the therapist determine the possibility of unresolved grief. If clients have suffered significant loss, always ask them what it was like for them at the time of that loss. If they avoided visiting the gravesite or participating in death-related rituals or activities, they may be harboring unresolved grief. This can also be true if they did not have family or other social support during the bereavement period.

With an understanding of diagnostic clues to complicated mourning, we can now move to a consideration of grief therapy itself. However, a caveat is important. I agree with Belitsky and Jacobs (1986), who advocate a cautious approach:

> Diagnostic decisions ought to be conservative in the circumstances of bereavement to avoid interference in a normal human process and iatrogenic complications with the associated introduction of professional interventions and their accompanying side effects. (p. 280)

This concern has recently been rearticulated by Jordan and Neimeyer (2003) in their much discussed research paper.

In chapter 6, we will look at specific techniques that the therapist can use to help people with complicated mourning resolve their grief and move through the four tasks of mourning to a more effective adaptation to the loss.

REFERENCES

Abraham, K. (1927). *Selected papers on psychoanalysis.* London: Hogarth.

Belitsky, R., & Jacobs, S. (1986). Bereavement, attachment theory, and mental disorders. *Psychiatric Annals, 16,* 276–280.

Boelen, P. A., & van den Bout, J. (2005). Complicated grief, depression and anxiety as distinct postloss syndromes. A confirmatory factor analysis study. *American Journal of Psychiatry, 162,* 2175–2177.

Boelen, P. A., van den Bout, J., & de Keijser, J. (2003). Traumatic grief as a disorder distinct from bereavement-related depression and anxiety. *American Journal of Psychiatry, 160,* 1339–1341.

Boelen, P. A., van den Hout, M. A., & van den Bout, J. (2006). A cognitive-behavioral conceptualization of complicated grief. *Clinical Psychology: Science & Practice, 13,* 109–128.

Bonanno, G. A., Wortman, C., Lehman, D., Tweed, R., Haring, M., Sonnega, J., et al. (2002). Resilience to loss and chronic grief: A prospective study from preloss to 18-months postloss. *Journal of Personality & Social Psychology, 83,* 1150–1164.

Bowlby, J. (1980). *Attachment and loss: Vol. 3. Loss, sadness, and depression.* New York: Basic Books.

Cerney, M. S., & Buskirk, J. R. (1991). Anger: The hidden part of grief. *Bulletin of the Menninger Clinic, 55*(2), 228–237.

Deutsch, H. (1937). Absence of grief. *Psychoanalytic Quarterly, 6,* 12–22.

Doka, K. (Ed.). (1989). *Disenfranchised grief: Recognizing hidden sorrow.* Lexington, MA: Lexington Books.

Freud, S. (1957). Mourning and melancholia. In J. Strachey (Ed. & Trans.), *The standard edition of the complete psychological works of Sigmund Freud* (Vol. 14, pp. 237–260). London: Hogarth. (Originally published 1917)

Geller, J. L. (1985). The long-term outcome of unresolved grief: An example. *Psychiatric Quarterly, 57,* 142–146.

Goldsmith, B., Morrison, R., Vanderwerker, L., & Prigerson, H. (2008). Elevated rates of prolonged grief disorders in African Americans. *Death Studies, 32,* 352–365.

Herrmann, N., & Eryavec, G. (1994). Delayed onset post-traumatic stress disorder in World War II veterans. *Canadian Journal of Psychiatry, 39,* 439–441.

Hogan, N., Worden, J. W., & Schmidt, L. (2004). An empirical study of the proposed Complicated Grief Disorder criteria. *Omega, 48,* 263–277.

Hogan, N. S., Worden, J. W., & Schmidt, L. A. (2005). Considerations in conceptualizing complicated grief. *Omega, 52,* 81–85.

Horowitz, M. J. (2005). Meditating on complicated grief disorder as a diagnosis. *Omega, 52,* 87–89.

Horowitz, M. J., Wilner, N., Marmar, C., & Krupnick, J. (1980). Pathological grief and the activation of latent self images. *American Journal of Psychiatry, 137,* 1157–1162.

Hughes, C., & Fleming, D. (1991). Grief casualties on skid row. *Omega, 23,* 109–118.

Jacobs, S., Hansen, F., Kasl, S., Ostfeld, A., Berkman, L., & Kim, K. (1990). Anxiety disorders during acute bereavement: Risk and risk factors. *Journal of Clinical Psychiatry, 51,* 269–274.

Jordan, J., & Neimeyer, R. A. (2003). Does grief counseling work? *Death Studies, 27,* 765–786.

Kastenbaum, R. (1969). Death and bereavement in later life. In A. H. Kutscher (Ed.), *Death and bereavement* (pp. 27–54). Springfield, IL: Thomas.

Lazare, A. (1979). Unresolved grief. In A. Lazare (Ed.), *Outpatient psychiatry: Diagnosis and treatment* (pp. 498–512). Baltimore: Williams and Wilkens.

Parkes, C. M. (1972). *Bereavement: Studies of grief in adult life.* New York: International Universities Press.

Parkes, C. M. (2006). *Love and loss: The roots of grief and its complications.* London: Routledge.

Paterson, G. W. (1987). Managing grief and bereavement. *Primary Care, 14,* 403–415.

Pincus, L. (1974). *Death and the family: The importance of mourning.* New York: Pantheon.

Prigerson, H. G., Bierhals, A., Kasl, S. V., & Reynolds, C. F. (1996). Complicated grief as a disorder distinct from bereavement-related depression and anxiety: A replication study. *American Journal of Psychiatry, 153,* 1484–1486.

Prigerson, H. G., Frank, E., Kasl, S. V., Reynolds, C. F., Anderson, B., Zubenko, G. S., et al. (1995). Complicated grief and bereavement-related depression as distinct disorders: Preliminary empirical validation in elderly bereaved spouses. *American Journal of Psychiatry, 152,* 22–30.

Prigerson, H. G., & Jacobs, S. (2001). Traumatic grief as a distinct disorder. In M. S. Stroebe, R. O. Hansson, W. Stroebe, & H. Schut (Eds.), *Handbook of bereavement research: Consequences, coping, and care* (pp. 613–645). Washington, DC: American Psychological Association.

Prigerson, H. G., Shear, M. K., Jacobs, S. C., Reynolds, C. F., III, Maciejewski, P. K., Davidson, J. R., et al. (1999). Consensus criteria for traumatic grief: A preliminary empirical test. *British Journal of Psychiatry, 174,* 67–73.

Randall, L. (1993). Abnormal grief and eating disorders within a mother-son dyad. *British Journal of Medical Psychology, 66,* 89–96.

Rosenman, S. J., & Tayler, H. (1986). Mania following bereavement: A case report. *British Journal of Psychiatry, 148,* 468–470.

Sahakian, B. J., & Charlesworth, G. (1994). Masked bereavement presenting as agoraphobia. *Behavioral and Cognitive Psychotherapy, 22,* 177–180.

Shoor, M., & Speed, M. N. (1963). Delinquency as a manifestation of the mourning process. *Psychiatric Quarterly, 37,* 540–558.

Simos, B. G. (1979). *A time to grieve.* New York: Family Service Association.

Vaillant, G. E. (1985). Loss as a metaphor for attachment. *American Journal of Psychoanalysis, 45,* 59–67.

Weisman, A. D., & Worden, J. W. (1980). *Psychological screening and intervention with cancer patients.* Boston: Massachusetts General Hospital.

Worden, J. W. (1996). *Children & grief: When a parent dies.* New York: Guilford Press.

Zerbe, K. J. (1994). Uncharted waters: Psychodynamic considerations in the diagnosis and treatment of social phobia. *Bulletin of the Menninger Clinic, 58*(2, Suppl. A), A3–A20.

Zisook, S., & DeVaul, R. A. (1977). Grief-related facsimile illness. *International Journal of Psychiatry in Medicine, 7,* 329–336.

6

Grief Therapy: Resolving Complicated Mourning

The goal of grief therapy is somewhat different from the goal of grief counseling. The goal in grief counseling is to facilitate the tasks of mourning in the recently bereaved so that the mourner makes a better adaptation to the loss. In grief therapy the goal is to identify and resolve the conflicts of separation that preclude the completion of mourning tasks in individuals whose grief is chronic, delayed, excessive, or masked as physical symptoms.

Grief therapy is most appropriate in situations that fall into one or more of these four categories: (1) the complicated grief reaction is manifested as prolonged grief, (2) it manifests as delayed grief, (3) it manifests as an exaggerated grief response, or (4) it manifests through some masked somatic or behavioral symptom. Let's briefly look at these individually.

Chronic grief can be defined as a deviation from the cultural norm in the duration or intensity of the symptoms of grief (Stroebe, Hansson, & Stroebe, 2001). Individuals who experience this difficulty are consciously aware that they are not coming to an adequate resolution of their grief, because the loss occurred many months, sometimes years, earlier. Often the reason behind this type of complicated grief reaction is a separation conflict leading to the incompletion of one or more of the tasks of mourning. Because these people are aware that there is a problem, they are generally self-referred. Much of the therapy involves ascertaining which of the grief tasks have yet to be completed and what the impediments to this completion are, then moving forward with that issue. Understanding the mediators of mourning outlined in chapter 3 can help identify most of these impediments.

Delayed grief does not mean absent grief. The person may have had an emotional reaction at the time of the loss, but it was not sufficient to the loss. Insufficient grieving can be due to a lack of social support, a lack of social sanction, the need to be strong for someone else, or feeling overwhelmed by the number of losses. One patient had seen his entire family shot by enemy soldiers when he was 10 years of age. He experienced very little grief due to the overwhelming number of losses and the circumstances. Years later, when he was 54, a current loss evoked all the pain that had been suppressed over the years. In therapy he was able to explore these earlier losses in a safe environment that allowed him to dose his pain.

Exaggerated grief is a specific psychological or psychiatric disorder that arises or is precipitated by the death of a loved one. The affect that is experienced is common to any loss but it is experienced to the degree that the person becomes dysfunctional and needs treatment. For example, it is normal to feel down and depressed after a loss. However, a depression that escalates into a major depressive episode after a death would fall into this category of exaggerated grief. It is common to feel anxious after losing someone to death. But anxiety that escalates into an anxiety disorder (panic attack, phobia, general anxiety disorder, etc.) is an example of exaggerated grief. Individuals falling into this category would be those with excessive depression, excessive anxiety, or some other feature usually associated with normal grief behavior manifested in an exaggerated way so that the person is dysfunctional and a psychiatric disorder diagnosis would apply. Psychiatric symptoms would be treated with standard intervention treatments for that disorder. Once the symptom (e.g., clinical depression) has lifted through clinical or pharmacological intervention, then the conflicts of separation can be addressed in the grief therapy.

When grief is *masked* as somatic or behavioral symptoms, patients are usually not aware that unresolved grief is the reason behind their symptoms. However, a peripheral diagnosis, such as the one described in chapter 5, reveals unresolved grief of a much earlier loss as the culprit. People usually experience this kind of complicated grief reaction because, at the time of the loss, the grief was absent or its expression was inhibited. Consequently, their grieving was never completed and this caused complications that surfaced later as somatic or behavioral symptoms.

GOALS AND SETTING OF GRIEF THERAPY

The goal of grief therapy is to resolve the conflicts of separation and to better adapt to the death. The resolution of these conflicts requires the patient to experience thoughts and feelings that he or she has been avoiding. The therapist provides the social support necessary for successful grief work and essentially gives the patient permission to grieve, permission that may have been lacking around the time of the death. Obviously, such permission or support implies an adequate therapeutic alliance. One way to enhance this alliance is to recognize and acknowledge the difficulty some people may experience when they reopen a past loss. The greater the underlying conflict with the deceased, the more resistance there will be to exploring painful thoughts and feelings. As in any good psychotherapy, resistances are constantly monitored and worked with as a part of the therapy process.

Grief therapy is usually conducted in an office setting and frequently on a one-on-one basis. This does not mean, however, that it cannot be done in other settings such as group therapy, particularly if an unresolved grief issue arises while the person is participating in a course of group therapy. In Germany, Wagner, Knaevelsrud, and Maercker (2005) have developed a treatment approach for complicated grief through the Internet. In an interesting paper, they outline the techniques as well as the caveats for such intervention, along with a case study.

The first step to grief therapy is to set up the contract with the patient. Usually grief therapy is set up on a time-limited basis; that is, the therapist contracts with the patient for 8 to 10 visits, during which they explore the loss and its relationship to the present pain or distress. In my experience, someone presenting with a focused, unresolved grief reaction without unusual complications can usually achieve a resolution of his or her problem within this limited time frame. Patients are usually seen once a week, but more frequent meetings are sometimes more effective.

Occasionally, during a contracted sequence of grief therapy sessions, more serious underlying pathology emerges that is of such substantial nature that it may require a prolonged period of non-grief treatment. "With people who are neurotically dependent personality types expert psychotherapeutic intervention is needed to deal with both the legitimate grief reactions as well as the underlying personality disorder" (Simos, 1979, p. 178). One way to identify any underlying pathology that may impair brief grief therapy is to screen for comorbidity in the initial interview. Initial screening for serious depression, anxiety disorders, trauma, or Axis II disorders can identify possible impairments to a brief treatment schema. Therapists who are doing a routine sequence of psychotherapy may turn up an unresolved grief issue and, in this case, do grief therapy within the context of a longer psychotherapy.

It is important to remember that in this type of treatment, as in any short-term psychotherapy treatment, the therapist must be knowledgeable and the sessions must be kept *focused*. One way the patient will express resistance is by not keeping the focus and going off on distracting issues that are unrelated to grief. In such cases, the therapist needs to remind the patient of the task at hand and explore this resistance and what is being avoided. A woman coming for brief grief therapy 2 years after the sudden death of her son agreed to an 8-week contract. After the third session she began complaining about how her husband was treating her. I reminded her of our contract to spend 8 sessions focusing on the death of her son. After we finished that, I would be more than happy to see her and her husband for marital therapy. Couples therapy never materialized because she was using her unhappiness with her husband as a deflection from the anger about the son that was emerging into her awareness.

PROCEDURES FOR GRIEF THERAPY

One can no more do good therapy by numbers than paint an artistic masterpiece by numbers. However, a listing of therapeutic procedures may help one to remember them. The assumption underlying these procedures is that they will be applied within each therapist's own theoretical framework and level of professional competence.

1. Rule Out Physical Disease

If the patient presents with a physical symptom, it is important to rule out physical disease. Although some symptoms do appear as grief equivalents, this is not true of all symptoms, and one should never enter a course of grief therapy when a physical symptom is the major presentation unless there is conclusive exclusion of physical disease behind the symptom. This would also be important during grief counseling if the person is manifesting physical complaints.

2. Set Up the Contract and Establish an Alliance

Here the patient agrees to explore his or her relationship with the person or people involved in the previous loss. The patient's belief that this will be beneficial is reinforced by the therapist, who agrees that this is a worthy area to explore. Some patients need more education than others—education about grief and the rationale for what we will be asking them to do. Keep in mind that this is brief therapy and the focus is specific. Past relationships are explored only if they directly affect the response to the immediate bereavement.

3. Revive Memories of the Deceased

Talk about the person who has died—who he was, what he was like, what the client remembers about him, what they enjoyed doing together, and so on. It is very important to begin to build groundwork of positive memories that will help the patient later on if he or she is resisting experiencing some of the more negative feelings. This will provide balance and will enable the patient to get in touch with some of these negative areas. Considerable time is spent in the early sessions talking about the deceased, particularly about positive characteristics and qualities and pleasant activities that the survivor enjoyed with the deceased. Gradually begin to talk about some of the more mixed memories. The technique mentioned in chapter 4 can be useful here. "What do you miss about him?" "What don't you miss about him?" "How did she disappoint you?" Finally, lead the person into a discussion of memories of hurt, anger, and disappointment. If the patient comes to treatment aware of only negative feelings, the process is reversed and positive memories and affects need to be retrieved, even if they are few in number.

If there have been multiple losses, you will need to deal with each one separately. In general, it is best to explore the loss that you believe has the fewest complicating factors first. One woman in her late 20s came for therapy after losing two brothers to suicide. While exploring both of these losses, it became clear that the first brother to take his own life was the one with whom she had the most unfinished business and the greatest attachment. Although we dealt with each loss, she reported the greatest sense of relief when she was able to deal with her anger and guilt about the first loss.

4. Assess Which of the Four Mourning Tasks the Patient Is Struggling With

If the struggle involves task I (to accept the reality of the loss), and the patient is saying to herself, "I won't have you dead," or "You can't be dead; you are just away," the therapy focuses on the fact that the person is dead and that the survivor is going to have to accept this reality. It is important to investigate dimensions of the loss that make it difficult to believe the person is gone and not coming back again. This can often be found in the nature of the attachment to the deceased.

If the difficulty lies in task II (to process the pain of grief), where the patient accepts the reality without the affect, then the therapy focuses on the fact that it is safe to feel both positive and negative emotions with regard to the deceased, and that one can come to a balance of these feelings. One of the key interventions needed to come to the completion of task II is the redefinition of the patient's relationship with the deceased, for example, "He did love me, but he just couldn't express it because of his upbringing."

If the difficulty lies around the first part of task III (external adjustments), then problem solving is a major part of grief therapy—the patient is taught to overcome his or her helplessness by trying out new skills and developing new roles through role-playing and, in general, is encouraged to get back to living. This was particularly true in the case of Margaret, a young widow who, prior to her husband's death, enjoyed going out to a club where people sat around a piano bar and sang show tunes. She and her husband had enjoyed this together, but 3 years after his death she still would not go there, not because she did not want to be reminded of him, but because she felt she lacked the social skills to go there alone. Part of the therapy involved helping Margaret to relearn these social skills, beginning with role-playing and then in an in vivo confrontation of the feared activity. I remember how pleased she was the day she came in and told me she had, after many failed attempts, gone to the club alone.

For those who are struggling to find meaning in the loss (the last two parts of task III: internal and spiritual), the therapist can help the patient in this search. Likewise, the patient can be helped to explore how the loss has affected his or her sense of self. A good resource for patients who are struggling to integrate their meaning of their loss into their current life is *Lessons of Loss: A Guide to Coping* by Robert Neimeyer (2003).

Finally, if the struggle is with mourning task IV, then the therapist can help the patient find some kind of enduring connection with the deceased and thus be free to embark on a new life and cultivate new relationships. This involves giving the patient permission to stop grieving and sanctioning new relationships and helping the patient to see that moving on with life is not an affront to the memory of the lost loved one.

5. Deal With Affect or Lack of Affect Stimulated by Memories

Often, when a patient is undergoing grief therapy and begins talking about the person who has died, the description of the deceased comes off bigger than life (e.g., "the best husband who ever lived"), and it is important for the therapist to allow the patient to describe the deceased in this way early in therapy. When there is this type of description, however, there is often considerable unexpressed anger beneath the surface, and exploring the more ambivalent feelings about the deceased and helping the patient to get in touch with his or her angry feelings are ways of gradually working through anger. Once angry feelings are identified, the patient needs to be helped to see that these do not obviate the positive feelings and indeed are there because he or she did care for the deceased.

The woman mentioned earlier whose son was killed in a midair collision described her son in this bigger-than-life way—he was a top cadet in the military, he was a graduate of an Ivy League school, he was the most wonderful son who ever lived. As we worked together in therapy, she began to get in touch with the fact that she did have some ambivalent feelings about him. Finally, she was able to allow into consciousness and to share with me the fact that shortly before he died, he had done something that had severely displeased her, and then he was gone and all her anger was suppressed. It was very important for her, as part of her therapy, to reexperience this anger and to see that the angry feelings did not preclude the positive ones, and vice versa, and to be able to express them to her son.

In a similar situation is Laura, a woman in her late 20s who came in for psychotherapy. During the course of the treatment, it seemed as though there were some unresolved issues concerning her father. He had died when she was 12 years old, and as she described him, he came off bigger than life, the greatest dad who ever lived. It was important for her to hold onto these positive feelings because underneath there was an incredible amount of anger that she was not in touch with. During therapy she went back to the old family homestead in the Midwest to visit the place where they had lived while he was alive. Then one day during one of our regular sessions, which just happened to fall on the anniversary of her father's death, the anger and rage erupted. She said that he had ruined her life by dying. She had to move out of her pleasant suburban home into a large city and share a room with her brother. Her anger at her father had gone underground and she was not aware of it, but it was the stimulus that lay behind the dysfunctional behavior that brought her into psychotherapy. Again, it was important to leave her with a balance between positive and negative feelings.

When the death has been a violent death, the patient may only focus on the disturbing aspects of the death and experience feelings that are mostly negative and disturbing. Here the goal is to help the patient remember the deceased in a more positive and comforting way. Before this can happen, the patient may need to focus on the most difficult images of the event and, through imagery exposure combined with systematic desensitization, defuse the pain associated with these images. Another useful approach to defusing these negative images and the eventual installation of positive images is the technique of EMDR (eye movement desensitization and reprocessing). Individuals trained in this approach will find it useful in defusing traumatic memories associated with the death so that these memories no longer evoke the level of affect that they did in the beginning (Solomon & Rando, 2007; Sprang, 2001).

Another affect that may come up frequently when one is stimulated by memories of the deceased is guilt. (Keep in mind we are talking about memories of someone who may have died a number of years earlier; this is grief therapy, not grief counseling.) As the patient begins to talk about the deceased, he or she becomes aware of some of the guilt he or she has concerning the former relationship. Again, once this guilt is identified, it is important to help the person reality test the guilt. As in acute grief, much guilt is irrational and doesn't hold up under reality testing or similar cognitive reappraisal.

Some guilt is real. Karen, a young mother whose 6-year-old son died of a long and complicated illness, felt very guilty about the fact that she had not stood between him and the physicians during his difficult final hospitalization. She had carried this guilt with her for nearly 7 years. Part of her treatment involved reality testing this guilt, which she determined was real. She was then able, through a psychodrama, to seek her son's forgiveness and understanding for her limitations. It is important when one is dealing with real guilt to facilitate the seeking and granting of forgiveness between the deceased and the patient. In the facilitation of this process, certain role-playing and imaging techniques may be useful, such as having the patient speak both for him- or herself and for the deceased by moving back and forth between two chairs while speaking from both awarenesses.

Not every mourner expresses affect of one kind or another, though most do. There is currently discussion as to whether the lack of expression of affect is healthy or not. This debate was sparked by the research finding that those who show strong early affect are those who are going to be expressing strong affect later in the bereavement (Bonanno & Papa, 2003; Wortman & Silver, 2001). Again, I would remind the reader that grief is a multidetermined phenomenon and that each person's grief is unique to him or her. Some with very little emotion after a death have very little attachment with the person who died. Still others who avoid affect don't want to deal with aspects about themselves with which the death confronts them. Avoidance of affect may help some deal with the traumatic components of the death, especially in cases of a violent death. Still others may show very little grief due to a lifetime of unresponsiveness from others when they were hurting. It is important for therapists to help mourners with whatever affect is being experienced in order to find a way of expression that is not going to cause them marked and persistent dysfunction in their everyday lives (Prigerson & Maciejewski, 2005–2006).

6. Explore and Defuse Linking Objects

In grief therapy, you may encounter cases in which linking objects play a role in the nonresolution of mourning. These are symbolic objects that the survivor keeps and that provide a means through which the relationship with the deceased can be maintained externally. This concept was developed by psychiatrist Vamik Volkan (1972), who has written widely on the issue of pathological grief.

It is important to be aware of and to understand this phenomenon because these objects can hinder satisfactory completion of the grieving process. After the death, the mourner may invest some inanimate object with symbolism that establishes it as a link between him or her and the dead individual. Most mourners are aware that they have invested the object with symbolism, and most are aware of some aspects of the symbolism without perhaps comprehending all that is symbolized. Generally, linking objects are chosen from one of four categories: (1) some belonging of the deceased's, such as something he or she wore, like a watch or a piece of jewelry; (2) something with which the dead person extended his or her senses, like a camera, which would represent a visual extension; (3) a representation of the deceased, such as a photograph; (4) something that was at hand when news of the death was received or when the mourner saw the dead body (Volkan, 1972).

For example, Donna, a young woman, was at her mother's bedside as she lay dying of cancer. When it was obvious that the death was very near, she began compulsively rummaging through her mother's jewelry box, picking out the pieces that she wanted to have as mementos. After her mother died, Donna wore the jewelry on a regular basis, and indeed, she found that she felt somewhat uncomfortable when she was not wearing it. Later on, as her grieving progressed, she found less and less need to wear her mother's jewelry. Volkan (1972) believes that these types of linking objects are used to handle separation anxiety and that they provide a "token of triumph" over the loss. He believes that linking objects mark a blurring of psychic boundaries between the patient and the one mourned, as if representations of the two individuals or parts of them merge externally through their use.

It is important for the person who possesses a linking object to know where it is at all times. One patient kept a tiny stuffed animal with him always. He and his deceased wife had given this animal a name, and he carried it with him in his pocket. One time, as he was flying home from a business trip, he felt in his pocket and discovered that the animal was missing. He was seized with panic, and in desperation he pulled the seat and carpeting up in an effort to find the missing linking object. He never found it, and his anxiety was the focus of many therapy sessions following that incident. Volkan (1972) believes that the need for such an object comes from the conflicting wish to annihilate the deceased and at the same time keep him or her alive. Both of these wishes are condensed in the linking object.

Linking objects are similar to transitional objects such as those that children hold on to as they grow away from their parents. As they grow older, they may hold on to a blanket, a stuffed animal, or some other object that makes them feel safe and secure during the transition between the safety and security associated with their parents and their need to grow and detach from the family and become their own person. In most cases transitional objects are dropped as children grow up. However, when they are needed, their absence can cause a tremendous amount of anxiety and uproar.

One patient disposed of all of her husband's clothing except for two or three items that she had given him. These items represented positive and happy times that they had had together. By holding on to them, she kept herself from being fully in touch with her negative feelings about the many unhappy times that they had together. In therapy she developed the awareness that this was one of the functions that her linking objects served.

Incidentally, linking objects are different from keepsakes. Most people keep something as a memento or token of remembrance when someone dies. Linking objects, however, are invested with much more meaning, and their loss creates a great deal more anxiety. Volkan (1972) talks about one of his cases in which the person holding the linking object was in an automobile crash. He made a desperate attempt to go back and retrieve this object, and it ended up being the only thing that was retrieved from the wreckage of this very serious accident.

It is important to ask patients about what items they have saved after the death, and if you determine that they are using something as a linking object, this should be discussed in therapy. Like Volkan, I encourage people to bring these objects to the therapy session. Doing this can be extremely helpful in facilitating the mourning and also helpful in pointing up the main conflicts causing people to get stuck in the grieving process. It is interesting to see what happens when people complete the course of grief therapy. Without external suggestion, they often put away or give away these objects in which they previously invested extreme amounts of meaning. One patient would not leave home without letters she had received from her husband while he was alive. As therapy progressed, she left the letters at home through her own initiative. Field, Nichols, Holen, and Horowitz (1999) see this patient as moving from getting comfort through an attachment to the deceased's possessions to maintaining an attachment through fond memories, a healthier type of continuing bond.

Keeping the clothing that the deceased wore at the time of death is another type of transitional object behavior that I see from time to time among survivors. This is particularly true in cases of sudden-death experiences. One woman whose husband died very unexpectedly found it important to keep the jacket he was wearing;

she held on to it until she was able to work through her grief. In the Harvard Child Bereavement Study a 9-year-old boy kept his dead father's baseball cap and during the first year after the death wore this cap all the time, including to bed. After the first year he wore the cap less and hung it on the bedpost in his room. By the second year after the death he still kept the cap but at this time was keeping it in his closet and not wearing it. Another patient and her husband had bought a small toy lobster together and had given this toy a name. Since they had no children, the lobster became a kind of pet or mascot for them. After the husband killed himself, she found it was important to sleep with this stuffed toy under her pillow and was very anxious when she did not have it. After we worked through a course of grief therapy, she was able to put the animal away in a drawer. She wanted to keep it because of the happy memories that it represented, but she no longer felt the need to have it as a source of comfort. Again, here was a person who had a very ambivalent relationship with her husband, and an important part of the therapy revolved around this ambivalence and her need to understand it better and to deal with it.

7. Help the Patient Acknowledge the Finality of the Loss

Although most people accomplish this during the early months after a loss, there are those who maintain long after that it is not final—that somehow the person is coming back in some form or another. Volkan (1972) calls this a chronic hope for reunion. Again, it is important to help these patients assess why they cannot acknowledge the finality of their loss. Carol was a young woman who came from a very puritanical, restrictive family background, and although she was a young adult at the time her father died, she would not allow herself, even after 5 years, to acknowledge the finality of her loss. To do so would mean that she would have to make her own choices and be subject to her own needs and impulses, something that scared her. She avoided making personal choices, maintaining, on one level of consciousness, the fantasy that her father was somehow still there, pulling the strings and providing external restraints on her behavior.

8. Help the Patient Design a New Life Without the Deceased

Keeping with task III (adjusting to a world without the deceased) and with the *restoration orientation of the dual-process model* helps the patient focus on personal goals. Shear (2006) has a technique that I find useful: therapists ask patients to envision what they would want for themselves if their grief could be magically removed and then work with them to articulate new life goals that might be done without the deceased. I recently asked a young widow this question, a woman with a close relationship to her husband, who died with a lingering and debilitating illness. We had worked for a year on her grief and adjustment to being a single parent of two teenage boys. When the boys left home for college, her grief was compounded as she found herself even more alone. She was able to envision a business activity that she had always wanted to do but didn't pursue because of her marriage at a young age. Her enthusiasm was palpable as she, for the first time since the death, could envision the framework for a new life.

9. Assess and Help the Patient Improve Social Relationships

Another restoration focus and a goal of mourning task III is to help the patient enhance and develop social relationships. Many of the bereaved move away from former friendships when they feel that their friends do not understand their grief and are trying to push them into a premature closure. Friends sometimes feel uncomfortable with the mourner's grief and stop calling or distance themselves from the friendship because they feel awkward around their grieving friend. Some widows who once participated in social activities with their spouses no longer feel comfortable attending dinner parties as the only unaccompanied person. Bereaved individuals often feel stigmatized or stigmatize themselves. Explore disappointments patients have with friendships, and through role-playing and small steps, encourage them to begin to connect with friends again, being candid about their disappointments with them and their hopes for a new chapter in their relationship. Some bereaved individuals and couples find new friendships with others who have experienced similar losses.

10. Help the Patient Deal With the Fantasy of Ending Grieving

One helpful procedure in doing grief therapy is to have patients explore their fantasies of what it would be like to complete the grieving or what would be in it for them. What would they lose in giving up their grief? Although this is a rather simple question, it often yields very fruitful results. Some are fearful that if they give up the grief they will forget the person who died (Powers & Wampold, 1994). They need to find ways of finding an enduring connection and appropriately memorializing the person, developing a continuing bond with the lost loved one. Still others are afraid that relinquishing the grief will give others the notion that they didn't care enough for the deceased. This idea needs to be reality tested.

SPECIAL CONSIDERATIONS FOR GRIEF THERAPY

There are several special issues that one needs to take into consideration when doing grief therapy. The first is the importance of completing the grief work so that the patient is not worse off than before he or she came to you for treatment. If the problem underlying the unresolved grief has been unexpressed anger, it is critical that once this anger is identified and felt, the patient is not left with guilt for the anger. If the therapist merely brings angry feelings to the surface without seeing them adequately resolved, the patient may be worse off than before, possibly even experiencing retroflected anger as depression.

Second, there is the issue of restraining overwhelming feelings. Parkes (2001) discusses the fact that grief therapy may unleash affective material that is overwhelming to the patient. In my clinical experience, this has occurred infrequently. Although patients may experience deep and intense sadness and anger during the course of therapy, it is rare that a patient cannot find the necessary boundaries for these feelings and hold them within an acceptable set of limitations. However, feelings need to be monitored. I use SUDS (subjective units of distress) to monitor affect, both its intensity and resolution. SUDS is a subjective report of a specific affect given by the patient on a scale from 0 (none) to 100 (the most of a specific feeling that one can imagine). I have also found that the concept of "dosing" feelings—or encouraging patients to handle as much of a feeling as they can at the time then back away from it and return to it later—can be useful to some clients. This gives patients control over feelings that sometimes threaten to overwhelm them. In the dual-process approach to grief therapy, the patient is encouraged to oscillate between deep feelings of grief (task II) and a restoration focus on things he or she needs to do to reconstruct his or her world (task III) (Stroebe & Schut, 1999). Related to this is the therapist's ability to tolerate intense feelings that may arise in grief therapy. This ability is obviously key to doing good treatment.

A third consideration is helping patients deal with the awkwardness that is often experienced during grief therapy. If patients sustained a loss several years earlier but have not adequately grieved that loss and through therapy are beginning to get in touch with the normal grief affects not previously experienced, they are going to feel considerable fresh and intense sadness. This may make it very difficult for them in social situations. One such patient was a young woman, an instructor at a local university. Although her father had been dead for 8 years, she had not grieved adequately, and during the course of grief therapy she began to feel all the intensity of the sadness she had not let herself feel before. While trying to perform her duties at the university, people would come up to her and say, "What's wrong? You look so sad. You look like somebody's died." She felt foolish and awkward telling them that yes, her father had died, when the death took place so many years earlier. It helps to give patients some warning that they may experience these kinds of social encounters and they will somehow be able to live around them. Sometimes I have, with the patient's permission, informed family members with whom the patient is living that grief therapy is being done and the patient may experience considerable fresh sadness. In this way the family is alerted to possible changes in behavior and misunderstandings are avoided.

Most of the time grief therapy is done in individual therapy sessions. Grief therapy can also be done in groups if run by competent therapists. McCallum, Piper, Azim, and Lakoff (1991) have an interesting approach to working with complicated grief in time-limited bereavement groups using a psychodynamic focus. Also, in the Netherlands, Schut, de Kiejser, van den Bout, and Stroebe (1996) have found good results from their program for inpatient grief therapy using groups.

TECHNIQUES AND TIMING

One technique that has been extremely helpful to me in doing grief therapy has been the Gestalt therapy technique of the empty chair (Barbato & Irwin, 1992). I've found it is important to have patients talk directly to the deceased person in the present tense rather than simply talk to me about the deceased. Talking *to* the deceased has a greater impact than talking *about* the deceased (Polster & Polster, 1973). I set up an empty chair in the office and have the patient imagine that the deceased is sitting in that chair. Then I have the patient talk directly to the deceased about his or her thoughts and feelings concerning the death and their relationship. I have never had a patient refuse to do this when it was adequately explained during the introduction to the procedure. Even the most hesitant patient has complied, with a little encouragement. This is a very powerful technique and is useful for completing unfinished business, handling guilt and regrets, and the like. You can increase the power of the technique by having the patient switch chairs and talk *for* the deceased as well as *to* the deceased. Like any other psychotherapeutic technique, this technique should not be used unless the therapist is adequately trained. Such a technique is obviously contraindicated with schizophrenic and borderline patients.

A related technique described by Melges and DeMaso (1980) involves having patients sit in chairs, close their eyes, and imagine they are talking to the deceased. This is an acceptable alternative to the empty chair, but what makes the technique important is not whether the person's eyes are opened or closed, but the fact that he or she is able to address the deceased directly in the first person and in the present tense. I was explaining this technique to a colleague of mine at Massachusetts General Hospital who is a prominent biological researcher trained in psychoanalytic psychiatry. I wondered how he would respond when I explained these Gestalt-oriented procedures, but he laughed and shared a personal experience with me. He said that his father had died 2 years earlier and from time to time he imagines that his father is there and holds conversations with him.

Another technique is the use of a role-playing psychodrama. On occasion I have had patients play both themselves and the role of the deceased person, talking back and forth until a particular conflict is resolved. Using pictures of the deceased can often facilitate the goals of therapy. The patient brings to the session a favorite photograph, which is then used to stimulate memories and affects and, on occasion, is used as the focus for discussions with the deceased in the present tense.

Homework is also useful in grief therapy. It is something that is used in other types of therapy, especially Gestalt psychotherapy and cognitive behavioral therapy. By assigning homework for the patient to do between therapy sessions, one can extend the benefits of a single weekly session and make the therapy shorter and more effective. This is particularly effective in briefer therapy. There is no limit on what can be assigned. Often it is the monitoring of affect and paying attention to the cognitions that stimulate the affect. Letters to the deceased can be written at home and brought into the session and shared with the therapist. There are two caveats to consider: Be sure to support the homework assignment so that patients know why you are asking them to do a particular task at home. Second, be sure to ask for a report on what they did at home. If you don't ask them for the results, they will assume that it is not important and will not complete the assignment.

With any technique, timing is essential. It is crucial that the therapist know how to time the interventions. Affect encouraged before a patient is ready will not be forthcoming. Ill-timed interpretations will fall on the floor. Training people to time psychotherapeutic interventions is always difficult. The best I can do is to reiterate that timing is extremely important because of the sensitive nature of the material and the time-limited nature of the contract.

DREAMS IN GRIEF COUNSELING AND THERAPY

The dreams of the bereaved frequently parallel the mourning process and often reflect the particular task of mourning that the grieving person is struggling with. One strategy in counseling is to link the dreams to these tasks. It is common for a mourner to dream that the dead loved one is alive only to wake up to the reality that the person is gone and will not be coming back. Such dreams can be seen as a struggle with the first mourning task to make the loss real.

Dream research shows that dreams can also help integrate troubling affects for the mourner. This relates to the second task of mourning—allowing feelings to be processed. Feelings of guilt, anger, and anxiety are common experiences after a loss, but there are times when these affects are so intense that they tend to impair the functioning of the bereaved person. Traumatic deaths can lead to considerable troubling affect, as seen in flashbacks and hyperarousal behavior. Dreams can help a person integrate these affects of trauma in a way that sometimes cannot be done in the waking state.

Adjusting to a world without the deceased (task III) can leave the mourner struggling with many problems to be solved. It is not unusual for the dreamer to experience the deceased returning to proffer advice on ways to deal with a particular problem. Such advice from the "other side" can help attenuate anxiety and move the mourner toward some possible solutions. Meaning making is also an important part of task III, and dreams can be useful in helping the bereaved to make sense of the loss.

How to go on without the deceased is a problem for many mourners who are struggling with task IV. One young man whose wife died suddenly found himself unable to establish a relationship with a new woman. He would date but then break off any developing relationship. After 5 years this became a problem for which he sought counseling. During the counseling he had a series of dreams in which the dead wife appeared and gave him permission to move on with his life and find someone new to love. He valued this permission but did not want to forget his wife when establishing a new relationship. One day when visiting her grave, he realized that whenever he wanted to remember her, he could go to her grave, and that gave him something concrete to hold onto as a way of memorializing her.

Since mourning is a process, one can get stuck anywhere in the process. Dreams can be a useful tool not only to show where one is stuck but also to identify what might be causing the impasse and why the person is stuck. For one mother whose young adult daughter was killed in a freak accident, a series of dreams found her searching for her daughter, wanting to find her and to know she was all right. She could not move forward with her life until she knew that her daughter was all right. In many of the dreams she could see her daughter, always at a distance and looking happy, but also leaving the mother with some uncertainty. Toward the end of counseling, she had a dream in which she grabbed a balloon that carried her high up to a cloud on which her daughter resided. Her daughter was surprised to see her, and they had a conversation in which her daughter assured her that she was all right. Relieved, the mother asked how she could get down. "Step down, Mother, and you will land where you need to be," said the daughter. From this dream the mother took the message that her daughter was all right and that she herself needed to be back on earth pursuing her own life. Many mourners have a strong wish to know that the loved one is all right, and many bereavement dreams reflect this.

SOME CONSIDERATIONS

Counselors who encourage clients to take note of their dreams and to share them in counseling sessions should note the following:

1. The deceased does not need to appear in the dream in order for the dream to be relevant to the mourning process. However, if the deceased appears in the dream, it is usually important to the grief, and one should not ignore the appearance of the deceased (alive, dead, etc.) or the activity in which the deceased is engaged.

2. Don't overlook dream fragments. Frequently a client will not feel that such fragments are important. However, if the coun-

selor and client are engaged in a mutual pursuit to understand the client's mourning, then putting the dream fragments together, much as one might put puzzle pieces together, can be useful.

3. Let the dreamer tell you the meaning of the dream (Barrett, 2002). Using dreams in grief work is not the same as in analytic work, where dreams are interpreted by the therapist. The woman who rose on the balloon to visit her daughter on a cloud mentioned that the color of the balloon was gold. Upon inquiry, she told me that the family would present family members with a gift of gold on each birthday and anniversary. Gold gave the event a special meaning in that family. The message she got from the dream was that her daughter was giving her the gift to go on with her life.

4. When a client has a series of dreams, look for the underlying themes that may tie all the dreams together. Often the same theme underlies each dream although the metaphors and images in the dream may vary (Belicki, Gulko, Ruzycki, & Aristotle, 2003).

5. It is not unusual for clients to have dreams of the deceased that occur around the anniversary of the death. This is true for those who have not dreamed regularly of the deceased. Anniversaries other than the death, such as birthdays, weddings, and other life transitions, can also trigger such dreams. Train clients to pay attention to these dreams and to use them as a way of understanding where they are in their grief.

6. Attachments are not all the same, and dreams can sometimes give one a clue as to the nature of the attachment. One mother whose young adult daughter was killed suddenly had grief that went on for years. Her family, who had done their grieving, could not understand the length of the mother's grief. In a series of dreams, the mother was seeking mothering from this oldest daughter—something that she never received from her own mother. This led her to an important awareness of the nature of this relationship and how letting go of her daughter would mean that she was letting go of the hope of ever being mothered again.

EVALUATING RESULTS

There are usually three types of change that help one evaluate the effectiveness of grief therapy. These are changes in subjective experience, behavior, and symptom relief.

Subjective Experience

People who complete a course of grief therapy report that they are different. They talk of increased feelings of self-esteem and less guilt. They make comments like "The pain, which has been tearing me to pieces, is now gone," "I feel like this time I have really buried my mother," and "I can speak of my father without getting choked up with watery eyes."

Another subjective experience that patients report is an increase in positive feelings about the deceased. They are able to think about the deceased and relate their positive feelings to positive experiences (Lazare, 1979). One woman who had great difficulty grieving the loss of her mother said at the end of treatment, "Now I just miss her. Before, it was anguish. I think mother would be happy with my progress. Her death revived a lot of childhood feelings of frustration and helplessness. I'm not that angry anymore. There are some days when I don't even think of mother, and that surprises me."

Behavioral Changes

Without suggestions from the therapist, many patients experience observable behavioral changes. Searching behavior stops, they begin to socialize again, or they begin to form new relationships. Patients who have previously avoided religious activities begin to return to them. People who have avoided visiting the gravesite now visit without it being suggested. One woman who had never changed her dead son's room came to the last session of grief therapy and said, "I'm going to dismantle my son's room and store his things in the basement. I don't think it will dishonor his memory to do this and to make a den out of his bedroom." I had never suggested this to her, but these kinds of behavioral changes are very common in somebody who has passed through a grief therapy sequence to the other side. A widow came on her own to the point where she removed her wedding ring, saying, "I'm not a married woman anymore." In still another case a woman who previously would not fly the flag that draped her son's casket began to fly it on appropriate holidays.

Symptom Relief

There are also measurable signs of symptom relief that occur when somebody has completed a sequence of grief therapy. Patients report fewer body aches and abatement of the symptom that originally brought them in for treatment. One patient exhibited gagging symptoms, which were giving her great difficulty. They turned out to be very similar to the symptoms that her father exhibited during the last 2 days of his life and that she had observed as a 5-year-old. These symptoms abated naturally after she had completed the grief therapy sequence and had taken care of the unfinished business with her dead father.

There are a number of clinical instruments that can be used with patients to help them make a more formal assessment of where they are in their grieving symptoms. In addition to using ratings like SUDS to measure relative distress, therapists can use the Beck Depression Inventory or the CES-D Depression measure to assess depression. The SCL-90 measures depression, anxiety, and general well-being. Grief can be assessed through scales like TRIG (Texas Revised Inventory of Grief); the Hogan Grief Inventory; and, of course, the latest version of the Inventory of Complicated Grief.

The point I would like to make here is that grief therapy works. Unlike some other psychotherapies, where the therapist may not be certain about its effectiveness, grief therapy can be very effective. The subjective experiences and observable behavioral changes lend credence to the value of such targeted therapeutic intervention.

REFERENCES

Barbato, A., & Irwin, H. J. (1992). Major therapeutic systems and the bereaved client. *Australian Psychologist, 27*, 22–27.

Barrett, D. (2002). The "royal road" becomes a shrewd shortcut: The use of dreams in focused treatment. *Journal of Cognitive Psychotherapy, 16,* 55–63.

Belicki, K., Gulko, N., Ruzycki, K., & Aristotle, J. (2003). Sixteen years of dreams following spousal bereavement. *Omega, 47,* 93–106.

Bonanno, G. A., & Papa, A. (2003). The social and functional aspects of emotional expression during bereavement. In P. Philippot (Ed.), *Nonverbal behavior in clinical settings* (pp. 145–170). London: Oxford University Press.

Field, N. P., Nichols, C., Holen, A., & Horowitz, M. J. (1999). The relation of continuing attachment to adjustment in conjugal bereavement. *Journal of Consulting & Clinical Psychology, 67,* 212–218.

Lazare, A. (1979). Unresolved grief. In A. Lazare (Ed.), *Outpatient psychiatry: Diagnosis and treatment* (pp. 498–512). Baltimore: Williams and Wilkens.

McCallum, M., Piper, W. E., Azim, H. F., & Lakoff, R. S. (1991). The Edmonton model of short-term group therapy for loss: An integration of theory, practice and research. *Group Analysis, 24,* 375–388.

Melges, F. T., & DeMaso, D. R. (1980). Grief-resolution therapy: Relieving, revising, and revisiting. *American Journal of Psychotherapy, 34,* 51–61.

Neimeyer, R. (2003). *Lessons of loss: A guide to coping.* New York: Routledge.

Parkes, C. M. (2001). *Bereavement: Studies of grief in adult life* (3rd ed.). Philadelphia: Taylor & Francis.

Polster, E., & Polster, M. (1973). *Gestalt therapy integrated.* New York: Brunner/Mazel.

Powers, L. E., & Wampold, B. E. (1994). Cognitive-behavioral factors in adjustment to adult bereavement. *Death Studies, 18,* 1–24.

Prigerson, H. G., & Maciejewski, P. K. (2005–2006). A call for sound empirical testing and evaluation of criteria for complicated grief proposed for *DSM-V. Omega, 52,* 9–19.

Schut, H., de Kiejser, J., van den Bout, J., & Stroebe, M. S. (1996). Cross-modality grief therapy: Description and assessment of a new program. *Journal of Clinical Psychology, 52,* 357–365.

Shear, K. (2006). Adapting imaginal exposure to the treatment of complicated grief. In B. O. Rothbaum (Ed.), *Pathological anxiety: Emotional processing in etiology and treatment* (pp. 215–226). New York: Guilford Press.

Simos, B. G. (1979). *A time to grieve.* New York: Family Service Association.

Solomon, R., & Rando, T. (2007). Utilization of EMDR in the treatment of grief and mourning. *Journal of EMDR Practice & Research, 1,* 109–117.

Sprang, G. (2001). The use of EMDR in the treatment of traumatic stress and complicated mourning: Psychological and behavioral outcomes. *Research on Social Work Practice, 11,* 300–320.

Stroebe, M. S., Hansson, R. O., & Stroebe, W. (2001). Introduction: Concepts and is-sues in contemporary research on bereavement. In M. S. Stroebe, R. O. Hansson, W. Stroebe, & H. Schut (Eds.), *Handbook of bereavement research: Consequences, coping, and care* (pp. 3–22). Washington, DC: American Psychological Association.

Stroebe, M. S., & Schut, H. (1999). The dual process model of coping with bereavement: Rationale and description. *Death Studies, 23,* 197–224.

Volkan, V. (1972). The linking objects of pathological mourners. *Archives of General Psychiatry, 27,* 215–221.

Wagner, B., Knaevelsrud, C., & Maercker, A. (2005). Internet-based treatment for com-plicated grief: Concepts and case study. *Journal of Loss & Trauma, 10,* 409–423.

Wortman, C. B., & Silver, R. C. (2001). The myths of coping with loss revisited. In M. S. Stroebe, R. O. Hansson, W. Stroebe, & H. Schut (Eds.), *Handbook of bereave-ment research: Consequences, coping, and care* (pp. 405–429). Washington, DC: American Psychological Association.

7 Grieving Special Types of Losses

There are certain modes and circumstances of death that require additional understanding and intervention modifications that go beyond the procedures described in the previous chapters. Losses from suicide, sudden death, sudden infant death, miscarriage and stillbirth, abortion, anticipated death, and AIDS can all create distinct problems for the survivors. The counselor should be aware of the special features and problems inherent in these situations and what they suggest with regard to counseling interventions.

SUICIDE

Nearly 750,000 people a year are left to grieve the completed suicide of a family member or loved one, and they are left not only with a sense of loss, but with a legacy of shame, fear, rejection, anger, and guilt. Edwin Shneidman, considered to be the father of the suicide prevention movement in the United States, has said:

> I believe that the person who commits suicide puts his psychological skeletons in the survivor's emotional closet—he sentences the survivors to deal with many negative feelings, and, more, to become obsessed with thoughts regarding their own actual or possible role in having

precipitated the suicidal act or having failed to abort it. It can be a heavy load. (Cain, 1972, p. x)

Richard McGee, who directed a large suicide prevention center in Florida, believes that "suicide is the most difficult bereavement crisis for any family to face and resolve in an effective manner" (Cain, 1972, p. 11). My own clinical experience with survivors of those who die by suicide confirms these observations. The person doing grief counseling must recognize in what ways this experience is unique in order to tailor intervention for maximum effectiveness. There is some evidence that the grief in suicide bereavement may be more intense and last longer than grief from other types of losses (Farberow, Gallagher-Thompson, Gilewski, & Thompson, 1992). There are others who argue that it is not different (Cleiren & Diekstra, 1995). Still others argue that suicide bereavement is a combination of grief and post-traumatic stress (Callahan, 2000). Despite these differences, there is general agreement that the three main themes found in suicide bereavement are generally not found in other kinds of death losses: Why did they do it? Why didn't I prevent it? How could he or she do this to me? (Jordan, 2001).

Of all the specific feelings the survivors of those who die by suicide experience, one of the predominant feelings is *shame.* In our society there is still a stigma associated with suicide (Houck, 2007). The survivors are the ones who have to suffer the shame after a family member takes his or her own life, and their sense of shame can be influenced by the reactions of others. "No one will talk to me," said one woman whose son killed himself. "They act as if it never happened." This added emotional pressure not only affects the survivor's interactions with society but can also dramatically alter relationships within the family unit (Kaslow & Aronson, 2004). It is not unusual for family members to acknowledge who knows and who does not know the facts surrounding the death and, almost with tacit agreement, adjust their behavior toward others based on this knowledge.

There is also a stigma for the victim of a suicide attempt that fails (Cvinar, 2005). One woman jumped from a 155-foot bridge and survived, something rarely done from such a height. But after her jump she experienced such a negative reaction from the people around her and was so filled with shame that she repeated the attempt. She jumped again from the same bridge and this time died.

Guilt is another common feeling among survivors of suicide victims. They often take responsibility for the action of the deceased and have a gnawing feeling that there was something they should or could have done to prevent the death. This feeling of guilt is particularly difficult when the suicide happened in the context of some interpersonal conflict between the deceased and the survivor.

We saw in chapter 1 that guilt is a normal feeling after any type of death, but in the case of death by suicide they can be seriously exacerbated. Survivors of suicide victims experience guilt more often than do those who survive those who have died from other causes (McIntosh & Kelly, 1992). Because of the intensity of the guilt, people may feel the need to be punished, and they may interact with society in such a way that society, in turn, punishes them. Children who turn to delinquency or who become involved in excessive use of drugs or alcohol are often examples of this self-punishing behavior. Whether or not survivors are successful in their need to be punished, the changes in their behavior patterns are significant and observable.

Sometimes survivors with this need go to extremes to get the punishment they think they deserve. I saw one woman in therapy who punished herself by eating excessively until she weighed more than 300 pounds. But, as if that were not enough, she then went through stages in which she would take a hammer and break her own bones. In time they would heal and then she would smash them again. Her particular problem arose after the suicidal death of her younger brother. She felt some of the normal responsibility for this, but her burden was increased when her grandparents told her outright that she was responsible for his death. She was young, and her inability to reality test the guilt led her to a long and bizarre sequence of self-destructive behavior.

Guilt can sometimes be manifested as *blame*. Some people handle their own sense of culpability by projecting their guilt onto others and blaming them for the death. Finding someone to blame can be an attempt to affirm control and to find a sense of meaning in a difficult-to-understand situation.

People who survive those who die by suicide usually experience intense feelings of *anger.* They perceive the death as a rejection; when they ask, "Why, why, why?" they usually mean, "Why did he do this to me?" The intensity of their rage often makes them feel guilty. A middle-aged woman whose husband killed himself paced through her house for nearly 6 months shouting, "Damn it, if you hadn't killed yourself, I would kill you for what you're putting me through." She needed to get the rage out of her system, and in a 2-year follow-up, she seemed to be doing very well.

A correlate of this anger is *low self-esteem.* Erich Lindemann and Ina May Greer (1953) emphasized this when they said, "To be bereft by self-imposed death is to be rejected" (p. 10). Survivors often speculate that the deceased did not think enough of them or they would not have committed suicide. This "rejection" can be an indictment of the survivor's self-worth, leading to low self-esteem and intense grief reactions (Reed, 1993). In such cases, counseling can be especially helpful.

Fear is a common response after a suicide. Farberow and colleagues (1992) found higher levels of anxiety among survivors of those who die by suicide than among survivors of those who died natural deaths. A common primary fear among survivors is their own self-destructive impulses. Many seem to carry with them a sense of fate or doom. This is especially true of sons of suicide victims:

> Characteristically they find life lacking a certain zing. They tend to feel more rootless than most, even in a notoriously rootless society. They are squeamishly incurious about the past, numbly certain about the future, to this grisly extent they suspect that they too will probably kill themselves. (Cain, 1972, p. 7)

I once followed a group of young men whose fathers killed themselves when the young men were in early adolescence. Each of these young men, followed into their 20s and 30s, believed that suicide would be his own fate. It is not unusual for the survivors of those who take their own lives to develop this preoccupation with suicide. But while some scare themselves with this, others cope by working as volunteers for suicide prevention groups such as the Samaritans.

In cases where there have been several suicides in one family, there may be anxiety concerning genetic transmission of the tendency. One young woman came for counseling prior to her marriage because of this fear. Two of her siblings had killed themselves, and she wondered if her offspring would have a tendency toward suicide or if she would fail as a parent, as she felt her parents had failed her brothers.

Distorted thinking is another feature found among survivors of suicide victims. Very often survivors, especially children, need to see the victim's behavior not as a suicide but as an accidental death. What develops is a type of distorted communication in families. The family creates a myth about what really happened to the victim, and anyone who challenges this myth by calling the death by its real name reaps the anger of the others, who need to see it as an accidental death or some other type of more natural phenomenon. This kind of distorted thinking may prove helpful on a short-term basis, but it is definitely not productive in the long run.

It is important to keep in mind that suicide victims often come from families in which there are difficult social problems such as alcoholism or child abuse. Within this context ambivalent feelings may already exist between family members, and the suicide only serves to exacerbate these feelings and problems. In order to maximize the effectiveness of grief counseling, the counselor must take into consideration the social and family difficulties that may exist as correlates to the suicide itself.

The issue of *assisted suicide* is under discussion more now than when I wrote the earlier editions of this book (Pearlman et al., 2005). Preliminary research has indicated that being involved in an assisted death can actually lead to positive outcomes for the survivor. However, if a person was not a part of the planning or enacting of an assisted death, then he or she may have reactions more similar to the typical survivor of someone who died by suicide (Werth, 1999). More research is obviously needed here.

COUNSELING SURVIVORS OF SUICIDE VICTIMS

When one is counseling survivors following a suicidal death, it is important to remember that death by suicide is one of those *socially unspeakable losses* mentioned earlier (Lazare, 1979). Both the survivors and others are hesitant to talk about such a death. A counselor or therapist can move in and help fill the gap caused by this loss of communication with others. Intervention with such survivors can include the following:

Reality Test the Guilt and Blame

This procedure, described in chapter 4, may take more time in the case of survivors of suicide victims. Again, much of the guilt may be unrealistic and will yield itself to reality testing, giving the person some sense of relief. One young woman who felt guilt over her brother's death was helped when she read a letter she had sent to him shortly before his suicide. The letter was among his effects, and it helped her see that she had reached out to him. There are some instances, however, in which the person really is culpable, and the counselor is challenged to help the person deal with these valid feelings of guilt. When blame is the predominant feature, the counselor can also promote reality testing. If the blame takes the form of scapegoating, family meetings can be an effective way to resolve this. A few survivors feel guilty because of their sense of relief. A long history of chronic problems with the deceased that included aberrant behavior and previous suicide attempts is now over because of the death (Hawton & Simkin, 2003).

Correct Denial and Distortions

Survivors need to face the reality of the suicide in order to be able to work through it. Using tough words with them such as "killed himself" or "hanged himself" can facilitate this. People who witnessed the suicide are sometimes plagued by intrusive images of the scene and show this and other signs of PTSD (Callahan, 2000). For people who were not present, the imagined scene can sometimes be worse than the actual one. Exploring graphic images can be difficult, but discussing them can help with reality testing. These images usually fade with time, but if not, special intervention may be required.

Another task is correcting distortions and redefining the image of the deceased, bringing it closer to reality. Many survivors tend to see the victim as either all good or all bad, an illusion that needs to be challenged. I worked with one young woman whose father committed suicide. During her therapy it was important for her to redefine his image from that of a "superdad" to that of a superdad who suffered from deep clinical depression, saw no way out, and in desperation took his own life.

Explore Fantasies of the Future

Use reality testing to explore the fantasies survivors have as to how the death will affect them in the future. If there is a reality involved, explore ways to cope with that reality by addressing questions the survivor may have, such as "When I have children, how can I tell them that their uncle killed himself?"

Work With Anger

Working with the anger and rage such a death can engender allows for its expression while reinforcing personal controls the survivor has over these feelings. A woman whose husband killed himself said at the final counseling session, "I've gotten through the hard part. It is a relief to be angry and you've given me permission to do this. There is still grief, but I feel it's okay."

Reality Test the Sense of Abandonment

Feeling abandoned is perhaps one of the most devastating results of a suicide. People who lose loved ones through a natural death feel abandoned, even though the death was neither desired nor caused by the deceased. However, in the case of death by choice, the sense of abandonment is extreme. There may be some reality in this feeling, but the level of reality can be assessed through counseling.

Help Them in Their Quest to Find Meaning in the Death

The existential quest for meaning is activated with any bereavement and is related to task III. Survivors of those who take their own lives are confronted additionally by a death that is sudden, unexpected, and sometimes violent (Range & Calhoun, 1990). There is a need to search for an answer to why the loved one has taken his or her life and, in particular, to determine the state of mind of the deceased before the death. Survivors frequently feel obliged to explain the suicide to others when such an explanation is typically beyond their own understanding (Moore & Freeman, 1995). In one study, Clark and Goldney (1995) found that soon after the loss many survivors could see no meaning in the tragedy. For some this changed over time, leading them to a sense of healing and the ability to make positive changes in their lives. Others remained devastated and bitter. Some found the medical model of mental illness and suicide helpful, particularly the neurotransmitter theory of depression. Making sense of suicide is a complex process and is not linear (Begley & Quayle, 2007).

Here are some additional intervention suggestions:

1. Contact the person or family right away, before distortions set in. Family myths begin early. Use the phrase "died by suicide" rather than "committed suicide," which connotes a more criminalized stigma (Parrish & Tunkle, 2003).
2. Watch for acting-out potential in counseling. The clients may try to get the counselor to reject them in order to fulfill their own negative self-image. Survivors should also be monitored for their suicide risk and risk for other psychiatric problems. Jordan and McMenamy (2004), quoting Shneidman, remind us that "postvention *is* prevention."
3. Many survivors of those who die by suicide feel that no one can understand them unless they have undergone a similar loss experience (Wagner & Calhoun, 1991). If there are a sufficient number of people grieving this type of loss, consider starting a group for survivors of suicide victims in your community. There is value in sharing with others who have experienced a similar loss. If you are doing a general bereavement group and have one survivor of a suicide victim in the group, try to include another to avoid the conclusion "Nobody in here can understand my loss." Mitchell, Gale, Garand, and Wesner (2003) used a narrative approach in an 8-week suicide bereavement support

group with good results. The focus was on closure around the *death* independent of the suicide itself.

4. Counseling should involve the family and the larger social system, if possible (Jordan, 2001). However, don't assume that all families will fall apart. Some families grow closer through this type of crisis (McNiel, Hatcher, & Reubin, 1988). See Kaslow and Aronson (2004) for intervention suggestions with suicidal families.

Although there are many common experiences that survivors of suicide victims go through, the counselor must constantly remind him- or herself that the experience of grief is multidetermined, and the mediators of mourning described in chapter 3 can account for striking individual differences.

SUDDEN DEATH

Sudden deaths are those that occur without warning and require special understanding and intervention. Although suicidal deaths fall into this category, there are other types of sudden deaths, such as accidental deaths, heart attacks, and homicides, that need to be discussed. Several studies have followed people for a number of months subsequent to such a loss to assess the resolution of bereavement. In most of these studies, the conclusions are similar—sudden deaths are often more difficult to grieve than other deaths in which there is some prior warning that death is imminent (Parkes, 1975). Over the past decade we have seen an increase in sudden deaths, especially violent deaths. Terrorist activities, school shootings, drive-by shootings, earthquakes, and airplane disasters all attest to this.

There are certain special features that should be considered in work with the survivors of those who die a sudden death. A sudden death usually leaves survivors with a sense of *unreality about the loss.* Whenever the phone rings and one learns that a loved one has died unexpectedly, it creates a sense of unreality, which may last a long time. It is not unusual for the survivor to feel numb and to walk around in a daze following such a loss. It is common for the survivor to experience nightmares and intrusive images after a sudden loss, even though they were not present at the time of the death. Appropriate counseling intervention can help the survivor deal with this manifestation of sudden death, reality test the event, and deal with the intrusive images from the trauma.

A second feature that is often found in cases of sudden death has to do with the exacerbation of *feelings of guilt*. Feelings of guilt are common following any type of death. However, in the case of a sudden death, there is often a strong sense of guilt expressed in "if only" statements such as "If only I hadn't let them go to the party," or "If only I had been with him." One of the main issues of counseling intervention is to focus on this sense of culpability and help the survivor reality test the issues of responsibility. A common phenomenon found in children after a sudden death is that of guilt associated with the fulfillment of a hostile wish. It is not uncommon for children to wish that their parents were dead or that their siblings were dead, and the sudden death of that person or people toward whom the hostile wish was directed can leave the child with a very difficult load of guilt (Worden, 1996).

Related to the guilt is the *need to blame,* and in the case of a sudden death, the need to blame someone for what happened can be extremely strong. Because of this, it is not unusual for someone within the family to become the scapegoat and, unfortunately, children often become easy targets for such reactions.

A fourth feature of sudden death is the frequent *involvement of medical and legal authorities*, especially in cases of accidents or homicide. For those whose loved one was the victim of homicide, getting on with the tasks of mourning is difficult, if not impossible, until the legal aspects of the case are resolved. For one family whose young adult daughter was murdered, the legal process went on for 6 years after the death, with no end in sight. Her father said, "Usually, when you have a death in the family, you have the death, you have the mourning, and slowly but surely you get on with your lives. But as long as this goes on, there is no end to the mourning, no time to put what happened behind" (Kerr, 1989). Some feel they have been victimized yet again by the systems that should be assisting them. These cases may need to be investigated, and because there is often some strong hint of culpability, this may lead to an inquest and to a trial. As everyone knows, the judicial system moves slowly, and these procedures often take a long time to reach completion. The delays can serve one of two functions. They can delay the grieving process; that is, people who are grieving may be so distracted by the details of the trial that they are kept from dealing with their own grief on a firsthand basis. However, there are times when these legal interruptions can play a positive role. When there is some adjudication of a case and the case is closed, this can help people move forward with their grieving.

A fifth special feature of sudden death is the sense of *helplessness* that it elicits on the part of the survivor. This type of death is an assault on our sense of power and on our sense of orderliness. Often this helplessness is linked with an incredible sense of rage, and it is not unusual for the survivor to want to vent his or her anger at someone. Occasionally, hospital personnel become the targets of violence or the survivor expresses a wish to kill certain people for having been involved in the death of a loved one. It is not uncommon to hear litigious accusations coming from survivors of those who die a sudden death. This expression of their rage may help counter the feelings of helplessness they are experiencing. The counselor should also be aware that the desire for retribution may be a defense against both the reality and the pain of the death (Rynearson, 1994).

A survivor can also exhibit manifest *agitation*. The stress of sudden death can trigger a flight-or-fight response in a person and lead to a very agitated depression. A sudden increase in levels of adrenalin usually is associated with this agitation.

Unfinished business is another special concern of survivors of those who die a sudden death. The death leaves them with many regrets for things they did not say and things they never got around to doing with the deceased. Counseling intervention can help the survivor to focus on this unfinished business and find some way to closure.

A final special feature of sudden death is an increased *need to understand*. In chapter 2 we discussed how in any death people are interested in why it happened. Meaning making is a large part of mourning task III. In the case of sudden death, there seems to be an especially strong need to find meaning. This search for meaning can be related to the need for mastery when a death has been traumatic.

Along with this, of course, is the need not only to determine the cause but to assign blame. At this point, some people find that God is the only available target for their recriminations, and it is not uncommon to hear people say, "I hate God," when they are trying to put together the pieces following the death.

Now let's look at some interventions that can be helpful to people after a sudden death. Intervention in these cases really becomes crisis intervention, and the principles of crisis intervention are appropriate here. It is of historical interest that the writing on crisis intervention actually began after Lindemann's (1944) publication of his work on the survivors of the Coconut Grove fire when he worked with a bereaved population.

Some counselors will be at the scene of the crisis. In many cases this will be the hospital. Help should be firmly offered. People in a state of numbness cannot always ask for help. Asking, "Do you need any help?" may get a negative reply. It is more productive for the intervener to say to the family, "I see people who have experienced this type of loss, and I'm here to talk and work with you. We need to call" family members, funeral homes, and so forth. Lending ego strength in the short haul can be useful, but reinforcing self-efficacy to minimize regression as soon as possible is the most salient intervention.

Help the survivors actualize the loss. There are several ways that this can be done. One is giving them a choice to see the body of the deceased to facilitate grief and actualization. I have found this to be a salutary experience on many occasions and advocate allowing people to see the body tastefully displayed, even in the case of death by automobile or other violent accidents. If the body is mutilated, the family should be informed of this before seeing the deceased. Being able to see the body, or part of the body, can help bring home the reality of the loss, which is mourning task I. I have spoken to people who didn't see the body after an accidental death and years later tell me that they wish they had. Another way to help actualize the loss is to keep them focused on the death (the loss), not on the circumstances of the accident or the blame.

Another intervention that the counselor can use to help the person come to the reality of the loss is to use the word "dead," for example, "Jenny is dead. Whom do you want to notify about her death?" Using this word helps bring home the reality of death as well as giving assistance with regard to arrangements that need to be made.

The counselor should be familiar with the hospital and ensure the physical comfort of the family members, enabling them to be with each other, if at all possible, in a place away from the hustle and bustle of the emergency care service. Everything should be done to make them physically comfortable.

As a caregiver, be careful not to handle your own sense of helplessness through the dispensation of platitudes. Occasionally we hear comments at the hospital that are meant to be helpful, like "You've still got your husband" or "You've still got your kids." Most survivors report that these comments are not comforting. For the caregiver to say, "It's going to be all right," is really to hold out false promise. However, for the caregiver to say, "You will survive this," is not a platitude but a matter of truth, and occasionally this comment can bring some comfort to a person in this type of crisis.

Finally, offer follow-up care, either from yourself or community or religious resources. For example, there are specialized support groups for the families and friends of those who have died by violence sponsored by Parents of Murdered Children (888-818-POMC). Be aware of these kinds of resources and make referrals to these specialized groups as part of the ongoing care for people whose family members or friends have died a sudden death.

In any discussion of sudden death, one should consider the issue of *trauma.* Certain deaths such as homicide can evoke trauma responses as well as grief responses. The central features of trauma are intrusive images; avoidant thinking; and hyperarousal, such as hearing a car backfire and thinking that it is a gunshot. Current wisdom suggests that post-traumatic stress symptoms should be clinically addressed before the grief work can be done (Parkes, 1993; Rando, 1993). Rynearson, who has pioneered research on bereavement after homicide, and McCreery (1993) state:

> Disintegratory effects of traumatic imagery and avoidance on cognition, affect, and behavior impair the more introspective and reflective demands of acknowledging and adjusting to the loss. While acknowledgment of the loss is a fundamental theme in therapy . . . the initial goal

of treatment includes moderation of the intrusive/avoidance response. (p. 260)

There are specific interventions aimed at those diagnosed with PTSD such as EMDR (Solomon & Rando, 2007). However, the initial treatment strategy must be supportive and focused on the reestablishment of resiliency, since most of these survivors are overwhelmed and reactive, rather than focusing the grief on mediators of mourning such as an ambivalent relationship and guilt.

SUDDEN INFANT DEATH SYNDROME (SIDS)

One type of sudden death that should be considered separately is sudden infant death. Seven to ten thousand babies die this way each year in the United States alone. SIDS occurs in infants less than 1 year of age, and most frequently among infants (often boys) ages 2 to 6 months. The causes of this phenomenon are not fully known, and the pathogenesis of SIDS has not been firmly established, although pediatric guidelines for parents to help prevent SIDS have been published (Task Force on Sudden Infant Death Syndrome, 2005). Parents who lose children to SIDS often think that the baby died of suffocation or choking or that the baby had some previously unsuspected illness.

There are several factors that complicate grieving this type of loss. First, the death occurs without warning in babies that appear healthy. Since it comes as a surprise, there is no opportunity to prepare for the loss, as there is in the case of infants and children who die of a progressive disease. Second, there is the absence of a definite cause, which gives rise to considerable guilt and blame. Family members and friends are always wondering, "Why did the baby die?" The absence of definitive information often creates suspicion that there was some type of neglect on the part of the parents. This lack of cause may also trigger a relentless search by the parents for the reason for the death. Adding to the guilt of some parents is interest in the possibility of maternal prenatal substance use as a factor in SIDS (Gaines & Kandall, 1992).

A third difficulty comes from the involvement of the legal system. As mentioned earlier, in the case of a sudden death, there is need for an investigation; very often the police investigate cases of SIDS. Many parents who have gone through this experience report that they had to endure insensitive interrogation and, in a few cases, even incarceration. With the increasing awareness of child abuse and child neglect, parents whose children have died of SIDS are now open to suspicion and legal investigation, which only adds to the stress of an already stressful situation.

Another issue is the impact of a SIDS death on *siblings*. It is not unusual for older siblings to resent the arrival of a new baby into the household, and when the baby dies they can experience guilt and remorse. One study of siblings found high levels of depression, aggression, and social withdrawal in siblings 4–11 years of age 2 years after the SIDS death (Hutton & Bradley, 1994).

The potential for partners suffering such a loss to break up is high. Tensions build up after the death, and couples may not have sexual relations because of the fear of pregnancy and a repeat of the experience. The wife may feel that her husband does not care enough about the death because he does not cry when she does. But what some wives do not realize is that the husband often does not cry because he does not want to upset her or he may be uncomfortable crying. Nevertheless, this type of misconception can place great strain on a relationship and is a good example of the communication breakdown that can occur between parents under such pressure. Not only is there sadness, but there is also much anger. One father whose child died of SIDS at 2 months of age said to me, "I let him into my life for 2 months and he left me." At first he felt guilty about these feelings, but through counseling, he was helped to understand that they were normal.

There are certain things we can do to help people better manage this type of loss. The first has to do with how the parents are treated in the hospital. Generally, after this type of death, the infant is rushed to the hospital, where death is pronounced. How this information is passed on to the parents is important in terms of helping them to adjust to the loss. At the hospital, a sensitive intervention on the part of the hospital staff is to allow the parents the option of spending time with the dead baby. This can be extremely important because often the parents want to be near their child, to hold their child, or to talk to their dead child. There is a difference of opinion among hospital personnel as to the value of this. But in my opinion, it is very important to let the parents have this option. A number of parents who have spent time with their dead babies have later reported that this helped them get through this very difficult experience. Second, the importance of autopsy permission in this type of death cannot be overemphasized. It provides the parents with some reality as to what really did or did not happen. Morgan and Goering (1978), writing on this subject, have suggested that "postmortem examination" is a more acceptable term to the layperson than "autopsy." Permission for autopsy is sometimes denied in cases where the parent feels some guilt about the loss. However, the person asking permission can mention a number of important reasons for doing the autopsy: it is the last chance to learn all the facts about the illness and cause of death; it is easier to accept death when we know that it was inevitable; knowledge of the exact cause of death is often necessary for settling insurance or legal matters. If the person requesting the autopsy is convinced of its importance, he or she is much more likely to obtain permission. Family members should not be bullied into giving permission but should be tactfully encouraged to do so.

It is very important for the physician to provide information to the family about sudden infant death syndrome. It is also important to give parents some information about the grief process so that they do not feel like they are going crazy or that their grief will never end. And the therapist should not overlook the siblings and their thoughts and feelings about the loss. This can be done within the context of family therapy as well as through the monitoring of their behavior following the death. Often trouble sleeping or problems in school will arise for these children.

Finally, parents can be counseled about subsequent pregnancies. Very often they are afraid of having another child because of the possibility of SIDS. Counselors should also be aware of the high probability for denial in this type of death due to the circumstances, the age of the child, and the suddenness of the death. Many parents feel a need to keep the room intact, to draw daily baths, and to keep on with the routine for a long time until they gradually come to the adaptation to grief task I, the awareness that the child is gone and is never coming back.

Counseling should take place over time because it is very difficult for the parents to absorb all the information at once. I think that an important part of counseling is encouraging patients to talk to other couples or families who have experienced similar trauma. Support groups are available for these parents. Such sharing helps them develop a growing awareness that it was not their fault that their baby died, that there was nothing more they could do. One comment often heard from parents whose infant died during the night is "I wish that I had been awake when she died." Referring parents to a local chapter of the national SIDS organization so they can share these feelings with others can be very helpful. The National SIDS and Infant Death Program Support Center operates a toll-free information service at 800-930-7437. They provide information about SIDS and can assist in the organization of local parent support groups.

MISCARRIAGES

Statistics for how many pregnancies end in a miscarriage vary, but a close estimate is about one-fifth to one-third. Parents who have experienced miscarriage may or may not receive support from family and friends. A miscarriage is often treated as a *socially negated loss*. Often the pregnancy is not common knowledge and the woman may be embarrassed to mention that she has lost a baby. She may experience a sense of isolation in a culture that emphasizes motherhood, which can make her grief more difficult to resolve (Frost & Condon, 1996). This and other common experiences that people go through make grieving more difficult.

Generally, when a woman has a miscarriage, everyone's first concern is for her health. It is only later that people begin to come to the full recognition of what has been lost. There are a number of concerns that come to the fore at such a time. For a woman who miscarries at her first pregnancy, there is her concern as to whether she will ever be able to have children. Physicians are usually fairly good at handling this concern, but the doctor's posture basically is one of focusing on statistics and probability levels of someone of her age and physical condition having a future successful pregnancy. Although this information can be helpful to the woman, it is also important that the doctor recognize that she has sustained a significant loss and not try to mask or minimize this loss by focusing on the possibility of future pregnancies. Future pregnancies are certainly a concern of the woman, but many physicians, in their discomfort over a miscarriage, may deal with this by focusing on this issue alone.

Self-blame is another major issue among woman who have experienced a miscarriage. The woman generally needs to blame someone and often the first focus of her recrimination is inward in self-directed anger. Was it caused by jogging, dancing, or some other physical activity? Women today may delay a first pregnancy, choosing instead to concentrate on career goals, and saving childbearing for later, when their careers are established. Losing a pregnancy under these circumstances can add to the degree of self-blame and the impact of the loss. Women also focus some of their blame on their husbands. "If only my husband hadn't been so eager for sexual relations, this wouldn't have happened," said one patient shortly after she miscarried. The man is often the target of the wife's anger. This happens because the woman blames him for not having the same feelings that she has, or at least she perceives that they are not the same. Generally, in the circumstances surrounding a miscarriage, the husband feels powerless and his need to act strong and to be supportive may be misinterpreted by the woman as not caring.

Out of this sense of helplessness, many husbands find an ally in the physician, who may be male and who focuses on the fact that the couple can conceive and have another child soon. Although this may make him feel less helpless and may be realistic in the situation, it may not be what the woman wants to hear at that particular time. Here, as in other losses, it is very important that people be able to talk openly and honestly about their feelings.

Studies show that both men and women grieve in the case of a miscarriage. In general, the longer the pregnancy, the more intense is the grief, especially for the father. Attachment is also an important mediator of grief with this type of loss (Robinson, Baker, & Nackerud, 1999). The grief of both men and women usually focuses on the lost dream of a wished-for future. The woman is usually more bonded to the fetus, but ultrasound imaging can initiate bonding for both men and women (Beutel, Deckardt, von Rad, & Weiner, 1995).

Because a miscarriage involves the loss of a person, it is important that grief work be done. There is mixed opinion as to whether or not the parents should see the fetus as part of the grieving process. I have spoken to several parents who have asked to see the fetus, and they have said that this was helpful. It helped them focus on the reality of the loss, enabling them to move forward and deal with their feelings about such a loss. "It helped me see this experience as a death," one woman said after she asked the physician to let her see her unborn baby. She was then able to say goodbye to the child, and she later told me that it helped her through her mourning.

As in other losses, there is an important need to be able to talk about the loss, but in the case of miscarriages, as in the case of abortions, friends and family members are often unaware of the pregnancy or uncomfortable talking about such an experience. Their discomfort does nothing to help the parents in the resolution of their grief.

If there are other children in the family, the problem of how to tell them about the death may arise. Generally, it is important to tell the older children about the experience and to allow them to talk about their thoughts and feelings regarding the loss and to help them to grieve for a lost sibling.

There are few established rituals for a miscarriage to help make the loss more tangible and facilitate the expression of grief. There are some things that the counselor can encourage, such as naming the fetus, having a memorial service in which a candle is lit or a tree is planted, and finding ways to put the hopes and dreams for the infant into words, such as writing a poem or letter to the baby (Brier, 1999).

STILLBIRTHS

For the most part, what is true for a miscarriage also pertains to still-births. If there is one thing that sums up the approach the health care professional should take to a husband and wife undergoing this kind of experience, it is recognizing that the parents have sustained a real loss, a death. Do not try to minimize the loss with an upbeat focus on the future and the possibility of other pregnancies and other children. Although it is not unusual for some couples to want to initiate a pregnancy immediately after experiencing a stillbirth, it is best to counsel them regarding acting with haste. It is often best to wait awhile until grieving is done for the child who was lost.

It is important to work with both partners involved in the loss. Fathers need to grieve too, and they do grieve, despite occasional comments to the contrary. Some men cry when they drive a car alone. Others visit the grave alone. Even though the role of the father in society is changing to be more nurturing and emotionally free, there is still pressure put on men to be strong and show less emotion in times of crisis (O'Neill, 1998). Studies show that the best adaptation to this type of loss comes when both parents have similar coping styles and more open communication (Feely & Gottlieb, 1988–1989). Work with the parents concerning their feelings about the loss, especially feelings of fear and guilt. Fears of special importance are the fear of future pregnancy, the fear of the impact of the loss on the marriage, and the fear of being a failure as a parent. Guilt can lead to blame or self-blame. Explore these tendencies and their resulting impact on self-esteem.

Look with the parents at their fantasies about the child they have lost. This includes looking at the meaning of the pregnancy. For example, was it planned and wanted by both partners, or was there ambivalence surrounding the pregnancy? Was it the result of infertility therapy, or a pregnancy late in their marriage? If the infant was deformed, the parents have two losses to grieve: the child they thought they had, and the child they actually lost.

Help families make the loss real by encouraging them to share decisions about disposition of the body, to name the baby, and to participate in rituals such as a funeral or memorial service. A meaningful collection of articles related to the baby, such as pictures of the baby, the birth certificate, a footprint, a lock of hair, a nursery bracelet, and cards received from friends can help make the loss real. Use the autopsy report to reality test the cause of death and to provide an opportunity for questions to be addressed.

Meaning making is an important task for mourning (see task III), and it is especially important after the death of a baby at birth. "Why did this happen?" is a universal cry of bereaved parents. Counselors can help bereaved parents struggle to find an answer, including the possibility that there may not be an answer.

Don't overlook the siblings. Perinatal death can be an invisible loss for the children at home. Not seeing the lost infant makes the death less real, a reality that is diminished even further if the loss is not acknowledged by the parents. A child's understanding of the loss will, of course, be influenced by his or her cognitive and emotional development. An inadequate understanding of the loss, coupled with magical thinking, can lead to a belief of personal culpability for the loss or lead the child to blame the loss on the lethality of the parents. The latter can increase the child's anxiety and personal vulnerability, resulting in a concern for his or her own safety and well-being. Supporting their other children can be difficult for parents when they are at their lowest. A 4-year-old boy whose brother was born dead said to his mother, "Don't be sad. I am your living boy" (Valsanen, 1998, p. 170). Recognizing and acknowledging the child's grief can be the most important means of supporting the child. Listening to and answering questions honestly is an important source of support (Wilson, 2001).

With this type of death, the family grieves as much for what they might have had as for what they've lost. The family unit should include grandparents, who also have sustained a loss. Consider referral to a support group with parents who have shared similar losses. If there are none in your area, you might want to help establish such a group. Do ongoing follow-up with the couple and with family members. We have a well-developed program at the Massachusetts General Hospital, and details about this program can be found in Reilly-Smorawski, Armstrong, and Catlin (2002).

For those doing prenatal counseling with a woman who has had a *previous* perinatal loss, Peterson (1994) offers some good counseling advice.

ABORTION

Many people take a casual attitude regarding the experience of abortion; at times this seems to border on the cavalier. When I worked at a university health service, I counseled many women who had had abortions, and they frequently did not recognize that the unresolved grief from a previous abortion lay behind what was currently troubling them. Abortion is one of those *unspeakable losses* that people would rather forget. The surface experience after an abortion is generally one of relief; however, a woman who does not mourn the loss may experience the grief in some subsequent loss.

The experience of Maria, a 27-year-old woman who was in a weekly therapy group, provides an example of this type of delayed grieving. One day she came to the group sad and upset because a friend and coworker had just lost a baby 6 months into the pregnancy. She was very distressed, and the group rallied to her support. At the next week's meeting she brought up the same issue, and the group again extended its support. However, after she had brought up the same issue for 5 or 6 weeks, it seemed to me that she was possibly more concerned over this loss than the mother herself. Her behavior seemed overreactive, and my hunch was that there might be an unmourned pregnancy in this woman's life. When I tactfully inquired, I found that this was the case. Several years earlier, when she was 24, Maria had become pregnant and had had an abortion and quickly put it out of her mind. Because of the casual relationship she had with the man, she did not tell him, and because of her Catholic upbringing, she did not tell her parents. She thought that the best way to cope, without any other emotional support, was to forget it as quickly as possible. However, by doing that, she robbed herself of the necessary grieving process. She was not aware of the necessity to grieve the loss, an awareness that only surfaced because of her friend's miscarriage. With help, she was able to work through her loss as part of her experience in the therapy group.

One of the ways to handle the issue of grief around abortion is to do more complete counseling before the abortion itself so that the person involved can explore ambivalent feelings, discuss various options, and receive emotional support. Most women seeking abortions tend to do so in haste and, because of the stigma and shame associated with abortion, they may make the decision without the emotional support of friends and family.

Post-abortion counseling can be effective, but many women do not seek it. Abortion in our society is often viewed as a *socially negated loss*. To view it as a death, and thus appropriate to grieve, could bring up profound feelings of guilt. Grief may appear years later when the woman reaches menopause, or if she learns that she is infertile (Joy, 1985). Such grief often manifests itself as anger or guilt, which results in self-punishing depression. Long-term consequences of abortion should be a part of post-abortion counseling (Broen, Moum, Bodtker, & Ekeberg, 2004).

Speckhard and Rue (1993) offer some guidelines for post-abortion counseling. They suggest:

> When a woman admits that there might be some merit to discussing her abortion(s) it is useful to ask her to relate how she became pregnant, when she first sensed her pregnancy (as opposed to having it medically verified), what her thoughts were about the developing embryo, if she personified it and referred to it with any referents of attachment (e.g., as "my baby"), and how she came to decide to have the abortion. This line of questioning typically begins to uncover the dual thought process of attachment and denial of attachment to the fetal child. (p. 23)

Adolescents are less likely to come in for post-abortion counseling, even though they find it more difficult to get emotional support. The adolescent's parents are usually angry at her because she got pregnant, and sometimes siblings are angry because they see their sister as having killed her baby. She often cannot turn to her peers because of the particular stigma attached to pregnancy at such an early age. In one study done in the Chicago area, Horowitz (1978) found that many of the teenagers she approached did not want to talk about their abortions or about their feelings surrounding the experience.

One of the ways that grief is managed by some teenagers is through a subsequent pregnancy. A common interpretation of a subsequent pregnancy is that it is an unconscious acting-out behavior. However, Horowitz (1978) found that many young women consciously got pregnant a second or third time as one way to handle their feelings about the first abortion. To put the experience of abortion out of mind is to minimize its importance, but I do not believe that it can be minimized, and adequate grieving is definitely necessary.

ANTICIPATORY GRIEF

The term "anticipatory grief" refers to grieving that occurs prior to the actual loss. It is distinguished from normal survivor grief, which we have been discussing up to this point. Many deaths occur with some forewarning, and it is during this period of anticipation that the individual begins the task of mourning and begins to experience the various responses of grief. Problems can arise that are specific to this situation and that may need specific types of intervention. While sudden death is exceedingly traumatic, prolonged grieving can produce resentment, which then can lead to guilt.

The term "anticipatory grief" was coined some years ago by Lindemann (1944) to refer to the absence of overt manifestations of grief at the actual time of death in survivors who had already experienced the phases of normal grief and who had freed themselves from their emotional ties with the deceased. The term was further developed by psychiatrist Knight Aldrich in a seminal paper entitled "The Dying Patient's Grief" (1963).

One of the first questions that comes to mind when one thinks about anticipatory grief is "Does it help post-death bereavement?" That is, do people who have sustained a period of pre-death bereavement handle their grief better and do they grieve for less time than those who do not begin grieving before the death? There does seem to be some evidence, particularly from the studies of Parkes (1975), that people who had some advance warning of a pending death did better when assessed at 13 months post-death than did people who did not have this advance warning. However, not all studies draw the same conclusions. Hogan, Morse, and Tason (1996) found that anticipatory grief did not ameliorate or foreshorten the bereavement process. The evidence is not all in. One should keep in mind that grief behavior is multidetermined, and as outlined in chapter 3, there are many mediators of this behavior, all contributing to its strength and to its outcome. Having some advance warning of death, some opportunity for pre-death bereavement, is one of these determinants. However, there are many more determinants, and it is too simplistic to look at this one variable alone.

It is important from a clinical standpoint for the practitioner who works with patients and families prior to an anticipated death to have an understanding of anticipatory grief in order to be helpful to both patients and family members (Rando, 2000).

In this type of situation, the mourning process begins early and involves the various tasks of mourning already discussed. With regard to task I, there is an awareness and acceptance of the fact that the person is going to die; hence the working through of this task begins early. However, in most cases the awareness of the inevitability of death alternates with experiences of denial that the event is really going to happen. Of all the tasks of mourning, perhaps task I is best facilitated by a period of anticipation, particularly when the person is dying of some progressive illness that causes him or her to deteriorate. Seeing the person go downhill brings the reality and inevitability of death closer. I have, however, seen some people hold out hope and reinforce denial when faced with extremes of visual evidence.

With regard to task II, there may be a whole variety of feelings associated with the anticipated loss, feelings that we generally associate with post-death bereavement. One feeling frequently observed during this period is an increase in anxiety. In chapter 3 we looked at separation anxiety—where it comes from and what it means. For many people, anxiety increases and accelerates based on the length of the period of anticipatory grief and the person's proximity to death. Aldrich (1963) likens this to a mother who is insecure about her child going to school for the first time and who feels more upset about it on Labor Day than she did on the Fourth of July.

In addition to the issue of separation anxiety, under these circumstances existential anxiety is exacerbated through an increase in personal death awareness (Worden, 1976). As you watch someone deteriorate during a progressive illness, you cannot help but identify with the process, having some awareness that this too may be your own fate. Also, watching your parents deteriorate and decline gives rise to the awareness that you are now moving up a generational step and will be the next one to face death in the overall order of things.

There is an interesting phenomenon that also occurs with regard to task III—the task of accommodating oneself to a world from which the deceased is missing. When there is some anticipation of death, it is common for survivors to do "role rehearsal" in their minds, that is, to run over the issues of "What will I do with the children?" "Where will I live?" "How will I manage without him?" This is what Janis (1958), in his study of surgical patients, has called "the work of worry." He found that those who do the work of worry prior to surgery do better in postsurgical responses. This type of role rehearsal is normal and plays an important part in overall coping. However, it can be viewed by others as socially unacceptable behavior. People who talk in detail about what they will do after the death may be perceived as insensitive, and their comments may seem premature and in bad taste. One of the things that the counselor can do is to help interpret this, both to the people exhibiting such behavior and to their friends and family members. Statements from well-meaning people such as "Oh, don't worry, things will work out" may cut off this very important process of the work of worry.

One of the difficulties in too long a time period of anticipatory grief is that someone may withdraw emotionally too soon, long before the person has died, and this can make for an awkward relationship. Michael's elderly mother was dying of a progressive disease. He anticipated her death, as did the other family members, and they had said the necessary goodbyes and made preparations. But the mother lived on and on, although in a seriously deteriorated stage. He came to the session one day expressing much turmoil and guilt over the fact that he wanted to make reservations to take his family away for a winter vacation, something they had done every year around the same time, yet he felt he could not go ahead and make the plans as long as she was still living. Under these circumstances Michael very much wished that she were dead, and he felt very guilty for having these feelings. This is not an unusual situation, particularly if the dying person is requiring much care and is in a seriously deteriorated condition. Weisman and Hackett (1961) talk about this withdrawal by family members and comment that such actions as drawing the shades, speaking in hushed voices, and presenting unnatural attitudes may suggest to the patient capitulation, abandonment, and premortem burial.

The opposite type of behavior can also occur; rather than moving too far away in terms of emotional detachment, the family members move too close to the dying patient. They move close to obviate feelings of guilt and loss, and in such cases they may want to overmanage the patient's medical care. This is particularly true when someone is trying to handle ambivalent feelings toward the dying person and the guilt that goes with such feelings. He or she may become overly caring of the patient or seek nontraditional treatments, and this can be a problem not only for the patient but also for the medical staff.

I observed one woman whose husband was a patient in the hospital's private service. She wanted to keep her husband alive and went to the most extreme means, extreme even to the most conservative of medical opinion. On the surface it looked to the nurses and other people caring for the patient like she cared so much for her husband that she wanted to keep him alive against all odds. But you only had to scratch the surface slightly to see that this woman had an extremely ambivalent relationship with her husband and she was expressing her ambivalence through this oversolicitation.

The time preceding a death can be used very effectively and can have an important impact on subsequent grief if the survivor is encouraged to take care of unfinished business. Unfinished business does not simply mean wills and other matters of estate, but being able to express both appreciation and disappointment, things that need to be said before the person dies. If the counselor can encourage family members and patients to have this kind of communication, this pre-death period can have a very salutary effect on all concerned. When these things are expressed, survivors do not have to spend time later on in grief counseling, where they might have to deal with regrets over things that were not ever said when they had the opportunity. So if you have access to patients and families in a situation prior to death, help them to see that even though this is a pending tragedy, it can also be an opportunity for them to take care of the things they want to deal with before the person dies. Often people need encouragement or permission to do this, but I think it is more often the exception than the rule that they will go ahead without the encouragement of the caregiving staff (Worden, 2000).

So far we have considered anticipatory grief of the survivor. But people who are dying can also experience this anticipatory grief, although they may feel it in ways that are somewhat different from survivors. The survivors are only losing one loved one. The person who is dying often has many attachments in his or her own life and, to that extent, will be losing many significant others all at once. The anticipation of loss can be overwhelming, and very often the patient will withdraw and turn his or her face to the wall in order to cope with the impact of this. A counselor can help interpret this kind of behavior both to the patient, who may be having trouble with it, and to the family and friends.

One more thing should be considered before we conclude this section on anticipatory grief. It concerns the use of support groups. There is one population that has a particularly difficult time with anticipatory grief and needs a lot of support—parents who are losing young children because of terminal illness. When one loses a child there is the sense of untimeliness about the death. Children are not supposed to die before their parents—it is not in the natural order of things. This, and a myriad of other kinds of experiences, which usually include a long series of medical treatments, puts great stresses on family members, not only the parents but the children as well (Davies, Gudmundsdottir, Worden, Orloff, Sumner, & Brenner, 2004).

There are support groups such as the Candlelighters available for parents whose children are very sick or dying. In these groups the parents can deal with some of their anticipatory grief in a social setting. Many parents who have participated in these groups have said that it was helpful to them because it gave them the opportunity to share their feelings with other parents who were going through the same thing. It also enabled them to cope better with some of the stresses in their marriages as well as some of the difficulties they were having with regard to the management of other children, especially the very common feeling that they were neglecting their other offspring because of the attention they were giving to the dying child.

The headquarters of one of these groups, the Candlelighters Childhood Cancer Foundation, is located at 3910 Warner Street, Kensington, MD 20895 (phone 800-366-2223). Another support group, Compassionate Friends, helps families after the death of a child. For information about this organization and local chapters, write: The Compassionate Friends, P.O. Box 3696, Oak Brook, IL 60522-3696 (phone 877-969-0010).

AIDS

The first edition of *Grief Counseling & Grief Therapy* appeared around the time that the HIV/AIDS pandemic began. Over the past 25 years an ever-increasing number of people have become afflicted with and died from acquired immune deficiency syndrome. There are, however, two major changes that need to be noted. First, the

HIV virus now affects a broader segment of society. In the early years, it was often seen as a gay disease. Now increasing numbers of women, children, and minorities have contracted the virus and have died or are living with the disease. Another affected group is the increasing number of children who have parents living and dying with AIDS (Rotheram-Borus, Weiss, Alber, & Lester, 2005). Aronson (1995) presents an effective school-based program for such children.

A second change is the new drugs and drug combinations that began to appear in the 1990s and have allowed those with HIV infection and AIDS to live longer. AIDS has become more of a *chronic disease*. This has been a mixed blessing (Demmer, 2000). When AIDS represented a terminal trajectory with little hope for remission, many patients could plan for deterioration and decline. Now lengthy remissions offer hope to those afflicted and their loved ones, but the less predictable course can present problems of its own, for example: "Do I return to work or stay on disability?" "Can I live until a cure is found?" For many, if not most, the sword of Damocles eventually falls, leaving a new circle of mourners to rejoice in the added time offered them but adding to their pain in hopes eventually dashed.

As the century turned, an estimated half-million people in the United States had died from AIDS-related disorders. Each of these left family and friends to face the consequences particular to this type of loss. Survivors of those who die from AIDS constitute a population of mourners who face very specific challenges. The fact that the syndrome is caused by an infectious virus, that it currently lacks a cure, that it carries a social stigma, and that it often leads to protracted illness can influence the mourning behavior of those who have sustained such a loss. Let us look at some features associated with AIDS that can affect the bereavement process.

Contagion

Because AIDS is transmitted through bodily fluids, the deceased's sexual partners may be anxious about their own health. Physical symptoms usually considered a normal part of the grieving process, such as fatigue, insomnia, and headaches, can be interpreted as symptoms associated with AIDS-related illnesses. The counselor needs to educate survivors regarding these physical aspects of bereavement so that these are not construed as AIDS and so that anxiety due to these physical symptoms can be diminished.

When the survivor is HIV positive, the feeling of vulnerability and the fear of developing AIDS can lead survivors to feel angry at the deceased. One survivor said, "I feel like a walking time bomb." Some of this vulnerability is real and not neurotic. Research has begun to look at how the stress of bereavement may affect the survivor's immune system, which may already be compromised by the virus (Kemeny, Weiner, Taylor, Schneider, Visscher, & Fahey, 1994).

Another aspect associated with the contagion factor is guilt. Some survivors feel guilty for transmitting the virus to their partner or for participating in activities or in a lifestyle that heightened the possibility of transmission. These feelings of guilt need to be addressed and evaluated. Contagion factors can also play a role when a survivor sets about to establish a new relationship. Some people reject relationships with individuals whose partners succumbed to AIDS-related illnesses, while in other cases survivors themselves may have doubts about forming new relationships.

Stigma

An AIDS-related death can be one of those *socially unspeakable losses* discussed earlier. Because of this stigma, which is often higher than for suicidal deaths (Houck, 2007), some survivors fear they will be rejected and judged harshly if the cause of death becomes known. So they may lie and attribute the death to cancer or something other than AIDS. This may get them off the "AIDS hook," but it takes another type of emotional toll in the form of fear of discovery and anger and guilt over what they have done. Helping survivors deal with the reality of the stigma and assisting them to find appropriate ways to share the circumstances of the loss can help to attenuate these feelings of anxiety and fear.

Lack of Social Support

Because of the stigma of AIDS, and because in our society kinship legitimizes grief, many survivors who had a nontraditional relationship with the deceased have difficulty finding the understanding and support they need after the death. Social support has been shown to reduce depression after an AIDS-related death (Ingram, Jones, & Smith, 2001). The mother of one of my clients, who did not know of her son's relationship with his lover, said after the death, "Why are you so sad? He was only your roommate." If a relationship is not socially sanctioned, it is less likely to be recognized as important by others or by the law. The family may exclude the deceased's partner and friends from participation in funeral planning and activities. Significant others in the deceased's life may also be prevented from inheriting property or otherwise benefitting from the settlement of the estate.

Folta and Deck (1976) make an important point about grief and nontraditional relationships:

> While all of these studies tell us that grief is a normal phenomenon, the intensity of which corresponds to the closeness of the relationship with the deceased, they fail to take friendship into account. The underlying assumption is that "closeness of relationship" exists only among spouses and/or immediate kin. (p. 239)

One group often hit hard by the stigma associated with AIDS is those families who learn of the illness of their child and his or her lifestyle at the same time. Because of the fear of stigma, such families can experience severe alienation from the ill family member. One Midwest family learned of their son's lifestyle and illness at the same time, very close to his death. They returned home and told friends that their son had died in an automobile accident, fearing that others would reject them. This dissimulation went on for several months until inner conflict led them to tell friends the truth about his death. Much to their surprise, rather than being rejected, these parents were embraced by friends and members of their church. Groups for families and friends of AIDS patients can be an excellent source of emotional support before and after the death (Monahan, 1994; Sikkema, Hansen, & Ghebremichael, 2006).

Untimely Deaths

Many of those who have succumbed to AIDS-related illnesses are young, between the ages of 20 and 35. Their deaths evoke the reactions that any untimely deaths evoke when parents outlive their children. Among friends and contemporaries, there can be an increase in the awareness of personal mortality and its attendant anxiety (Worden, 1976). Many survivors are faced with these issues at an age when people are not usually confronted with mortality.

Multiple Losses

In the gay community many people have lost a number of friends and significant others to AIDS. As noted earlier, multiple losses can lead to bereavement overload and may cause the grieving process to shut down or to manifest itself in various somatic symptoms. One study in New York City found that the number of distress symptoms varied with the number of friends the bereaved had lost to AIDS, and this was especially true for seropositive men (Martin & Dean, 1993). More recent studies in California found little relationship between the number of losses and the frequency of depressive symptoms, suggesting that the death of friends and lovers may have become almost "normal" in the gay community (Cherney & Verhey, 1996; Folkman, Chesney, Collette, Boccellari, & Cooke, 1996; Summers et al., 1995). However, multiple losses have been associated with grief symptoms such as preoccupation with the deceased and searching behavior (Neugebauer, Rabkin, Williams, Remien, Goetz, & Gorman, 1992). Those providing bereavement services need to be aware of this association and reach out to those with multiple losses.

Multiple losses that can lead to massive bereavement can also leave a person with the sense of being a repeated survivor. Survivor guilt is possible following survival of any catastrophe, and survivor guilt can also be found in those who see themselves as repeated survivors (Blechner, 1993; Boykin, 1991).

When grieving multiple losses, one cannot be certain for whom one is grieving. All the losses tend to blend together. At times a recent loss may trigger feelings associated with an earlier and more significant loss. The counselor needs to be flexible with the client whose grief focus shifts between prior and current losses (Nord, 1996).

Individuals experiencing multiple losses may hesitate to share their feelings and feel isolated because they sense the larger community does not want to know their feelings. Support groups can be especially helpful here. Some may not want to participate in groups lest some members die during their group participation.

The impact of multiple losses can also be a problem for those care-givers who are working with large groups of AIDS patients. One counselor working with AIDS patients in San Francisco said, "I reached a saturation point in my personal and professional life where I could not fit in another death." The cumulative deaths have an effect (Bell, 1988). Those caring for people with AIDS need to be able to release their grief and sorrow and stay connected with life-affirming activities in order to avoid burnout (Bennett, Kelaher, & Ross, 1994).

Protracted Illness and Disfigurement

The HIV virus compromises the immune system so that a number of opportunistic infections can invade the body. Many of these infections lead to progressive physical and mental deterioration. People with AIDS-related illness often experience wasting of their physical and mental capacities. Formerly youthful and attractive, they can take on the appearance of death camp victims. Because of this deterioration, some people find it difficult to be around those with AIDS whose illness is progressing. I have worked with a few survivors who felt intense guilt after a loss because they were not present when the person was dying. Others who are present through the dying process find it difficult to relinquish memories of a friend or family member in such an impaired condition. The realization that such a phenomenon is normal and that they will gradually be able to recapture a more balanced set of memories can be helpful.

Neurological Complications

Another feature of AIDS that affects loss are the neurological complications often caused by the illness. Several studies have found that autopsies show that up to 80% of AIDS patients suffered some kind of damage to the central nervous system. Sometimes the damage makes for subtle changes in behavior, but more often one sees a higher level of impairment, depending on the area of the brain that is under attack by the virus. These deteriorations of mental function can look like the impairments suffered by the Alzheimer's patient. Once dementia progresses, family and friends begin to lose the person they once knew, and these losses, as in the case of Alzheimer's disease, can precipitate an early grieving response (McKeough, 1995).

At this point in time it looks like the AIDS virus will continue to affect a broader segment of society, and those working with grief issues can expect to see more AIDS-related bereavement in the coming years.

REFERENCES

Aldrich, C. K. (1963). The dying patient's grief. *Journal of the American Medical Association, 184,* 329–331.

Aronson, S. (1995). Five girls in search of a group: A group experience for adolescents of parents with AIDS. *International Journal of Group Psychotherapy, 45,* 223–235.

Begley, M., & Quayle, E. (2007). The lived experience of adults bereaved by suicide. *Crisis, 28,* 26–34.

Bell, J. P. (1988). AIDS and the hidden epidemic of grief: A personal experience. *American Journal of Hospice Care, 5,* 25–31.

Bennett, L., Kelaher, M., & Ross, M. W. (1994). The impact of working with HIV/AIDS on health care professionals: Development of the AIDS Impact Scale. *Psychology and Health, 9,* 221–232.

Beutel, M., Deckardt, R., von Rad, M., & Weiner, H. (1995). Grief and depression after miscarriage: Their separation, antecedents, and course. *Psychosomatic Medicine, 57,* 517–526.

Blechner, M. J. (1993). Psychoanalysis and HIV disease. *Contemporary Psychoanalysis, 29*(1), 61–80.

Boykin, F. F. (1991). The AIDS crisis and gay male survivor guilt. *Smith College Studies in Social Work, 61*(3), 247–259.

Brier, N. (1999). Understanding and managing the emotional reaction to a miscarriage. *Obstetrics & Gynecology, 93,* 151–155.

Broen, A. N., Moum, T., Bodtker, A. S., & Ekeberg, O. (2004). Psychological impact on women of miscarriage versus induced abortion: A 2-year follow up study. *Psychosomatic Medicine, 66,* 265–271.

Cain, A. C. (Ed.). (1972). *Survivors of suicide.* Springfield, IL: Thomas.

Callahan, J. (2000). Predictors and correlates of bereavement in suicide support group participants. *Suicide & Life-Threatening Behavior, 30,* 104–124.

Cherney, P. M., & Verhey, M. P. (1996). Grief among gay men associated with multiple losses from AIDS. *Death Studies, 20,* 115–132.

Clark, S. E., & Goldney, R. D. (1995). Grief reactions and recovery in a support group for people bereaved by suicide. *Crisis, 16,* 27–33.

Cleiren, M., & Diekstra, R. (1995). After the loss: Bereavement after suicide and other types of death. In B. Mishara (Ed.), *The impact of suicide* (pp. 7–39). New York: Springer Publishing.

Cvinar, J. (2005). Do suicide survivors suffer social stigma: A review of the literature. *Perspectives in Psychiatric Care, 41,* 14–21.

Davies, B., Gudmundsdottir, M., Worden, J. W., Orloff, S., Sumner, L., & Brenner, P. (2004). "Living in the dragon's shadow": Fathers' experiences of a child's life-limiting illness. *Death Studies, 28,* 111–135.

Demmer, C. (2000). Grief and survival in the era of HIV treatment advances. *Illness, Crisis & Loss, 8,* 5–16.

Farberow, N. L., Gallagher-Thompson, D. E., Gilewski, M. J., & Thompson, L. W. (1992). Changes in grief and mental health of bereaved spouses of older suicides. *Journals of Gerontology, 47,* 357–366.

Feely, N., & Gottlieb, L. N. (1988–1989). Parents' coping and communication following their infant's death. *Omega, 19,* 51–57.

Folkman, S., Chesney, M., Collette, L., Boccellari, A., & Cooke, M. (1996). Postbereavement depressive mood and its prebereavement predictors in HIV+ and HIV– gay men. *Journal of Personality and Social Psychology, 70,* 336–348.

Folta, J., & Deck, E. (1976). Grief, the funeral, and the friend. In V. Pine, A. II. Kutscher, D. Peretz, & R. Slater (Eds.), *Acute grief and the funeral.* Springfield, IL: Thomas.

Frost, M., & Condon, J. T. (1996). The psychological sequelae of miscarriage: A critical review of the literature. *Australian & New Zealand Journal of Psychiatry, 30,* 54–62.

Gaines, J., & Kandall, S. R. (1992). Counseling issues related to maternal substance abuse and subsequent sudden infant death syndrome in offspring. *Clinical Social Work Journal, 20,* 169–177.

Hawton, K., & Simkin, S. (2003). Helping people bereaved by suicide. *British Medical Journal, 327,* 177–178.

Hogan, N., Morse, J., & Tason, M. (1996). Toward an experiential theory of bereavement. *Omega, 33,* 43–65.

Horowitz, N. H. (1978). Adolescent mourning reactions to infant and fetal loss. *Social Casework, 59,* 551–559.

Houck, J. (2007). A comparison of grief reactions in cancer, HIV/AIDS, and suicide bereavement. *Journal of HIV/AIDS & Social Services, 6,* 97–112.

Hutton, C. J., & Bradley, B. S. (1994). Effects of sudden infant death on bereaved siblings: A comparative study. *Journal of Child Psychology and Psychiatry and Allied Disciplines, 35,* 723–732.

Ingram, K. M., Jones, D. A., & Smith, N. G. (2001). Adjustment among people who have experienced AIDS-related multiple loss: The role of unsupportive social interactions, social support, and coping, *Omega, 43,* 287–309.

Janis, I. L. (1958). *Psychological stress.* New York: John Wiley.

Jordan, J. (2001). Is suicide bereavement different? A reassessment of the literature. *Suicide & Life-Threatening Behavior, 31,* 91–102.

Jordan, J., & McMenamy, J. (2004). Interventions for suicide survivors: A review of the literature. *Suicide & Life-Threatening Behavior, 34,* 337–349.

Joy, S. S. (1985). Abortion: An issue to grieve? *Journal of Counseling and Development, 63,* 375–376.

Kaslow, N., & Aronson, S. (2004). Recommendations for family interventions following suicide. *Professional Psychology: Research & Practice, 35,* 240–247.

Kemeny, M. E., Weiner, H., Taylor, S. E., Schneider, S., Visscher, B., & Fahey, J. L. (1994). Repeated bereavement, depressed mood, and immune parameters in HIV seropositive and seronegative gay men. *Health Psychology, 13,* 14–24.

Kerr, P. (1989, March 2). As murder case drags on, the mourning never ends. *New York Times.* Retrieved April 14, 2008, from http://query.nytimes.com/gst/fullpage.html?res=950DE0D7113CF931A35750C0A96F948260

Lazare, A. (1979). Unresolved grief. In A. Lazare (Ed.), *Outpatient psychiatry: Diagnosis and treatment* (pp. 498–512). Baltimore: Williams and Wilkens.

Lindemann, E. (1944). The Symptomatology and management of acute grief. *American Journal of Psychiatry, 101,* 141–148.

Lindemann, E., & Greer, I. M. (1953). A study of grief: Emotional responses to suicide. *Pastoral Psychology, 4,* 9–13.

Martin, J. L., & Dean, L. (1993). Effects of AIDS-related bereavement and HIV-related illness on psychological distress among gay men: A 7-year longitudinal study, 1985–1991. *Journal of Consulting & Clinical Psychology, 61,* 94–103.

McIntosh, J. L., & Kelly, L. D. (1992). Survivors' reactions: Suicide vs. other causes. *Crisis, 13,* 82–93.

McKeough, M. (1995). Dementia in HIV disease: A challenge for palliative care? *Journal of Palliative Care, 11,* 30–33.

McNiel, D. E., Hatcher, C., & Reubin, R. (1988). Family survivors of suicide and accidental death: Consequences for widows. *Suicide & Life-Threatening Behavior, 18,* 137–148.

Mitchell, A. M., Gale, D. D., Garand, L., & Wesner, S. (2003). The use of narrative data to inform the psychotherapeutic group process with suicide survivors. *Issues in Mental Health Nursing, 24,* 91–106.

Monahan, J. R. (1994). Developing and facilitating AIDS bereavement support groups. *Group, 18,* 177–185.

Moore, M. M., & Freeman, S. J. (1995). Counseling survivors of suicide: Implications for group postvention. *Journal for Specialists in Group Work, 20,* 40–47.

Morgan, J. H., & Goering, R. (1978). Caring for parents who have lost an infant. *Journal of Religion and Health, 17,* 290–298.

Neugebauer, R., Rabkin, J. G., Williams, J. B., Remien, R. H., Goetz, J., & Gorman, J. M. (1992). Bereavement reactions among homosexual men experiencing multiple losses in the AIDS epidemic. *American Journal of Psychiatry, 149,* 1374–1379.

Nord, D. (1996). Issues and implications in the counseling of survivors of multiple AIDS-related loss. *Death Studies, 20,* 389–413.

O'Neill, B. (1998). A father's grief: Dealing with stillbirth. *Nursing Forum, 33,* 33–37.

Parkes, C. M. (1975). Determinants of outcome following bereavement. *Omega, 6,* 303–323.

Parkes, C. M. (1993). Psychiatric problems following bereavement by murder or manslaughter. *British Journal of Psychiatry, 162,* 49–54.

Parrish, M., & Tunkle, J. (2003). Working with families following their child's suicide. *Family Therapy, 30,* 63–76.

Pearlman, R. A., Hsu, C., Starks, H., Back, A. L., Gordon, J. R., Bharucha, A. J. et al. (2005). Motivations for physician-assisted suicide. *JGIM: Journal of General Internal Medicine, 20,* 234–239.

Peterson, G. (1994). Chains of grief: The impact of perinatal loss on subsequent pregnancy. *Pre- and Perinatal Psychology Journal, 9,* 149–158.

Rando, T. A. (1993). *Treatment of complicated mourning.* Champaign, IL: Research Press.

Rando, T. A. (Ed.). (2000). *Clinical dimensions of anticipatory mourning.* Champaign, IL: Research Press.

Range, L. M., & Calhoun, L. G. (1990). Responses following suicide and other types of death: The perspective of the bereaved. *Omega, 21,* 311–320.

Reed, M. D. (1993). Sudden death and bereavement outcomes: The impact of resources on grief symptomatology and detachment. *Suicide & Life-Threatening Behavior, 23,* 204–220.

Reilly-Smorawski, B., Armstrong, A. V., & Catlin, E. A. (2002). Bereavement support for couples following the death of a baby: Program Development and 14-Year Exit Analysis. *Death Studies, 26,* 21–37.

Robinson, M., Baker, L., & Nackerud, L. (1999). The relationship of attachment theory and perinatal loss. *Death Studies, 23,* 257–270.

Rothcram-Borus, M. J., Weiss, R., Alber, S., & Lester, P. (2005). Adolescent adjustment before and after HIV-related parental death. *Journal of Consulting & Clinical Psychology, 73,* 221–228.

Rynearson, E. K. (1994). Psychotherapy of bereavement after homicide. *Journal of Psychotherapy Practice and Research, 3,* 341–347.

Rynearson, E. K., & McCreery, J. M. (1993). Bereavement after homicide: A synergism of trauma and loss. *American Journal of Psychiatry, 150,* 258–261.

Sikkema, K. J., Hansen, N. B., & Ghebremichael, M. (2006). A randomized controlled trial of a coping group intervention for adults with HIV who are AIDS bereaved: Longitudinal effects of grief. *Health Psychology, 25,* 563–570.

Solomon, R., & Rando, T. (2007). Utilization of EMDR in the treatment of grief and mourning. *Journal of EMDR Practice & Research, 1,* 109–117.

Speckhard, A., & Rue, V. (1993). Complicated mourning: Dynamics of impacted post abortion grief. *Pre- and Perinatal Psychology Journal, 8,* 5–32.

Summers, J., Zisook, S., Atkinson, J. H., Sciolla, A., Whitehall, W., Brown, S., et al. (1995). Psychiatric morbidity associated with acquired immune deficiency syndrome–related grief resolution. *Journal of Nervous & Mental Disease, 183,* 384–389.

Task Force on Sudden Infant Death Syndrome. (2005). The changing concept of sudden infant death syndrome: Diagnostic coding shifts, controversies regarding the sleeping environment, and new variables to consider in reducing risk. *Pediatrics, 116*(5), 1245–1255.

Valsanen, L. (1998). Family grief and recovery process when a baby dies. *Psychiatria Fennica, 29,* 163–174.

Wagner, K. G., & Calhoun, L. G. (1991). Perceptions of social support by suicide survivors and their social networks. *Omega, 24,* 61–73.

Weisman, A. D., & Hackett, T. P. (1961). Predilection to death. *Psychosomatic Medicine, 23,* 232–255.

Werth, J. (1999). The role of the mental health professional in helping significant others of persons who are assisted in death. *Death Studies, 23,* 239–255.

Wilson, R. (2001). Parents' support of their other children after a miscarriage or perinatal death. *Early Human Development, 61,* 55–65.

Worden, J. W. (1976). *Personal death awareness.* Englewood Cliffs, NJ: Prentice-Hall.

Worden, J. W. (1996). *Children & grief: When a parent dies.* New York: Guilford Press.

Worden, J. W. (2000). Towards an appropriate death. In T. Rando (Ed.), *Clinical dimensions of anticipatory mourning* (pp. 267–277). Champaign, IL: Research Press.

8   Grief and Family Systems

Up to this point, our primary focus has been the grief reactions of an individual and how this relates to his or her relationship with the deceased. However, most significant losses occur within the context of a family unit, and it is important to consider the impact of a death on the entire family system.

Most families exist in some type of homeostatic balance, and the loss of a significant person in the family group can unbalance this homeostasis and cause the family to feel pain and to seek help. Murray Bowen (1978), a well-known family therapist, says that knowledge of the total family configuration, the functioning position of the dying person in the family, and the overall level of life adaptation is important for anyone who attempts to help a family before, during, or after a death.

Specific factors that affect the mourning process and influence the degree of family disruption have been identified. These include stages in the family life cycle; roles played by the deceased; power, affection, and communication patterns; and sociocultural factors (Davies, Spinetta, Martinson, & Kulenkamp, 1986; Vess, Moreland, & Schwebel, 1985–1986; Walsh & McGoldrick, 1991).

My purpose here is to discuss how family dynamics can hinder adequate grieving. This chapter is not intended to be a treatise on family therapy. I will assume that the reader has some understanding of and skill in the administration of this type of therapy. For those less familiar with this area who want an overview, I suggest *Handbook of Clinical Family Therapy* by J. L. Lebow (2005). A family therapy approach for use with bereaved families can be found in Kissane and Bloch's *Family Focused Grief Therapy* (2002).

The concept of family therapy is based on the belief that the family is an interactional unit in which all members influence each other. Therefore, it is not sufficient to treat each individual in relationship to the deceased and to deal with his or her grief without relating it to the total family network. The characteristics of individual family members help determine the character of the family system, but this family system is more than the sum of its individuals' characteristics. The grief reactions of a family deserve assessment apart from those of its individual members (Rosen, 1990). One reason it is necessary to look at family grief as well as individual grief is the impact of family myths. These myths work in a similar fashion as defenses for the individual, and they give the family group definition and identity. In addition, each change that occurs following the death of a family member is symbolic of the death of the family itself, making the primary task the establishment of a new family from the old (Greaves, 1983).

Families vary in their ability to express and tolerate feelings. If openly expressed feelings are not tolerated, this may lead to various types of acting-out behavior that serve as grief equivalents. Families that cope most effectively are open in their discussions about the deceased, whereas closed families not only lack this freedom but provide excuses and make comments that allow and encourage other family members to remain quiet. Functional families are more likely to process feelings about the death, including admitting to and accepting feelings of vulnerability (Davies et al., 1986).

One important reason for looking at a family systems approach is that unresolved grief may not only serve as a key factor in family pathology but contribute to pathological relationships across the generations (Gajdos, 2002). Walsh and McGoldrick (1991) have noted that postponed mourning in the family of origin impedes one from experiencing emotional loss and separation within the current family. Reilly (1978), who has looked at this phenomenon in relationship to drug abuse, believes that parents of youthful drug abusers have never fully mourned or resolved their ambivalent ties to their own parents.

Therefore, they tend to project their conflicts over loss and abandonment onto their present-day families. In order to assess the impact of intergenerational conflict, Bowen (1978) encourages counselors to take an extensive family history, which should cover at least two generations, as part of the intake procedure.

In the assessment of grief and family systems, at least three main areas need to be considered. The first is the *functional position* or role the deceased played in the family. There are various roles played by family members, such as the sickly one, the value setter, the scapegoat, the nurturer, and the clan head. To the extent that the deceased had a significant functional position, his or her death is going to create a corresponding disturbance of functional equilibrium. Bowen (1978) sees the family unit as having stasis and calm when each member is functioning at reasonable efficiency. But the addition or loss of a family member can result in disequilibrium. Through death, the family can be deprived of an important role, and another member might be sought out to fill the role vacancy.

Children play important roles in the family, and their deaths upset family balance. I saw an adolescent, the youngest of three children, before he died of leukemia. He had required numerous hospitalizations and subsequent care. This boy was resented by his brother, the oldest child, and after the death, the brother would not let his parents dismantle the room or store or give away his dead brother's belongings. He would become very angry when this was mentioned by his family because to do so would mean he would have to face the finality of the loss and his unresolved ambivalence toward his brother.

The mother suffered because she had an unusually close relationship with the dead child. In a reversal of dependency, she leaned on him to bolster her sagging self-esteem, placing him in a role that would have been more appropriate for her husband. The husband, who had never given his wife much attention, gave her even less attention after the death and refused to talk about his feelings. He spent increasingly long periods away from home. The middle child, a girl who lived away from home, was the only one who seemed to be doing well. Individual counseling for the members of this family could have been done with some success, but it is my belief that three or four individual counselors would not be as effective as family therapy, where these various conflicts and issues could be worked out within the purview of each other. In fact, psychiatrist Norman Paul (1986) believes that grief work confined to an individual and the therapist may deaden the relational possibilities for the individual and his or her family.

The death of either parent when the family is young can have long-range effects. "This not only disturbs the emotional equilibrium, but it removes the function of the breadwinner or the mother at a time when these functions are most important" (Bowen, 1978, p. 328). Another important death with widespread ramifications is the death of a patriarchal clan head who has been serving the decision-making function in family affairs for a long time. One woman had a grandfather who ran the family with an iron fist. Within 2 years of his death, her parents had divorced, the family business had crumbled, and the family members had scattered to different parts of the country. But it is important to realize that many people play only peripheral roles in family affairs. One might consider such a person somewhat neutral; therefore, deaths of these more neutral figures are not as likely to affect current or future family functioning with quite the same intensity.

A second area to assess is the *emotional integration* of the family. A well-integrated family will be better able to help each other cope with the death, even that of a significant family member, with little outside help. A less integrated family may show minimal grief reaction at the time of a death, but members may respond later with various physical or emotional symptoms or some type of social misbehavior. It is important that the counselor understand this, because merely getting the family to express feelings after a death does not necessarily increase the level of emotional integration (McBride & Simms, 2001).

Since affective expression is so important in the mourning process, a third area to assess is *how families facilitate or hinder emotional expression.* In order to see this, one needs to understand the value families place on emotions and the kinds of communication patterns that give a person permission to express feelings or not express feelings. Davies and associates (1986) found that in some less functional families, sadness is equated with craziness, a feeling that is manifested in comments such as "I've seen enough tears." They also found that in more functional families the father was able to express grief openly instead of hiding his feelings or praising his son for not crying at the funeral. The latter behavior reinforces gender role rigidity and is a characteristic of less functional families. Because a death can trigger varied and intense feelings, a context in which these feelings can be experienced, identified, and brought to completion is important. Families that conspire to keep feelings down or at a distance may ultimately keep the individual from an adequate resolution of grief (Traylor, Hayslip, Kaminski, & York, 2003).

For example, Karen was the youngest of five children when her father, a ne'er-do-well alcoholic, was found dead in a local hotel. Because he had long been an embarrassment to the family, they opted for immediate cremation, and his ashes were disposed of unceremoniously. Karen wanted to provide some kind of marker for her father, but no one in the family agreed with her, and being the youngest, she had little clout. She thought this was a "crummy way to die" and she was unable to detach herself from her father. She kept him with her through a type of pathological identification that developed over the years, and her family would often say, "You're just like your father." As a young woman Karen developed a serious drinking problem, which turned out to be related in part to this pathological identification with her father. Through grief therapy she was able to see the connection, to say a final goodbye to her father, to deal with the other family members concerning his death, and over time to see her problem with alcohol resolved.

This family would probably not have seen the need for family therapy, believing, or wanting to believe, that the father's death had little impact on them or on the family system. But this case also suggests why those who have access to families after a death would be wise to assess the fantasies and feelings of all family members, including the younger ones.

Like the tasks of mourning outlined in chapter 2, there are essential tasks for families making an adaptation to the loss: there must be a recognition of the loss and acknowledgment of the unique grief experiences of each family member (healthy families can define these differences as strengths); the family must reorganize, with roles reassigned to other family members or abandoned, thus reducing the sense of chaos; and the family members must reinvest in this "new" family while maintaining a sense of connection with the deceased (McBride & Simms, 2001; Walsh & McGoldrick, 1991). Open and honest communication plus appropriate rituals and ceremonies can assist the family to accomplish each of these tasks (Gilbert, 1996; Rotter, 2000).

An added task for the family, based on the important work of Janice Nadeau, is meaning making. Individuals in the family hold unique beliefs and understandings of the loss. A sharing of these individual awarenesses with others in the family helps the family as a unit to develop their own meaning. The way in which a family construes the loss of a family member greatly influences how they grieve. A family that understands the death of a family member as a long-awaited relief from pain is likely to grieve differently from the family who construes a death as something that should have been prevented (Nadeau, 1998, 2001).

Research has shown that families who cope the best after the death of a family member are more cohesive; are more able to tolerate individual differences among family members; have more open communication, including more open emotional sharing; find more support from within the family as well as outside the family; and cope more actively with problems (Greeff & Human, 2004; Kissane, McKenzie, McKenzie, Forbes, O'Neill, & Bloch, 2003; Worden, 1996). Not all these characteristics can be influenced by family intervention, but many can. Kissane and Bloch (2002) have shown the effectiveness of family bereavement interventions directed toward a subset of families identified by screening procedures.

DEATH OF A CHILD

One very difficult loss that impinges heavily on family equilibrium and can sometimes cause complicated grief reactions is the death of a child. Surviving siblings frequently become the focus for unconscious maneuvers designed to alleviate feelings of guilt experienced by the parents and are used as a way to control fate. One of the most difficult positions in which parents put surviving siblings is that of the substitute for the lost child. This often involves endowing the surviving child with qualities of the deceased. In some cases it may even result in a child born later being named the same or a similar name as the dead child. Davies and her colleagues (1986) found that healthy families were able to acknowledge the loss of a child without expecting other children to fill the empty space. The ability of the parents to help siblings communicate within the family unit and the opportunity to directly express feelings lead to the healthy negotiation of grieving tasks (Schumacher, 1984).

Some families cope with their feelings about the death of a child by suppressing the facts surrounding the loss so that children born after the death may not know anything about their predecessors and in some cases not even know there were predecessors at all. This happened to Judy. Her parents' first child was a boy who died in early infancy. They subsequently had another child, a girl, and then a third child, Judy, who was supposed to be the replacement for the dead son. This was never directly verbalized and obviously not communicated to her. But over the years, even though the parents did not talk about the dead brother, an awareness of him always hung in the back of her mind. Subconsciously she attempted to make up for all the things that he might have been by engaging in a lot of "masculine" interests, activities, and hobbies.

But many years later, as her mother lay dying of cancer, Judy insisted that her parents discuss the dead brother—their disappointments in him and their expectations for her. This was not an easy thing for her to do, but she persisted until her parents could consciously admit to their disappointments and expectations. Even though this took a great deal of effort and she met with considerable resistance, she felt it was important to clear things up before her mother's death. Fortunately, she was successful in this effort and was then able to move beyond this legacy and start being more her own person.

It is common for siblings of the lost child to be overlooked during the time immediately following the death (Worden, Davies, & Mc-Cown, 2000). Sometimes it is assumed that children are simply too young to comprehend the loss or that they need protection from what is perceived as a morbid situation. More often, children are not given the attention they need because their primary caregivers are in a state of trauma and are simply not able to extend themselves to help. This is when support networks can be helpful in alleviating some of the common reactions and feelings a child experiences when a sibling dies (Worden, Davies, & McCown, 2000).

Children have a difficult time trying to sort out what their friends should be told and how to deal with the discomfort of other people in relation to the death. Many times, as a result of this discomfort, they are afraid to play or be happy because they don't want others to think they didn't care about their lost sibling (Schumacher, 1984).

In the absence of open and honest communication, children seek their own answers to questions that are often beyond their ability to understand. It is particularly important for parents to dispel magical and erroneous thinking regarding death in order to establish an emotional link between the remaining siblings and the parents. This is a crucial time that may affect their personality development and their ability to form and maintain future relationships (Schumacher, 1984).

The experience of the bereaved parents is central to the loss of a child and its impact on the family. Losing a child of any age can be one of life's most devastating losses and its impact lingers for years. Sanders (1979) identified this in her oft-cited classic study, and recently in Australia, Middleton, Raphael, Burnett, and Martinek (1998) replicated her findings. Parental bonds are strong. They reflect aspects of the parent's personality as well as historical and social dimensions. Klass and Marwit (1988–1989) write:

> The child represents to the parent both the parent's best self and the parent's worst self. Difficulties and ambivalence in the parent's life are manifest in the bond with the child. The child is born into a world of hopes and expectations, into a world of intricate psychological bonds, into a world that has a history. The parent-child bond can also be a recapitulation of the bond between the parent and the parent's parent, so the child can be experienced as praising or judging the parent's self. From the day the child is born, those hopes and expectations, bonds, and history are played out in the parent's relationship with the child. (p. 33)

Friends and family may not know how to respond to such a loss and how to be supportive. This can be especially true when more time has passed since the loss. I have worked with several bereaved mothers whose friends comment that they should be getting over the loss, since it has been over a year since their child died.

The mediators of mourning discussed in chapter 3 affect the experience of this type of loss. Such deaths are often sudden and untimely— parents are supposed to outlive their children. Many children die in accidents, which heightens the challenge to the parent's sense of competency, since part of the parental role is to keep the child safe. This may also lead to strong feelings of guilt (Davies, Gudmunds-dottir, Worden, Orloff, Sumner, & Brenner, 2004).

Guilt can have multiple sources. Miles and Demi (1991–1992) have posited five types of guilt that bereaved parents may experience. The first is *cultural guilt*. Society expects parents to be guardians of their children and take care of them. The death of one's child is an affront to this social expectation and may lead to this type of guilt. Causal guilt is a second type. If the parent was responsible for the death of the child through some real or perceived negligence, the parent may experience causal guilt. *Causal guilt* can also be a part of the parent's experience when the death occurs from an inherited disorder. *Moral guilt* is characterized by the parent's feeling that the death of the child was due to some moral infraction in his or her present or earlier life experience. There are a variety of such presumed infractions. One frequently seen is residual guilt from a terminated pregnancy: "Because I elected to terminate a pregnancy, I am now being punished for that act by losing my child." *Survival guilt* may also be found among bereaved parents: "Why did my child die and I am still alive?" Survival guilt is more frequently found when the parent and child have been involved in the same accident and the parent survives when the child does not. Finally, there is *recovery guilt*. Some parents feel guilty when they move through their grief and want to get on with their lives. They believe that such recovery somehow dishonors the memory of their dead child and that society may judge them negatively. One parent said, "To relinquish my guilt means giving up a way I can be attached to my child" (Brice, 1991, p. 6).

Bereaved parents frequently have the need to blame someone for the death of their child and to seek retribution. This is especially true of bereaved fathers. Such a need is strong when the child dies in an accident or by suicide or homicide. But the same anger can be found when the child dies of natural causes. Sometimes this need to blame is targeted at a marriage partner or other family member and places stress on the family system. It is also possible for a family member, such as a child, to become a scapegoat after a death. Counselors need to be aware of these dynamics and help the family to find the most appropriate place to place their anger and their blame (Drenovsky, 1994).

Both parents have sustained a loss, but the grief experience may be different for each, due to their different relationships with the child and their own different coping styles. These differences can put a strain on a marital relationship, and this in turn can cause tensions and alliances among family members (Robinson & Marwit, 2006).

Each parent needs to understand his or her own way of expressing grief as well as his or her partner's grieving style (Littlewood, Cramer, Hoekstra, & Humphrey, 1991). One partner may be more facile than the other at expressing and discussing emotions. An open expression of feelings may intimidate the other partner, close that partner off to communication, and thus drive the parents farther away from each other. When a counselor is working with a couple, it is important not to appear to be siding with the more emotionally expressive partner. If this happens, the less expressive parent may feel left out and become frustrated with the counseling process. At the onset of counseling, the couple's communication with each other may be through the counselor. One parent may attend reluctantly or be there "just to help" the other. Often this will be the father. Some people believe that it does not help to dwell on the past, especially the painful past. For this reason they will not speak of the grief they are experiencing (Worden & Monahan, 2001).

There are also gender differences that play out in the expression of grief (Polatinsky & Esprey, 2000; Schwab, 1996). These gender role expectations are part of the socialization process of our society and its culture. Studies reveal that men are more likely than women to fear the consequences of emotional expression in a social context. Men disclose far less intimate information to others than do women. For men, close friendships are based on shared activities rather than intimacy, and assumed loyalties rather than shared feelings. Bereaved fathers are faced with several double binds as they struggle to cope with their child's death. First, fathers are given little social support, while they are expected to be a major source of support for their wives, children, and other family members. Second, fathers are simultaneously confronted with the culturally idealized notions that grief is best handled through expressiveness and that they need to control such frightening and overwhelming expressions of grief (Cook, 1988). These conflicts between social and personal expectations can lead men to feel frustration, anger, and aloneness in grief.

Parents are often surprised at their own needs and responses when a child dies. The severity of the loss elicits a longing for closeness and intimacy, but some parents are surprised or feel guilty when they find themselves attempting to meet these needs sexually. It is important for parents to recognize and understand these needs and feelings as part of the normal life process. Sexual abstinence is frequently reported by couples due to a lack of sexual interest resulting from overwhelming grief. This lack of interest may be true for one partner but not the other, which places strain on the relationship (Lang, Gottlieb, & Amsel, 1996).

The opposite can also be true. Sexual activity may be sought out by some couples shortly after the death. For these couples, sexual intimacy serves as a reaffirmation of life and supports their strong need to be close to each other and take care of each other (Hagemeister & Rosenblatt, 1997). Johnson (1984) studied bereaved couples and noted that some men who previously could not be close to their wives without sexual activities could, after the loss, be close without sex. This was a surprise to some of the men who now understood why their wives enjoyed and were comforted by hugging.

Divorce has frequently been associated with parental bereavement. The Compassionate Friends (1999) conducted a survey and found that there was no conclusive evidence that showed an increased divorce rate resulting directly from parental grief. However, there is sufficient anecdotal evidence to suggest potential for an increased divorce rate among this population. Klass (1986–1987) gives an excellent description of the paradoxical effect of the death of a child on the relationship of the parents:

> The shared loss creates a new and very profound tie between them at the same time that the individual loss each of them feels creates an

estrangement in the relationship. The paradox is expressed differently in couples with different relationships prior to the death. (p. 239)

Klass concludes that the divorce rate may indeed be higher, but any increase in the divorce rate may not be a direct result of the death of the child but due to preexisting factors.

Grieving the loss of a child may become even more complicated when the parents of the child are already divorced. Parents are often brought together in this time of crisis, and this coming together can evoke strong emotions and extreme behaviors, from empathy and caring to an all-out struggle for power and control. But in this situation it is impossible to gain the type of control that is really desired—the recovery of the deceased.

Parents should be encouraged not to have more children until they have worked through the loss of the first child. Otherwise, they may not do the necessary grief work, or they may work out their grief issues on the replacement child (Reid, 1992). I once saw a couple shortly after their child died of SIDS. They wanted to have another child immediately, but I cautioned them against this. Not heeding my advice, they left their 4-year-old son with a babysitter and headed for the Caribbean to get pregnant. Fortunately, their attempts did not work. Two years later they were able to have another child and, in my opinion, were better able to see the child for what she was and not as a replacement for her sister.

The child who is placed in this role is also at a distinct disadvantage. Being a replacement child can interfere with cognitive and emotional development. It may lead to a relative absence of the sense of individuality, as the child is treated as the deceased's sibling and not themselves (Legg & Sherick, 1976). The development of the replacement child is further complicated because replacement children are often overprotected by fearful parents and raised in homes dominated by images of the dead child (Poznanski, 1972). Replacement children are expected to emulate the deceased child—who can be easily overidealized—and are not allowed to develop their own identity.

Bereaved parents face two issues: (1) learning to live without the child, which involves learning a new form of interacting with the social network, and (2) internalizing an inner representation of the child that brings comfort (Klass, 1988). The various tasks of mourning (described in chapter 2) address these issues and need to be worked through. For many parents who have lost children, the reality of the loss (task I) is a struggle between belief and nonbelief. On one hand, they know that the child is gone, and on the other hand they don't want to believe it. Dealing with the possessions of their lost child is often a reflection of this struggle. Parents sometimes keep a child's room intact for many years after the death so that if the child returns it will be ready.

Strong feelings, including anger, guilt, and blame, are frequently present. Processing these is the second task of mourning. Such feelings are often processed best in groups like Compassionate Friends, where empathic listening is available from those with similar experiences. Many who have not undergone this type of loss believe that the last thing grieving parents want to do is to talk about their child, but this is exactly what most want to do (Wijngaards-de Meij, Stroebe, & Schut, 2005).

One dimension of the third task of mourning for many parents is finding some kind of meaning from the death of their child (Brice, 1991; Wheeler, 2001). There are various ways parents may go about this. Some find meaning in adherence to religious and philosophical beliefs. Others find meaning through identification of the child's uniqueness and by finding some appropriate memorialization for the child. Parents who lost a college-age son in a terrible accident created a foundation in his honor. Every year a college scholarship is awarded to a graduate of the high school attended by their son. Still others find meaning by becoming involved in activities that can help individuals and society (Miles & Crandall, 1983). Klass (1988) found that parents who could transform the parental role of helping and nurturing their child to helping and nurturing others in a self-help group had more positive and less stressful memories of the deceased child.

Working through task IV issues can be very difficult for bereaved parents. "The same ambivalence and multiple representations that were part of the living relationships with the child are part of the search for equilibrium when the child dies" (Klass & Marwit, 1988–1989, p. 42). However, it is possible, and for some, this struggle with repositioning the lost child can lead to important self-awareness and personal growth coming out of this very difficult experience (Klass &

Marwit, 1988–1989; Riley, LaMontagene, Hepworth, & Murphy, 2007). One such parent eventually found an effective place for the thoughts and memories of her dead son so she could begin reinvesting in life. She said:

> Only recently have I begun to take notice of things in life that are still open to me. You know, things that can bring me pleasure. I know that I will continue to grieve for Robbie for the rest of my life and that I will keep his loving memory alive. But life goes on, and like it or not, I am a part of it. Lately, there have been times when I notice how well I seem to be doing on some project at home or even taking part in some activity with friends.

Here is a bereaved parent who is moving through her grief and carrying on with her life without feeling that she is dishonoring the memory of her child. This is the ultimate and the most challenging goal for any bereaved parent.

CHILDREN WHOSE PARENTS DIE

Another significant family area that needs to be addressed is that of children who lose a parent to death. When this occurs in childhood or adolescence, the child may fail to adequately mourn and later in life may present with symptoms of depression or the inability to form close relationships during the adult years. As described in chapter 6, intervention focuses on the reactivation of the mourning process, with the result that patients improve symptomatically and are able to resume life tasks that were previously arrested.

There has been considerable controversy over the years, particularly stemming from psychoanalytic schools, as to whether or not children are capable of mourning. On one side, you find people like Martha Wolfenstein (1966), who says that children cannot mourn until there is a complete identity formation, which occurs at the end of adolescence, when the person is fully differentiated. On the other hand, people like Erna Furman (1974) take the opposite position and say that children can mourn as early as 3 years of age, when object constancy is achieved. Bowlby (1960) pushes the age back to 6 months.

There are those, like myself, who take a third position—that children do mourn and what is needed is a model of mourning that fits children rather than the imposition of an adult model on children. A key component in children's grief is their emotional reaction to separation. Such reactions exist very early and may predate a realistic concept of death. Although young children show grief-like behavior when attachments are broken, they may not have the cognitive development to understand death. They cannot integrate something that they do not understand. Some of the cognitive concepts that are necessary in order to fully understand death are finality, transformation, irreversibility, causality, inevitability, and concrete operations (Smilansky, 1987). In his studies, Piaget suggests that concrete operations are developed only in children beyond the ages of 7 or 8 (Piaget & Inhelder, 1969).

In the Harvard Child Bereavement Study, Phyllis Silverman and I followed 125 school-age children from 70 families for 2 years after the death of one parent. These families were from communities selected for their varying demographics. Non-bereaved children matched for age, gender, grade in school, family religion, and community were also followed for the same period. Assessments were made of the children, their surviving parents, and the family. We wanted to study a group of children from the community to see what the natural course of bereavement would be for children from 6 to 17 years of age (Silverman, 2000; Worden, 1996). Here are some of the important findings from this study:

1. Most bereaved children (80%) were coping well by the first and second anniversaries. However, the 20% who were not coping well exceeded the percentage of matched controls not coping well during that period. Differences between bereaved children not doing well and their control counterparts were greater at 2 years than at 1 year, which makes a case for a late effect of the loss on these children.

2. Children doing well tended to come from more cohesive families where communication about the dead parent was easy, and where fewer daily life changes and disruptions took place. Families who coped actively rather than passively and who

could find something positive in a difficult situation had children who made a better adaptation to the loss.

3. Children not doing as well tended to come from families experiencing a large number of stressors and changes as the result of the death and have a surviving parent who was young, depressed, and not coping well. These children showed lower self-esteem and felt less able to control what happened to them in life.

4. The functioning level of the surviving parent was the most powerful predictor of a child's adjustment to the death of a parent. Children with a poorly functioning parent showed more anxiety and depression as well as sleep and health problems.

5. In general, the loss of a mother was worse for most children than the loss of a father. This was especially true during the second year of bereavement. The death of a mother portends more daily life changes and, for most families, the loss of the emotional caretaker of the family. Mother loss was associated with more emotional/behavioral problems, including higher levels of anxiety, more acting-out behavior, lower self-esteem, and weaker belief in one's own self-efficacy.

6. Most children were given the choice of participation in the funeral and opted to do so. Better outcomes were seen in the children who were prepared beforehand for the service. The ability to recapture memories of the funeral and talk about it increased over time. Including children in the planning of the funeral had a positive effect, helping them to feel important and useful at a time when many are feeling overwhelmed.

7. Many children remained connected to their dead parent through talking to them, feeling watched by them, thinking about them, dreaming about them, and locating them in a specific place. Children with strong continuing bonds to the deceased parent seemed better able to show their emotional pain, to talk with others about the death, and to accept support from families and friends.

8. Three things children need after the death of a parent are support, nurturance, and continuity. Providing these may be difficult for a surviving parent, and particularly difficult for a

surviving father. Childhood grief is best facilitated in the presence of a consistent adult who is able to meet the child's needs and help the child express feelings about the loss.

9. Bereaved teenagers frequently feel different from their friends because of the loss and often feel that their friends do not understand how it is to lose a parent to death. One particularly vulnerable group is teenage girls whose mothers die and who are left with a father.

10. Parental dating in the first year of bereavement was associated with withdrawn behavior, acting-out behavior, and somatic symptoms, especially if the parent was a father. Engagement or remarriage after a suitable bereavement period had a positive influence on the children, leading to less anxiety, depression, and worry about the safety of the surviving parent.[1]

From this study we identified a number of needs that bereaved children have. Counselors working with bereaved children should be aware of these needs and target specific interventions toward meeting these needs (Saldinger, Porterfield, & Cain, 2005; Worden, 1996).

Bereaved children need to know that they will be cared for. "Who will take care of me?" is a question on the minds of most children, whether articulated or not. The death of a parent touches primitive anxiety that one cannot survive without a parent, something that is true for the very young, but a feeling that all can experience even into adulthood. In our study, half the children still expressed a concern for the safety of the surviving parent 2 years after the death. Children need to know that they will be safe and cared for, and this can be addressed directly even if the child is not asking it directly. Some children act out to see if they are cared for, and consistently applied discipline can help children feel safer.

Bereaved children need to know that they did not cause the death out of their anger or shortcomings. The question "Did I cause it to happen?" may be on the child's mind. We learn early in life that strong feelings can injure others. Opportunities to talk about the deceased can often reveal this sense of culpability. A particularly vulnerable age for this kind of thinking is 4–5 years, when children believe in magic, thinking that they have the power to cause things to happen.

Bereaved children need clear information about the death—its causes and circumstances. "Will it happen to me?" is on the mind of many children. Contagion must be explained to some children, for example, "If we go to visit Grampa in the hospital, you can't catch cancer." If children are not given information in terms they can understand, they will make up a story to fill in the blanks, a story often more frightening or bizarre than the truth. Children need to be told these things in age-appropriate terms. One mother preparing her 5-year-old to attend the funeral told him that Daddy's body would be in the casket. Upon hearing that, the child left the room screaming. It was only later that the mother discovered that the child made a distinction between the body and the head. If the body was in the casket, where was the head?

Children need to feel important and involved. Including children in decisions about the funeral and in the funeral or memorial service itself can be useful. Children who have never attended a funeral need to be coached ahead of time as to what will happen at the service and what they might see. It is helpful to assign an adult who is not a family member to look out for younger children in case these children need to leave the service before it is concluded. Involving children in decisions about holiday and anniversary activities as well as cemetery visits can help children feel included while making such memorials a family activity.

Bereaved children need continued routine activity. Children in the study who did best were those whose daily routine could be kept as consistent as possible—mealtimes, bedtime, homework assignments, and the like. Sometimes bereaved adults do not understand why children go play when the rest of the family is grieving and may need a reminder that children cope through play activity.

Bereaved children need someone to listen to their questions. It is not unusual for a grieving child to ask the same question repeatedly, much to the frustration of the adults. Children may want to see if the adult response is consistent as they are struggling with their own feelings. Some questions from younger children may be annoying. The question "Can Grandma still pee in heaven?" may be met with derision by older siblings, but children's questions should be answered with respect.

Bereaved children need ways to remember the dead person. An excellent way to do this is to make a memory book in which the children can put pictures, stories, photographs, and other items memorializing the person who died and the events the child shared with that person. This is best done as a family activity and can be done in a simple inexpensive scrapbook. It is my experience that children, as they grow older, revisit the memory book to see who that person was and to speculate who that person would have been now had he or she lived.

The mental health practitioner needs to be aware of several things when dealing with children who have lost parents.

1. Children do mourn, but differences in mourning are determined by both the cognitive and emotional development of a child.

2. The loss of a parent through death is obviously a trauma but does not in and of itself necessarily lead to arrested development.

3. Children between the ages of 5 and 7 years are a particularly vulnerable group. They have developed cognitively enough to understand some of the permanent ramifications of death but they have very little coping capacity; that is, their ego skills and social skills are insufficiently developed to enable them to defend themselves. This particular group should be singled out for special concern by the counselor.

4. It is important also to recognize that the work of mourning may not end in quite the same way for a child as it does for an adult. Mourning for a childhood loss can be revived at many points in an adult's life when it is reactivated during important life events. One of the most obvious examples is when the child reaches the same age as the parent who died. When this mourning is reactivated, it does not necessarily portend pathology but is simply a further example of working through.

The same tasks of mourning that apply to the adult obviously apply to the child, but these tasks have to be understood and modified in terms of the child's cognitive, personal, social, and emotional development. It is important for the mental health worker to develop preventive mental health approaches for bereaved children. Offering early intervention to the child identified as at risk for later poor adaptation to the loss is one way to do preventative mental health work. A screening instrument for the early identification of the at-risk child can be found in Worden (1996).

FAMILY INTERVENTION APPROACHES

After a death, ask to meet with survivors both individually and as a family unit. The focus of such family meetings is not only to facilitate tasks I and II, with the special focus on the expression of both positive and negative affects about the deceased, but also to identify what roles the deceased played and the ways these roles are being taken up or rejected by surviving family members—task III. In the case of the death of the father, some of these roles may be assigned to the eldest son. The eldest son will either take up the cudgel and suppress a lot of himself and his own feelings or back away from this demand, often to the frustration of the surviving parent or other relatives who are fostering this role expectation.

Identifying the restructured roles within the family is particularly helpful when there are teenage children involved. Their fears and their willingness to pick up various tasks can often be negotiated. However, it is often very difficult for surviving parents to negotiate these on their own after the death. Frequently the family ends up in a situation of bickering and conflict, or with various family members withdrawing emotionally. Helping them sort out the real issues and the peripheral issues is a very important aspect of this kind of family therapy (Traylor et al., 2003).

Role assignments are usually made subtly and nonverbally, but there are times when there is a direct verbal assignment. Jerry arrived home from school at age 15 to find the house full of neighbors and family members surrounding his mother, who was trying very hard not to cry. His uncle told him that his father had died suddenly and also told him that he was going to be "the man in the family" because he was the oldest male. This was due in part to Jewish family tradition. Because he was now designated the man of the house, this overwhelmed boy was asked to make decisions regarding the funeral such as whether or not to have an open casket. He was able to make these decisions, but what the family did not know was how responsible and burdened he felt because of his brother, who was 4 years his junior. These feelings were aggravated because his mother offered little support during the time of death. It was only as an adult of 30 that Jerry became aware of how destructive this situation had been over the years in his relationship with his brother and he was able to verbalize how much of a burden this was.

When Jerry finally confessed this to his mother, she told him that he was not responsible and freed him from this encumbrance. Shortly thereafter, through therapy, he was able to see how this sense of overresponsibility for his brother had colored all his relationships with women over the years in terms of his limited commitment. If this pattern had not been broken, he doubts that he could have the satisfying relationship he enjoys at present. No one, including the patient, blames the uncle or believes he had bad intentions, but it is a difficult legacy to carry for 15 years, and it points up the need to talk with children about their feelings and fantasies when there is a death in the family.

Related to roles is the issue of alliances. In any family situation there are various dyadic alliances formed. Usually these serve the various needs for power that individuals experience. They can also serve the need to reinforce self-esteem. Anyone who is studying families from a sociometric point of view can diagram these very important alliances. When a significant family member dies, upsetting the equilibrium of the family unit, new alliances need to be formed. The maneuvering for these new alliances may cause considerable tension and distress in the family.

Bowen (1978) suggests that many dyadic relationships become triangulated in order to remove some of the anxiety or the pressure of a dyadic relationship. After someone dies, there is a need to shift and reequilibrate family triangles. Various alliances that have formed need to be altered. However, if no substitute is found, then the deprived member may seek homeostasis through various social, physical, or emotional illnesses (Kuhn, 1977; McBride & Simms, 2001).

Another problem that can arise in families after a death is that of making someone a scapegoat. Throughout this book we have looked at the issue of anger and the importance of the ways in which it is handled by the bereaved. One way that anger is handled ineffectively is through displacement; likewise, one of the least effective ways of handling anger vis-à-vis displacement in the family is through scapegoating—one of the family members becomes the target of the wrath and the blame and the anger for the death. Sometimes one of the younger and more vulnerable members of the family becomes the scapegoat. I once saw a 6-year-old girl whose mother blamed her for the death of her infant brother and sent her off to live with relatives.

Like individuals, bereaved families also struggle with making meaning out of the loss, and this is an important feature of family grief. Meanings are critical to how families grieve (Sedney, Baker, & Gross, 1994). Nadeau (1998), in her excellent book on this subject, suggests that counselors listen and encourage families to tell their stories. In this way one can enter into the world of grieving families and stand by them in moments of great pain and, through talking and listening, facilitate their quest for meaning so that they can go on living.

Finally, family therapy can address the impact of incomplete mourning on subsequent family life and interaction. Incomplete mourning is a pervasive defense against further losses and disappointments and can be transmitted unwittingly to other family members, especially to offspring. To overcome this, psychiatrist Norman Paul and his colleagues have developed what he calls "operational mourning" and have used it in conjoint family therapy (Paul, 1986; Paul & Grosser, 1965).

Operational mourning consists of inducing the mourning response by directly asking one family member about reactions to actual losses the family has sustained. Then the other family members who are present are asked to talk about the feelings that have been stimulated through their observations of the grief reaction of the first person. In this way children, often for the first time, observe their parents expressing intense emotions. This gives the therapist an opportunity to assure them of the normality of these feelings. It also gives the therapist the opportunity to review the episodic threats of abandonment by a parent or other family member that have been an important influence in current family life. During these periods of activated mourning, family members are encouraged to share their affective experiences and to react empathetically to affects expressed by the other family members. In using this procedure, Paul finds an enormous amount of resistance and denial on the part of the family, but if this resistance is overcome, the intervention is very beneficial.

GRIEF AND THE ELDERLY

Still another issue that affects the family system is the increase in the elderly bereaved population. While the maximum age for human beings has not increased significantly in recent years, the number of people living into their 70s and 80s has grown and will continue to grow through the 21st century. With this increase comes a larger number of elderly who have experienced bereavement, especially the loss of a spouse. Widowhood affects three out of four women. (In 1998 there were 7.8 million widowed women age 65 and older in the United States and 1.5 million widowed elderly men.) Although the mourning process is shaped by the mediators discussed in chapter 3, several features of grief in the elderly deserve to be noted (Moss, Moss, & Hansson, 2001).

Interdependence

Many elderly widows and widowers were married for a long time, which leads to deep attachments and to the entrenchment of family roles. There is interdependence in any marriage. However, in these lengthy marriages, it is possible that the spouses were highly dependent upon one another. To the extent that the bereaved were highly dependent on their spouses for certain roles or activities, this makes for a more difficult adjustment after the loss, especially the accomplishment of task III (Ott, 2007). Parkes (1992) observes that the person who died is often the one who previously helped the bereaved person handle crises. Therefore, the bereaved frequently find themselves turning to someone who is not there.

Multiple Losses

With age, the number of deaths of friends and family members that one experiences increases. This increased number of losses in a brief period can cause a person to be overwhelmed and possibly not to grieve. Concurrent with the loss of friends, relatives, and family members are other losses the aging person may experience. These can include the loss of occupation; loss of environment; loss of family constellations; loss of physical vigor, including physical disabilities; the diminishing of one's senses; and for some, the loss of cerebral functioning. All these changes, added to losses through death, need to be grieved. But the ability one has to grieve may be lessened as a result of many losses in an abbreviated time period (Carr, Nesse, & Wortman, 2006). There was one hopeful note from a study that showed that older women who had a physical disability prior to the death of their spouse were amazingly resilient in handling the death, compared to non-bereaved matched controls (Telonidis, Lund, Caserta, Guralnik, & Pennington, 2005).

Personal Death Awareness

Experiencing loss of contemporaries such as a spouse, friends, or siblings may heighten one's personal death awareness. This increase in the awareness of personal mortality can lead to existential anxiety (Worden, 1976). Counselors need to be comfortable discussing the bereaved's personal sense of mortality and explore the extent to which this death awareness might be troublesome (Fry, 2001).

Loneliness

Many bereaved elderly live alone. A study done by Lopata (1996) showed that younger widows and widowers were more likely to move after the loss, whereas older ones were more likely to remain in the home they lived in at the time of the death. Living alone can lead to intense feelings of loneliness, which may be particularly intensified if one continues to live in the physical surroundings shared with the spouse. Van Baarsen, Van Duijn, Smit, Snijders, and Knipscheer (2001) make the distinction between social loneliness and emotional loneliness, the latter being the most perduring among the elderly. There is some evidence that those who had more harmonious marriages experience the most emotional loneliness (Grimby, 1993). Some elderly cannot continue to live alone after the death of a spouse and may require institutional care. There is anecdotal evidence to support the contention that elderly people who are forced to move out of their homes after losing a spouse may be at higher risk for mortality.

Role Adjustment

The loss of a spouse and its effect on day-to-day living may be more disruptive for elderly men than for women. Many men face new roles, particularly homemaking, and may need help adjusting to these roles. When a woman loses her husband, there often is not the same level of disruption in terms of her ability to keep house and her self-reliance as a homemaker. There are certain counseling interventions such as skill building that can be useful in work with the elderly bereaved, especially men.

Support Groups

Support groups for the bereaved can be useful at any age, but it is particularly important for elderly individuals, whose network of support is often diminished and whose isolation is often pronounced (Cohen, 2000; Moss et al., 2001). Support groups can offer important human contact to those who are experiencing high levels of social loneliness. In one study, Lund, Dimond, and Juretich (1985) discovered that both elderly men and women would be willing to participate in support groups. Those whose main confidant was less available than previously, those with more depression and less life satisfaction, and those who perceived that they were not coping well were most eager to participate in a support group. There was also more willingness among those between the ages of 50 and 69 to participate in groups than among those of more advanced age. One should note that perception of support both before and after the death may be more important than objectively measured social network characteristics in assessments of support satisfaction (Feld & George, 1994).

Touch

Another useful intervention is touch. Many men and women, but particularly men, who've been married for a long time and then lose their spouse have a strong need to be touched. Without their spouse, they may find it difficult to get this need met. A counselor who is comfortable with physical contact can include touching in working with the elderly bereaved. However, any time touch is used therapeutically, the counselor must be clear as to its suitability and must also attend to whether or not the person is willing or ready to be touched.

Reminiscing

Another intervention technique is reminiscing, something that is common among the elderly and can be stimulated therapeutically in an elderly bereaved population. Reminiscing is sometimes called life review. It is a naturally occurring process that brings the person to a progressive return to consciousness of past experiences and, in particular, to the resurgence of unresolved conflicts. It is generally assumed that reminiscing serves an adaptational function for the aging person and that it is not a sign of intellectual decline.

Siblings can often serve as a major resource for life review because they may be the elderly person's longest-lived relationship. However, the older one becomes, the less likely it is that one's siblings will also be alive (Hays, Gold, & Peiper, 1997).

Reminiscing contributes to the maintenance of identity. Even though a person may have lost loved ones, the mental representations of these people endure. Through the process of reminiscing, the past can be reworked. The counselor can encourage the client to reminisce, and this can have a salutary effect, particularly with conjugal bereavement. Elderly individuals never truly lose the deceased, since so much of what the deceased represented is internalized and significant in the present (Moss et al., 2001). In recent years we have recognized the importance of continuing bonds with the deceased through internal representations of them (Klass, Silverman, & Nickman, 1996). See task IV in chapter 2.

Discussing Relocation

The counselor can help elderly individuals decide whether they should move from their home. This decision, of course, depends on the ability of the person to take care of him- or herself. However, one should never underestimate the importance of a home, where the bereaved may have lived for a long time and which may represent a whole scrapbook of meanings for the older person. Moving from the house may reduce a person's sense of self as well as dilute the tie with the deceased spouse. Being able to remain in their homes gives elderly people a sense of personal control and offers an arena in which they can recall the cherished past.

Skill Building

It is possible for some of the bereaved elderly to become too dependent on their adult children. Though bereaved, these people have the capacity to develop new skills and, in doing so, can benefit from the sense of self-esteem that comes through mastery. One bereaved elderly woman called her adult children constantly and wanted them to come to her home to fix things, such as the furnace, even when these repairs were needed in the middle of the night. The children were happy to do this for awhile, but it became clear to them that their mother needed to learn to call the electrician and to take care of those things that, prior to the death, her husband would have handled. She was very resistant to the suggestion and felt her children were rejecting her. However, reason finally prevailed, and when she did learn how to handle some of these day-to-day activities, she felt good that she had developed some of these skills. The counselor needs to keep in mind that mastery and self-esteem go together, and this is true for the elderly and the elderly bereaved. However, time for adjustment may be required. Parkes (1992) reminds us that both grieving and relearning take time, so a period of dependency on others may be required to help elderly individuals through this period of transition.

In any discussion of the bereaved elderly, it is important to keep in mind that research has shown that stresses experienced by this population may be stronger prior to the death than afterward. This is particularly the case when one has been the primary caretaker of a sick spouse. If this is true, then one might want to begin interventions early and not wait until after the death has occurred.

While most of the focus in this discussion of elderly bereavement has been on spousal loss, other family deaths are also frequently experienced. Among these are the deaths of siblings and the deaths of grandchildren. In the latter case, bereavement support is often focused on the bereaved parents to the exclusion of the grandparents' grief.

It is important not to assume that all elderly bereaved are in need of counseling. Caserta and Lund (1992) found that many bereaved elderly showed strong resilience. Those coping well had better self-confidence, optimism, self-efficacy, and self-esteem than those who coped less well. To this I would add that they also had better health. With the elderly, as with other age groups, it is important to keep in mind that there is no universal experience of grief and no universal way of dealing with it (Bennett & Bennett, 2000). Remember Allport's dictum that "each man is like no other man"!

FAMILY VERSUS INDIVIDUAL NEEDS

Before concluding this chapter on grief and the family system, there are two points I want to emphasize. First, it is important to recognize that not everyone in a family will be working on the same tasks of mourning at the same time. Individual family members will process tasks at their own rate and in their own way. For example, it may be that bereavement in the elderly takes a long time, and to some extent, it may not have an end point. Miller and colleagues (1994) talk about a "timeless attachment" to the deceased. Some elderly, particularly the "old-old," may be at a stage in their lives at which it is best for them to consolidate their memories and draw on them for sustenance throughout their remaining years.

Families need to be encouraged not to rush a person through the grief experience. I spoke recently with a woman whose father had died 4 months earlier. She was very upset with her mother for continuing to have long crying spells. I tried to help her see that this was a very natural thing and that in time her mother would probably cry less.

An important second point is that individual members of a family will sometimes be reluctant to come in for counseling with the entire group. But even when met with resistance, it is important for the counselor to try to include the entire family in the sessions. I like to have at least one session with the entire family. That way I can see how the family interacts as a unit, each individual influencing the others. When the counselor can assess the feelings of all the family members, the probability is greater that the grief counseling will be effective and that equilibrium will be restored to the family unit.

If family members are reluctant to attend, the counselor can still use a family systems approach to work with an individual. Bloch (1991) reminds us that the issue is not the number of people in the counseling room but whether the counselor helps the client to understand family dynamics so that he or she can transmit this to other relevant members of the system.

NOTE

1. Additional information on this Harvard study can be found in: Worden, J. W. (1996). *Children & grief: When a parent dies.* New York: Guilford; and Silverman, P. R. (2000). *Never too young to know: Death in children's lives.* New York: Oxford.

REFERENCES

Bennett, K. M., & Bennett, G. (2000). "And there's always this great hole inside that hurts": An empirical study of bereavement in later life. *Omega, 42,* 237–251.

Bloch, S. (1991). A systems approach to loss. *Australian & New Zealand Journal of Psychiatry, 25,* 471–480.

Bowen, M. (1978). *Family therapy in clinical practice.* New York: Aronson.

Bowlby, J. (1960). Grief and mourning in infancy and early childhood. *Psychoanalytic Study of the Child, 15,* 9–52.

Brice, C. W. (1991). Paradoxes of maternal mourning. *Psychiatry, 54*(1), 1–12.

Carr, D., Nesse, R., & Wortman, C. (Eds.). (2006). *Spousal bereavement in late life.* New York: Springer Publishing.

Caserta, M. S., & Lund, D. A. (1992). Bereavement stress and coping among older adults: Expectations versus the actual experience. *Omega, 25,* 33–45.

Cohen, M. (2000). Bereavement groups with the elderly. *Journal of Psychotherapy in Independent Practice, 1,* 33–41.

Compassionate Friends. (1999). *When a child dies: A survey of bereaved parents.* Author.

Cook, J. A. (1988). Dad's double binds: Rethinking fathers' bereavement from a men's studies perspective. *Journal of Contemporary Ethnography, 17,* 285–308.

Davies, B., Gudmundsdottir, M., Worden, J. W., Orloff, S., Sumner, L., & Brenner, P. (2004). "Living in the dragon's shadow": Fathers' experiences of a child's life-limiting illness. *Death Studies, 28,* 111–135.

Davies, B., Spinetta, J., Martinson, I., & Kulenkamp, E. (1986). Manifestations of levels of functioning in grieving families. *Journal of Family Issues, 7,* 297–313.

Drenovsky, C. K. (1994). Anger and the desire for retribution among bereaved parents. *Omega, 29,* 303–312.

Feld, S., & George, L. K. (1994). Moderating effects of prior social resources on the hospitalizations of elders who become widowed. *Journal of Aging and Health, 6,* 275–295.

Fry, P. (2001). The unique contribution of key existential factors to the prediction of psychological well-being of older adults following spousal loss. *Gerontologist, 41,* 69–81.

Furman, E. (1974). *A child's parent dies: Studies in childhood bereavement.* New Haven, CT: Yale University Press.

Gajdos, K. C. (2002). The Intergenerational effects of grief and trauma. *Illness Crisis & Loss, 10,* 304 317.

Gilbert, K. R. (1996). "We've had the same loss, why don't we have the same grief?" Loss and differential grief in families. *Death Studies, 20,* 269–283.

Greaves, C. C. (1983). Death in the family: A multifamily therapy approach. *International Journal of Family Psychiatry, 4,* 247–259.

Greeff, A., & Human, B. (2004). Resilience in families in which a parent has died. *American Journal of Family Therapy, 32,* 27–42.

Grimby, A. (1993). Bereavement among elderly people: Grief reactions, post-bereavement hallucinations and quality of life. *Acta Psychiatrica Scandinavica, 87,* 72–80.

Hagemeister, A., & Rosenblatt, P. (1997). Grief and the sexual relationship of couples who have experienced a child's death. *Death Studies, 21,* 231–252.

Hays, J. C., Gold, D. T., & Peiper, C. F. (1997). Sibling bereavement in late life. *Omega, 35,* 25–42.

Johnson, S. (1984). Sexual intimacy and replacement children after the death of a child. *Omega, 15,* 109–118.

Kissane, D., & Bloch, S. (2002). *Family focused grief therapy: A model of family-centered care during palliative care and bereavement.* Birmingham, UK: Open University Press.

Kissane, D., McKenzie, M., McKenzie, D. P., Forbes, A., O'Neill, I., & Bloch, S. (2003). Psychosocial morbidity associated with patterns of family functioning in palliative care: Baseline data from the family focused grief therapy controlled trial. *Palliative Medicine, 17*, 527–537.

Klass, D. (1986–1987). Marriage and divorce among bereaved parents in a self-help group. *Omega, 17*, 237–249.

Klass, D. (1988). *Parental grief: Solace and resolution.* New York: Springer Publishing.

Klass, D., & Marwit, S. J. (1988–1989). Toward a model of parental grief. *Omega, 19*, 31–50.

Klass, D., Silverman, P., & Nickman, S. (Eds.). (1996). *Continuing bonds: New understandings of grief.* Washington, DC: Taylor & Francis.

Kuhn, J. S. (1977). Realignment of emotional forces following loss. *Family, 5*, 19–24.

Lang, A., Gottlieb, L. N., & Amsel, R. (1996). Predictors of husbands' and wives' grief reactions following infant death: The role of marital intimacy. *Death Studies, 20*, 33–57.

Lebow, J. L. (Ed.). (2005). *Handbook of clinical family therapy.* Hoboken, NJ: John Wiley.

Legg, C., & Sherick, I. (1976). The replacement child: A developmental tragedy. *Child Psychiatry & Human Development, 7*, 113–126.

Littlewood, J. L., Cramer, D., Hockstra, J., & Humphrey, G. B. (1991). Gender differences in parental coping following their child's death. *British Journal of Guidance and Counseling, 19*, 139–148.

Lopata, H. Z. (1996). *Current widowhood: Myths and realities.* Thousand Oaks, CA: Sage.

Lund, D. A., Dimond, M. F., & Juretich, M. (1985). Bereavement support groups for the elderly: Characteristics of potential participants. *Death Studies, 9*, 309–321.

McBride, J., & Simms, S. (2001). Death in the family: Adapting a family systems framework to the grief process. *American Journal of Family Therapy, 29*, 59–73.

Middleton, W., Raphael, B., Burnett, P., & Martinek, N. (1998). A longitudinal study comparing bereavement phenomena in recently bereaved spouses, adult children and parents. *Australian & New Zealand Journal of Psychiatry, 32*, 235–241.

Miles, M. S., & Crandall, E. K. B. (1983). The search for meaning and its potential for affecting growth in bereaved parents. *Health Values, 7*, 19–23.

Miles, M. S., & Demi, A. S. (1991–1992). A comparison of guilt in bereaved parents whose children died by suicide, accident, or chronic disease. *Omega, 24*, 203–215.

Miller, M., Frank, E., Cornes, C., Imber, S., Anderson, B., Ehrenpreis, L., et al. (1994). Applying interpersonal psychotherapy to bereavement-related depression following loss of a spouse in late life. *Journal of Psychotherapy Practice and Research, 3*, 149–162.

Moss, M. S., Moss, S. Z., & Hansson, R. O. (2001). Bereavement and old age. In M. S. Stroebe, R. O. Hansson, W. Stroebe, & H. Schut (Eds.), *Handbook of bereavement research: Consequences, coping, and care* (pp. 241–260). Washington, DC: American Psychological Association.

Nadeau, J. W. (1998). *Families making sense of death.* Thousand Oaks, CA: Sage.

Nadeau, J. W. (2001). Meaning making in family bereavement. In M. S. Stroebe, R. O. Hansson, W. Stroebe, & H. Schut (Eds.), *Handbook of bereavement research: Consequences, coping, and care* (pp. 329–347). Washington, DC: American Psychological Association.

Ott, C. (2007). Spousal bereavement in older adults: Common, resilient, and chronic grief with defining characteristics. *Journal of Nervous and Mental Disease, 195,* 332–341.

Parkes, C. M. (1992). Bereavement and mental health in the elderly. *Reviews in Clinical Gerontology, 2,* 45–51.

Paul, N. L. (1986). The paradoxical nature of the grief experience. *Contemporary Family Therapy, 8,* 5–19.

Paul, N. L., & Grosser, G. H. (1965). Operational mourning and its role in conjoint family therapy. *Community Mental Health Journal, 1,* 339–345.

Piaget, J., & Inhelder, B. (1969). *The psychology of the child.* New York: Basic Books.

Polatinsky, S., & Esprey, Y. (2000). An assessment of gender differences in the perception of benefit resulting from the loss of a child. *Journal of Traumatic Stress, 13,* 709–718.

Poznanski, E. O. (1972). The replacement child: A saga of unresolved parental grief. *Journal of Pediatrics, 81,* 1190–1193.

Reid, M. (1992). Joshua—life after death: The replacement child. *Journal of Child Psychotherapy, 18,* 109–138.

Reilly, D. M. (1978). Death propensity, dying, and bereavement: A family systems perspective. *Family Therapy, 5,* 35–55.

Riley, L. P., LaMontagene, L. L., Hepworth, J. T., & Murphy, B. A. (2007). Parental grief responses and personal growth following the death of a child. *Death Studies, 31,* 277–299.

Robinson, T., & Marwit, S. J. (2006). An investigation of the relationship of personality, coping, and grief intensity among bereaved mothers. *Grief Studies, 30,* 677–696.

Rosen, E. J. (1990). *Families facing death.* Lexington, MA: Lexington Books.

Rotter, J. (2000). Family grief and mourning. *Family Journal of Counseling & Therapy for Couples & Families, 8,* 275–277.

Saldinger, A., Porterfield, K., & Cain, A. (2005). Meeting the needs of parentally bereaved children: A framework for child-centered parenting. *Psychiatry, 67,* 331–352.

Sanders, C. (1979). A comparison of adult bereavement in the death of a spouse, child, and parent. *Omega, 10,* 303–322.

Schwab, R. (1996). Gender differences in parental grief. *Death Studies, 20,* 103–113.

Schumacher, J. D. (1984). Helping children cope with a sibling's death. In J. C. Hansen & T. Frantz (Eds.), *Death and grief in the family* (pp. 82–94). Rockville, MD: Aspen.

Sedney, M. A., Baker, J. E., & Gross, E. (1994). "The story" of a death: Therapeutic considerations with bereaved families. *Journal of Marital and Family Therapy, 20,* 287–296.

Silverman, P. R. (2000). *Never too young to know: Death in children's lives.* New York: Oxford University Press.

Smilansky, S. (1987). *On death: Helping children understand and cope.* New York: Peter Lang.

Telonidis, J. S., Lund, D. A., Caserta, M. S., Guralnik, J. M., & Pennington, J. L., Jr. (2005). The effects of widowhood on disabled older women. *Omega, 50,* 217–235.

Traylor, E., Hayslip, B., Jr., Kaminski, P., & York, C. (2003). Relationships between grief and family system characteristics: A cross lagged longitudinal analysis. *Death Studies, 27,* 575–601.

Van Baarsen, B., Van Duijn, M., Smit, J., Snijders, T., & Knipscheer, K. (2001). Patterns of adjustment to partner loss in old age: The widowhood adaptation longitudinal study. *Omega, 44,* 5–36.

Vess, J., Moreland, J., & Schwebel, A. (1985–1986). Understanding family role realloca- tion following a death: A theoretical framework. *Omega, 16,* 115–128.

Walsh, F., & McGoldrick, M. (1991). *Living beyond loss: Death in the family.* New York: Norton.

Wheeler, I. (2001). Parental bereavement: The crisis of meaning. *Death Studies, 25,* 51–66.

Wijngaards-de Meij, L., Stroebe, M. S., & Schut, H. (2005). Couples at risk following the death of their child: Predictors of grief versus depression. *Journal of Consulting & Clinical Psychology, 73,* 617–623.

Wolfenstein, M. (1966). How is mourning possible? *Psychoanalytic Study of the Child, 21,* 93–123.

Worden, J. W. (1976). *Personal death awareness.* Englewood Cliffs, NJ: Prentice-Hall.

Worden, J. W. (1996). *Children & grief: When a parent dies.* New York: Guilford Press.

Worden, J. W., Davies, B., & McCown, D. (2000). Comparing parent loss with sibling loss. *Death Studies, 23,* 1–15.

Worden, J. W., & Monahan, J. (2001). Caring for bereaved parents. In A. Armstrong- Daily & S. Goltzer (Eds.), *Hospice care for children* (2nd ed., pp. 137–156). New York: Oxford University Press.

9   The Counselor's Own Grief

Grief counseling presents a special challenge to the mental health worker. Most of us go into mental health professions in order to benefit the people who come to us for help, but there is something about the experience of grief that precludes our ability to help. Bowlby (1980) touches on this when he says:

> The loss of a loved person is one of the most intensely painful experiences any human being can suffer, and not only is it painful to experience, but also painful to witness, if only because we're so impotent to help. (p. 7)

Parkes (1972) echoes this sentiment when he says:

> Pain is inevitable in such a case and cannot be avoided. It stems from the awareness of both parties that neither can give the other what he wants. The helper cannot bring back the person who's dead, and the bereaved person cannot gratify the helper by seeming helped. (p. 175)

Because the experience of grief makes it difficult for us to be or feel helpful to the person experiencing bereavement, the counselor can easily feel frustration and anger. Or the counselor may be so uncomfortable witnessing the pain in the other person that this discomfort causes him or her to cut the relationship short (Hayes, Yeh, & Eisenberg, 2007).

251

In addition to challenging our ability to be helpful, the experience of bereavement in others also touches the counselor personally in at least three ways. First, working with the bereaved may make us aware, sometimes painfully so, of our own losses. This is particularly true if the loss experienced by the bereaved is similar to losses that we have sustained in our own lives. If the loss in the counselor's life is not adequately resolved, it can be an impediment to a meaningful and helpful intervention. If it has been adequately integrated, the counselor's experience with a similar loss can be beneficial and useful in work with the client. The counselor who has lost a spouse through death or divorce, and for whom the loss is very recent, will find it difficult, if not impossible, to work with a person who has sustained a similar loss. However, if this counselor has moved through his or her own bereavement and found a good adaptation on the other side of the loss, this can be useful and helpful in the counseling intervention. "Treatment of the bereaved needs to emerge from a compassion based on recognition of the common vulnerability of all human beings in the face of loss" (Simos, 1979, p. 177).

A second area where grief may get in the way is the counselor's own feared losses. All of us who work in this area have sustained various losses in our lifetimes, but we also come to the counseling situation with apprehension over pending losses—for example, our parents, our children, our partners. Usually this apprehension is at a low level of awareness. However, if the loss our client is experiencing is similar to the one we most fear, our apprehension can get in the way of an effective counseling relationship (Saunders & Valente, 1994).

For example, if a counselor is overanxious about the possible death of his children, and if this anxiety is translated into an overprotective relationship, the counselor may have a great deal of difficulty working with someone whose child has died. This is especially true if the counselor has not adequately brought his anxiety into consciousness and addressed the issue.

Existential anxiety and one's own personal death awareness are a third area in which grief counseling presents a special challenge to the mental health worker. In an earlier book, I addressed this issue and how this type of awareness can make a person more effective or less effective as a human being (Worden, 1976). When a client comes for grief counseling, the counselor is put in touch with the inevitability of death and with the extent to which he or she is uncomfortable with this inevitability in his or her own life. This situation is especially difficult when the person who's being grieved is similar to the counselor in terms of age, sex, or professional status, all of which can greatly increase the anxiety of the counselor. All of us are anxious to one degree or another about our own mortality, but it is possible to come to terms with this reality and for it not to be a closet issue that makes us uncomfortable and hinders our effectiveness.

Because grief counseling presents a special challenge to the mental health worker, we encourage the counselors in our training programs to explore their own histories of losses. We believe that this can make them more effective counselors. In the first place, it can help the counselor to better understand the process of mourning, what it is like to go through the experience of grief, and how the curative process of mourning takes place. There is nothing like looking at a significant loss in one's own life to bring home the reality of the grief process. It also gives the counselor an understanding of coping strategies and an idea of how long the process can go on before it comes to an adequate resolution (Redinbaugh, Schuerger, Weiss, Brufsky, & Arnold, 2001).

Second, by exploring his or her personal history of losses, the counselor can get a clear sense of the kinds of resources available to the bereaved. This includes not only what was helpful when one was undergoing a specific loss, but also what was not helpful. An exploration of this can make for more creative intervention on the counselor's part, helping the counselor know not only what to say, but also what not to say. When looking at personal losses, the counselor can identify his or her own coping style and how this personal coping style affects behavior in a counseling intervention.

The counselor can also identify any unfinished business that is still present from prior losses. The Zeigarnik psychological principle suggests that a task will be remembered until it is completed. The counselor who has a grasp on his or her own life knows about and is able to face honestly and squarely those losses that have not been adequately grieved at this particular time, and what he or she still needs to do to resolve these particular losses. Not only is it important to identify currently unresolved losses, but it is also important to identify the conflict that loss portends for the counselor and the way that conflict can be identified and dealt with (Muse & Chase, 1993).

Finally, looking at his or her own grief helps the counselor or therapist know his or her limitations with respect to the kinds of clients and the kinds of grief situations that he or she is able to deal with. Once Elisabeth Kübler-Ross and I surveyed 5,000 health professionals on issues of terminal care (Worden & Kübler-Ross, 1977–1978). One of the areas we were interested in concerned difficulties caregivers had with dying patients. Ninety-two percent of the respondents to our inquiry reported that there was at least one type of dying patients with whom they had special difficulty. The types of patients varied widely, although there was a certain clustering among the various professional groups. Because not everyone can work adequately with all types of dying patients, it is important for the caregiver to recognize personal limitations and make referrals to other colleagues who can handle certain cases more effectively.

Similar limitations hold true for the grief counselor. It is important for the grief counselor to know the kind of grieving person with whom he or she cannot work effectively and to be able to make a referral or share the support when faced with such a client. One of the subtle seductions in the mental health professions is the notion that one is capable of handling all situations. This obviously is not so, and the mature counselor knows his or her own limitations and knows when to refer. The type of client the grief counselor has personal difficulty with is usually related to the counselor's own area of unresolved conflict.

LOSS HISTORY

At this point, let me suggest that you look at your own history of losses. Below you will find a series of incomplete sentences. Complete the sentences either in the book or on a separate sheet of paper, and spend some time reflecting on your answers. If possible, talk this over with a friend or colleague. This reflection on your own life can pay dividends later on in helping to make you more effective in your own work.

1. The first death I can remember was the death of:
2. I was age:

3. The feelings I remember I had at the time were:
4. The first funeral (or wake or other ritual service) I ever attended was for:
5. I was age:
6. The thing I most remember about that experience is:
7. My most recent loss by death was (person, time, circumstances):
8. I coped with this loss by:
9. The most difficult death for me was the death of:
10. It was difficult because:
11. Of the important people in my life who are now living, the most difficult death for me would be the death of:
12. It would be the most difficult because:
13. My primary style of coping with loss is:
14. I know my own grief is resolved when:
15. It is appropriate for me to share my own experiences of grief with a client when:

STRESS AND BURNOUT

There is much current interest in the problem of professional burnout and stress management among health care providers. The concept of professional burnout was proposed by Freudenberger (1974) and later developed by Maslach (1982) to describe the progressive professional ineffectiveness of medical and mental health care workers when they are under too much stress that is badly managed. One focus of this interest has been the health care providers who work with terminally ill patients and their families. A recent book entitled *When Professionals Weep* (Katz & Johnson, 2006) outlines many of the stress/grief issues of those working in this area. Many bereavement counselors also work with the terminally ill and have contact with the deceased as well as the family prior to the actual death. Mary Vachon (1979) has compared staff stress among those working in a hospice setting and those working with the seriously ill in a general hospital. She finds stress in both settings and concludes that the best care can be given if caregivers are cognizant that they too have needs.

Since much of my work at Massachusetts General Hospital as well as several hospices in California has been with terminal patients as well as with the families' bereavement issues, I have also been interested in this issue of staff stress. There are three guidelines that I would like to suggest to the counselor who may be working with dying patients. The first is to *know your own personal limitations* in terms of the number of patients with whom you can work intimately and be attached at any given point in time. One can work with a number of patients and do an adequate job, but there is a definite limit to the number of dying patients with whom one can work and have any kind of in-depth attached relationship. This number, of course, varies from person to person, but it is extremely important for the counselor to recognize personal limitations and not be overly involved and attached to too many dying people. To the extent that there is an attachment, there is going to be a loss that the counselor will need to grieve.

In the second place, a counselor can avoid burnout by *practicing active grieving*. When a patient dies, it is important for the counselor to go through this period of active grieving. One thing I find personally helpful and recommend to our staff is that they attend the funeral service of the person with whom they were working. It is also important that they allow themselves to experience their sadness and other feelings after someone dies and not to feel guilty if they do not grieve the same way for each death.

Third, the counselor should know how to *reach out for help* and know where his or her own support comes from. Sometimes this can be a very difficult thing for health care workers to do. After lecturing to a group of funeral directors in the Midwest, I was approached by a funeral director's wife who was very concerned about her husband. He had sustained an important loss and was not doing well. He was able to help others with their grief but found it very difficult to reach out for help himself. This man's experience is similar to that of many counselors. Counselors are well known for their inability to negotiate their own help and support systems. Therefore, those of you doing grief counseling and grief therapy need to know where you get emotional support, what your limitations are, and how to reach out for help when you need it (Papadatou, 2006).

For those working in institutional settings such as hospitals, nursing homes, and hospices, support often comes from others on the caregiving team, and a team leader can be responsible for facilitating this support. Regular staff meetings where participants are encouraged to talk about problems that arise in the care of the dying and their families, and their own feelings, can help prevent excessive stress and can facilitate the feelings associated with grief and loss. Mental health professionals who are not a part of the management team can also be available to others for private consultation, or to the team, should it need help. I provided such consultation to the gynecologic service staff at Massachusetts General Hospital for several years. Parkes (1986), in speaking of support for staff who work in settings where there are a number of deaths, says, "With proper training and support we shall find that repeated griefs, far from undermining our humanity and our care, enable us to cope more confidently and more sensitively with each succeeding loss" (p. 7). I believe this is true.

Psychologist Danai Papadatou, who works in a pediatric unit and teaches nurses in Athens, Greece, has developed a series of six rules for her pediatric unit that set the guidelines for staff members on how to handle grief on the unit. I find these particularly useful:

Rule No. 1—Health professionals are expected to invest in and develop close relationships with seriously ill and dying children.
Rule No. 2—Health professionals are expected to be affected and express their grief reactions in anticipation, at the moment of death, or after it. The intensity and expression of their grief, however, must be tempered and controlled.
Rule No. 3—The grief of health professionals must never be so intense as to impair clinical judgment or lead to an emotional breakdown.
Rule No. 4—The grief of professionals must never exceed the grief of family members.
Rule No. 5—The grief of professionals should never be apparent to other sick or dying children or to their parents, who should be protected at all costs.
Rule No. 6—Team members are expected to support each other in their grief. They can share feelings and thoughts with

colleagues, such sharing, however, must be limited to specific times of formal or informal gatherings and must be suppressed when tending to the care of other children. (Papadatou, 2000, pp. 71–72)

A Canadian psychologist, Mary Vachon (1987), outlined a grief-sharing procedure that has been useful in some institutional settings. After a patient dies, the attending nurse tape-records the circumstances of the death, who was present and their reactions, and an informal assessment of which family members might be at risk following the loss. The nurse also shares personal feelings that he or she may be having at the time. Later in the week others on the team listen to the tape during rounds set-up for the entire caregiving team to discuss deaths on the unit. The tape is used not only to provide information to those not present at the death, but also to stimulate a discussion about the loss, to share feelings that have been engendered by the death, and to assess how treatment could have been different or improved. Each of the staff signs a sympathy card that is sent to the survivors about a month after the death.

As part of this discussion of the counselor's own grief, I want to comment on the use of volunteers as lay counselors. Personal bereavement has often motivated people to serve as volunteers in the various bereavement outreach programs that have proliferated in the past three decades. Most hospice programs, both here and abroad, use volunteers in some capacity to work with the dying and their families. The same holds true for the many widow-to-widow programs stemming from the early work of Phyllis R. Silverman (1986) that have been so effective. These use widows as volunteers to befriend and offer counsel to those more recently bereaved.

Volunteers can be effective, but it is my strong conviction that lay counselors should be people who have worked through their own grief and have experienced some degree of resolution. I have noticed that some of the people attending the various training workshops I have conducted across the country are experiencing acute grief, and their interest in further training in grief counseling comes from a need to work through their own grief. I do not believe that grief counseling is the place for a counselor to work through a recent bereavement—there are too many blind spots that hinder effective counseling. However, a person who has gone through a grief experience and come to some resolution has the potential to do more significant intervention than someone who has never experienced loss and grief (Nesbitt, Ross, Sunderland, & Shelp, 1996).

Charles Garfield, founder of the Shanti Program in the San Francisco Bay Area, found that the volunteers who do the most effective work are those who have a history of mutually satisfying interpersonal relationships and whose motivations for work are personally relevant. He and his colleagues recommend that programs that use volunteers be set up to offer training, supervision, support, and the opportunity to explore one's style of coping and its effectiveness. The same would be advisable for professionals working in this field (Garfield & Jenkins, 1981–1982).

REFERENCES

Bowlby, J. (1980). *Attachment and loss: Vol. 3. Loss, sadness, and depression.* New York: Basic Books.

Freudenberger, H. (1974). Staff burnout. *Journal of Social Issues, 30,* 159–165.

Garfield, C. A., & Jenkins, G. J. (1981–1982). Stress and coping of volunteers counseling the dying and the bereaved. *Omega, 12,* 1–13.

Hayes, J. A., Yeh, Y., & Eisenberg, A. (2007). Good grief and not-so-good grief: Countertransference in bereavement therapy. *Journal of Clinical Psychology, 63,* 345–355.

Katz, R., & Johnson, T. (2006). *When professionals weep: Emotional and countertransference responses in end-of-life care.* New York: Routledge.

Maslach, C. (1982). *Burnout: The cost of caring.* Englewood Cliffs, NJ: Prentice-Hall.

Muse, S., & Chase, E. (1993). Healing the wounded healers: "Soul" food for clergy. *Journal of Psychology and Christianity, 12,* 141–150.

Nesbitt, W. H., Ross, M. W., Sunderland, R. H., & Shelp, E. (1996). Prediction of grief and HIV/AIDS-related burnout in volunteers. *AIDS Care, 8,* 137–143.

Papadatou, D. (2000). A proposed model of health professionals' grieving process. *Omega, 41,* 59–77.

Papadatou, D. (2006). Caregivers in death, dying, and bereavement situations. *Death Studies, 30,* 649–663.

Parkes, C. M. (1972). *Bereavement: Studies of grief in adult life.* New York: International Universities Press.

Parkes, C. M. (1986). Orienteering the caregiver's grief. *Journal of Palliative Care, 1,* 5–7.

Redinbaugh, E., Schuerger, J., Weiss, L., Brufsky, A., & Arnold, R. (2001). Health care professionals' grief: A model based on occupational style and coping. *Psycho-Oncology, 10,* 187–198.

Saunders, J. M., & Valente, S. M. (1994). Nurses' grief. *Cancer Nursing, 17,* 318–325.

Silverman, P. R. (1986). *Widow to widow.* New York: Springer Publishing.

Simos, B. G. (1979). *A time to grieve.* New York: Family Service Association.

Vachon, M. L. S. (1979). Staff stress in the care of the terminally ill. *Quality Review Bulletin, 251,* 13–17.

Vachon, M. L. S. (1987). *Occupational stress in the care of the critically ill, the dying, and the bereaved.* Washington, DC: Hemisphere.

Worden, J. W. (1976). *Personal death awareness.* Englewood Cliffs, NJ: Prentice-Hall.

Worden, J. W., & Kübler-Ross, E. (1977–1978). Attitudes and experiences of death workshop attendees. *Omega, 8,* 91–106.

10   Training for Grief Counseling

In 1976 Mary Conrad, who was then director of programming at the University of Chicago Center for Continuing Education, and I decided to offer a 2-day grief counseling program for health professionals. We had previously presented workshops geared to help health professionals deal with various aspects of terminal illness care, but we shared the belief that our efforts to train people in this type of care would not be complete until we addressed the issues of grief counseling and grief therapy.

We decided on a 2-day format so that we could make the program as comprehensive as possible, not only to present didactic material but also to help the participants increase their skills in dealing with bereaved individuals. It was necessary to address a wide variety of issues related to the general area of bereavement. Not only did we want to present information about the theory of mourning and why it is necessary, but we also wanted to address issues of differential diagnosis of normal and pathological grief and to look at some of the special interventions surrounding grief, such as grief from sudden death and from partial losses such as amputations.

One aspect unique to our program proved to be a very successful training technique. At the beginning of the 2-day program we divided the attendees into groups of 10 that met throughout the program. At their first meeting, after introductions, they shared aspects of their own grief history. Each member was encouraged to do this, and although on the surface, their experiences of grief were different, there was an underlying awareness that each had experienced the pain of loss and bereavement. This awareness of similar experiences contributed to group dynamics and brought the groups close together in a relatively short period of time. On the second day, a great deal of time was given over to role-playing various grief-related situations. To facilitate this, I had developed a series of vignettes based on cases in my files that represented a variety of situations and grief-related issues. They are included in this chapter and can be used in training. The role-playing was set up in a format similar to one we used at Harvard Medical School to train medical students in their counseling skills, particularly with dying patients and bereaved families.

The procedure requires members of the group to volunteer to play the various roles, which may include family and friends but always include a counselor in some capacity. The roles are assigned, and the volunteers are asked to read their parts carefully and adhere to the script. They are also asked not to discuss their parts among themselves. It is very important that each individual know only his or her part and not the whole vignette because this stimulates creativity and adds considerably to the vitality and realism of the role-playing situation. While the volunteers are out of the room, the group leader reads only the counselor's part to the remaining members of the group. The players are then called back into the room, and the session is ready to begin.

The group leader allows the role-playing to go on as long as it seems productive and then rotates the part of the counselor to another member of the group. This is done several times so that at least two or three people are able to try their skills as a counselor. Then the whole process is critiqued and evaluated. The various people playing the counselor are asked to explain the direction they took and what they had in mind, and the people who played the bereaved talk about which interventions were helpful and which were not. The observing group members share their observations, and the group leader can add his or her own suggestions. After the critique, the same situation can be role-played again, or the group can go on to a different situation. The participants in the role-playing, particularly those playing the counselors, are reminded that they are not expected to be perfect and that they are there because they wanted to further their skill development.

Although 2 days is obviously not enough time to develop experienced grief counselors, this did seem to be a favorable format, and we have repeated the program for various health professionals across the country. The basic assumption behind such a workshop is that the participants already have certain understandings and skills as mental health practitioners. The purpose of the workshop is to give them further information about the special aspects related to bereavement as well as to give them some hands-on experience doing counseling and having it critiqued in front of a peer group.

Most of the vignettes are set up to address the issue of grief counseling, not the issue of grief therapy. Grief therapy is a much more complicated procedure and cannot be addressed in such an abbreviated manner. Again, as I have emphasized throughout this book, people should not attempt grief therapy unless they have the necessary education and training. This includes a thorough knowledge of psychodynamics, including the ability to assess the decompensating potential of the patient. There are many people who attempt psychotherapy without adequate background and training. One of the most valuable qualities of a good therapist is knowing one's own limitations and knowing when to refer or to consult with a more experienced professional.

Grief Sketch 1

Woman: Twelve weeks ago your husband of 33 years left to drive to an appointment 100 miles from your home. He was to stay overnight and return home the next day, but he never returned. Several days later his dead body was found in his car on a remote road, where he apparently died of a heart attack. Decomposition was rapid because of the heat, and you were advised not to see his body. You attended the funeral and burial in his home state, a great distance from your home. Even now you cannot believe he is dead and you wait for him to come home. You cry all the time and don't know what to do, so you seek counseling.

Counselor: A 58-year-old woman lost her husband to a heart attack while he was away on a business trip. She never saw his body and is having difficulty believing he is really dead. Assist her with this first task of mourning and in any other way she may need your help.

From *Grief Counseling and Grief Therapy* (4th ed.), by J. William Worden, PhD. Copyright © 2009 by Springer Publishing Company, LLC.

Grief Sketch 2

Widow: You are a widow age 75 whose husband died 6 months ago. You are ill and in a nursing home. You feel sad and lost without your husband. Your children are living on the coast, and you feel all alone. You have a very strong desire to give up and die so you can join your husband. You see nothing left to live for. You just keep telling the staff taking care of you, "Leave me alone and let me die."

Social Worker: In a nursing home you are assigned to take care of a 75-year-old widow who lost her husband 6 months ago. Your task is to help her with her grief, to get over the loss, and to get back to living again.

From *Grief Counseling and Grief Therapy* (4th ed.), by J. William Worden, PhD. Copyright © 2009 by Springer Publishing Company, LLC.

Grief Sketch 3

Woman: You are 38 and single. Three months ago your alcoholic stepfather died suddenly of a heart attack. He had come into your life when you were 3 years old, and over the years he had been physically and sexually abusive to you until you left home at age 17. You were happy to hear of his death, are glad that he is finally out of your life, and can only remember negative things about him. Since his death, you have had several dreams of him with his arms outstretched to you. You are not sure of the meaning of the dreams, but you awake from them upset and are unable to go back to sleep. Your disturbed sleep is beginning to affect your work performance so you have decided to seek counseling.

Counselor: A 38-year-old single woman has been experiencing sleep difficulties over the past 3 months since her stepfather died suddenly of a heart attack. Explore her symptoms in light of her recent loss. If there is grief work to be done, help her to identify and facilitate it.

Grief Sketch 4

Woman: You are a 51-year-old single woman whose mother has died. The two of you always lived together and had a close but ambivalent relationship. You cared for your mother during her lengthy illness, which involved several hospitalizations. Your mother was not an easy person to get along with, and several times during her final years you told her in anger that if she didn't shape up, you would send her off to a nursing home. You really wouldn't have, but now that she is dead, you miss her terribly and you're feeling very guilty about having said these things.

Counselor: A 51-year-old single woman has approached you for help with the guilt she has been feeling since her mother's death. Your task is to help her reality test her guilt and to find a better way to cope with it.

From *Grief Counseling and Grief Therapy* (4th ed.), by J. William Worden, PhD. Copyright © 2009 by Springer Publishing Company, LLC.

Grief Sketch 5

Widower: You are 29 and your wife of 6 years died of cancer 4 months ago, leaving you with a 3-year-old son and a 5-year-old daughter. You had a good marriage and are hurting a great deal and want to find something to help cut the pain you are now feeling. You believe if you can only get remarried, all this will be over and behind you. You have dated several women, but each one has left you feeling more depressed than before. Nevertheless, you still believe if you can get remarried soon, your kids will have a new mother, you will feel better about yourself, and your pain will be gone. You will see the bereavement counselor from the hospice that took care of your wife.

Counselor: You have been asked to see a 29-year-old man whose wife died of cancer in your hospice program 4 months ago. You did not work with the family before the death but will now see the husband as part of your bereavement follow-up.

From *Grief Counseling and Grief Therapy* (4th ed.), by J. William Worden, PhD. Copyright © 2009 by Springer Publishing Company, LLC.

Grief Sketch 6

Woman: Over the past 3 years you have lost your mother, your father, a brother, and a close friend. All these losses have left you feeling numb. When you do feel, you are more aware of feelings of anxiety than you are of sadness. The anxiety has been increasing in recent months and you have seen your physician several times to check out heart palpitations. The physician says you are all right physically but that your symptoms are associated with stress and anxiety. She has sent you to see a counselor to help you better manage your stress.

Counselor: A physician colleague has referred a woman to you who needs help to better manage her stress. She has lost several family members and friends to death during the recent past. Evaluate the relationship of these losses to her stress and intervene appropriately with her around these issues.

From *Grief Counseling and Grief Therapy* (4th ed.), by J. William Worden, PhD. Copyright © 2009 by Springer Publishing Company, LLC.

Grief Sketch 7

Wife: Your 8-year-old child died of leukemia 2 years ago. You are adjusting to the loss but fear that over time you might forget some of the important details of your child's life and your time together. In order to keep this from happening, you have kept your child's room intact, just as it was when he died. Your husband is upset about this. He feels that after 2 years the room should be dismantled, a few things kept, and the room put to other uses. Every time you and he discuss this, you end up in a fight and feel estranged from him.

Husband: After your 8-year-old child died of leukemia 2 years ago, nothing was changed in his room. This presented no problems for you then, but now, since 2 years have passed, you are pushing your wife to dismantle the room, save a few important memorabilia, and rearrange the room to serve another purpose. To you, keeping the room as it is just adds to your painful memories. Your wife will not listen to reason and will not change the room.

Counselor: A couple has approached you to help them arbitrate a dispute they are having regarding their dead child's room and possessions. The husband wants to dismantle the room and the wife doesn't. Help them to resolve this problem and to get in touch with their underlying fears and feelings engendered by this situation.

From *Grief Counseling and Grief Therapy* (4th ed.), by J. William Worden, PhD. Copyright © 2009 by Springer Publishing Company, LLC.

Grief Sketch 8

Wife: Seven months ago your father, age 78, committed suicide by shooting himself in the head. This came as a complete shock to you, and he left no note explaining his actions. Your mother had died the previous year, and though your father lived far away from you, you spoke often with him by phone and believed that he was making an adequate adjustment to his loss. Since the death, you have been irritable and short with everyone, especially with your husband. He is losing patience with you and has threatened to move out. You reluctantly agree to go with your husband to see a counselor.

Husband: Your father-in-law shot himself recently within a year of losing his wife. This came as a shock to both you and your wife, and he left no note to explain his suicide. Since his death, your wife has been unbearable to live with. She is irritated with every little thing you do. You are so fed up with this behavior that you have threatened to leave. Before you do, you want to give counseling a chance, but you are not too hopeful.

Counselor: You will see a couple on the verge of splitting up. You know from the initial phone contact with the husband that his wife's father recently died. In your evaluation, see to what extent grief issues may or may not be contributing to their marital disharmony.

From *Grief Counseling and Grief Therapy* (4th ed.), by J. William Worden, PhD. Copyright © 2009 by Springer Publishing Company, LLC.

Grief Sketch 9

Mother: Your child died in the hospital after living for 3 months. It has been 15 months since the death, and you are still feeling very depressed. You attended one group session for bereaved parents but left saying, "Story swapping is not what I need." You feel a lot of anger toward your husband for not being there when the baby died and for paying more attention to your two living children than he does to you. Your own father abandoned you and the family when you were 5 years old. Recently you have been dreaming of your dead child, who says in the dream, "You didn't give me a chance." A friend suggested you see a counselor.

Father: After living only 3 months, your newborn died in the hospital from congenital complications. You feel some guilt over this death, and now you give your two living children more attention than you gave them before the death. Your wife has been depressed for the past 15 months since the loss. Her sadness bothers you and gives you a sense of helplessness. The only way you know how to help her is to appear strong and confident. This hasn't helped. She is going to see a counselor and wants you to go with her. You feel that you are okay but agree to go if it will help her.

Counselor: A couple lost their baby 3 months after birth. The wife has been depressed for the past 15 months since this happened. The couple has two other children. Both the husband and wife will attend the first counseling session. Your task is to see where they are in their grief and decide whether to work with them individually, as a couple, or as an entire family.

From *Grief Counseling and Grief Therapy* (4th ed.), by J. William Worden, PhD. Copyright © 2009 by Springer Publishing Company, LLC.

Grief Sketch 10

Father: Your wife died of cancer 10 months ago, leaving you with three children: a 14-year-old daughter and two sons ages 11 and 6. You are doing your best to manage as a single parent, but your work requires long hours and a lengthy commute. You thought that your children would pull together after the death, but they seem to be going separate ways. You are especially annoyed at your daughter, who resents taking on household chores, something you feel she should do because she is a girl and the oldest child. When the school counselor called to report her truancy, you agreed to see a family counselor.

Sister: You are 14 and lost your mother to cancer 10 months ago. You miss her and find your father has become a first-class pain since she died. He expects you to fix breakfast and dinner, to shop, and to baby-sit your 6-year-old brother. You resent this, are doing poorly in school since your mother died, and prefer hanging around the mall with your friends to going to class. You see this as your only private time, since your household responsibilities don't leave you any other time just for you. You reluctantly agree to go see the family counselor.

Brother: Ten months ago, when you had just turned 11, your mother died of cancer. Since then things have been chaotic at home and you prefer to be out of the house. You spend most of your time with your friends, hanging out and playing hacky sack down at the park. Your older sister is bossy, and you resent her telling you what to do. You like your 6-year-old brother but do not share an interest in many of the same activities.

Brother: You are 6 years old. Since your mother died of cancer 10 months ago, you have felt abandoned. You don't really understand what happened to your mother or where she is now. You were not included in the funeral service. At night you have dreams of her and find these somewhat comforting. You have few friends to play with, and after school and on weekends you spend most of your time watching TV.

Counselor: The school has referred a family to you for family counseling, which may include family grief counseling. The mother died of cancer

10 months ago, leaving her husband and three children—a 14-year-old daughter, an 11-year-old son, and a 6-year-old son. The daughter has been truant and is not doing well in school. The boys are not having difficulty in school, but according to his teacher, the 6-year-old seems lost, and she is not sure what to do with him. Evaluate this family and develop an intervention strategy.

Grief Sketch 11

Young Man: Your lover of 8 years died 6 months ago of AIDS. You shared a house and cared for him until he died at home. You feel that you did a lot of grieving during his 18-month illness. His older sister calls you frequently for emotional support. Although you like her and would like to help, her calls make you feel sad, and you would prefer that she not call so often. Her brother was an important chapter in your life and you miss him, but you now want to move on with your life. You reluctantly agree to a single visit with her counselor in the hope that she will back off.

Sister: Your brother, who was 7 years younger than you, died 6 months ago from AIDS. You helped his lover of 8 years care for him during the 18-month-long illness. You are familiar with this role as caretaker, as your mother died when you were 12, leaving you, the oldest, to care for the rest of the family. You feel unsupported and alone in your grief. You are angry at your brother's lover and at your husband for wanting to put this difficult death behind them and move forward with life.

Husband: Your wife lost her brother to AIDS 6 months ago. You liked her brother and were sympathetic and supportive of your wife during his 18-month illness, but you felt real relief after he died. To you that meant the ordeal was over and you could get back to normal living. However, your wife cries a lot and refuses to return to work, and you are feeling frustrated, angry, and helpless. You reluctantly agree to go visit a counselor, with the hope that it will bring an end to all this.

Counselor: You have an appointment with a woman whose younger brother died of AIDS 6 months ago. She is bringing along her husband and her brother's lover. Your task is to bring the grief issues to light and to facilitate their discussion within this family context.

From *Grief Counseling and Grief Therapy* (4th ed.), by J. William Worden, PhD. Copyright © 2009 by Springer Publishing Company, LLC.

Grief Sketch 12

Mother: Your son, age 15, was killed suddenly one evening a year ago. He was a passenger in a car driven by his 16-year-old friend, and the car went out of control. Since that time you have been inconsolable. This boy was your firstborn, talented, and clearly your favorite. You cannot understand why your husband and two other children are not as grief stricken as you are. You have moments of deep rage that are targeted either at your husband, the boy who drove the car, or your younger son, who won't talk about his dead brother.

Father: You lost your 15-year-old boy in a car accident a year ago. For the first couple of months you felt devastated and cried a lot when you were alone. Although you still miss him, you believe that you, your wife, and your two remaining children need to move on with your lives. Your wife cries much of the time, and you feel tension in the family. Because of this, you have contacted a family counselor to straighten all this out.

Brother: You are 13, and your 15-year-old brother died in a car accident a year ago while riding with a friend. You always felt inferior to your brother, and you felt somewhat relieved when he died. Now you feel guilty about these feelings. His memory and presence linger around the house, but when people talk about him, you get up and leave the room. This behavior upsets the rest of the family, but you don't care.

Sister: You are the 9-year-old sister of a boy, age 15, who was killed when the car he was riding in went out of control. You feel sad and miss your brother. Your sadness is even worse because your mother is not as close to you as before, and you feel you have lost her too. You are not sure what to do to get your mother back.

Counselor: You have been contacted by the father of a 15-year-old boy who was killed a year ago in a car accident to do family grief counseling. Your role is to see them, assess the issues, and suggest an appropriate mode of intervention. (This scenario could be played out over several therapy sessions.)

Grief Sketch 13

Son: You are 20. Your dad committed suicide 3 months ago in the garage. You have been experiencing many feelings, especially anger, because he killed himself. However, most of the time you just feel depressed. You are drinking a lot and you find that it helps you feel better. You still live at home, and your mother is concerned about your drinking. When she mentions it, you either get angry at her or withdraw. You are really not sure at this point what you feel about your dad. There is some guilt mixed in with your feelings of sadness and anger. You reluctantly agree to go with your mother to a counselor.

Wife: Your husband killed himself by carbon monoxide poisoning 3 months ago. You feel both guilt and anger along with the sadness. Sometimes you get so mad that you find yourself saying, "Damn it, Harold, if you hadn't died, I'd kill you for putting me through all this!" You are concerned about your son's drinking, which has increased since his father's death, so you have sought out a counselor to help the two of you with your problems.

Counselor: A woman and her 20-year-old son have come to you following the death of her husband by carbon monoxide poisoning. She is upset and not functioning well. Her son has been drinking heavily since his father's suicide. She finally got him to agree to see you along with her. He is somewhat reluctant. Your task is to help them sort out their feelings and deal with unfinished business regarding the deceased.

From *Grief Counseling and Grief Therapy* (4th ed.), by J. William Worden, PhD. Copyright © 2009 by Springer Publishing Company, LLC.

Grief Sketch 14

Father: Your only child, 8-year-old Timothy, died of leukemia 3 months ago. You handle your grief by keeping busy both at work and in leisure-time pursuits. This annoys your wife, but you feel that keeping busy is all that is holding you together. You would like to have another child soon, but your wife is not interested in any more children, who might put her through another loss like the one you've both just experienced. You ask her to go with you to a minister for counseling.

Mother: Your only child, 8-year-old Timothy, died of leukemia 3 months ago. Since then you have been depressed and you often cry. You have lost interest in most of your friends and spend your time alone. You are angry at your husband, because since Timothy's death, he has kept himself busy and is unavailable to you. You are also angry because he wants another child right away. You feel this is insensitive and your relationship is becoming strained. You agree to go with him to your minister for counseling.

Nurse: You nursed young Timothy, age 8, through his long bout with leukemia, and you stop by to visit his parents, whom you got to know during Timothy's illness. You sense that all is not right between them, and you try to help them with their sense of loss and with their relationship with each other.

Minister: A husband and wife lost their only son, Timothy, age 8, to leukemia 3 months ago. They are coming to see you at the husband's insistence. The wife is reluctant. He wants you to help him with the feelings that he is experiencing concerning his wife and son. He hopes you will convince his wife to have another child soon. They are members of your church, but you have had minimal contact with them.

From *Grief Counseling and Grief Therapy* (4th ed.), by J. William Worden, PhD. Copyright © 2009 by Springer Publishing Company, LLC.

Grief Sketch 15

Son: Your father has just died after a year-long struggle with cancer. It is only a few weeks before you are to enter college as a freshman, and you are feeling anxious about leaving home for the first time and have experienced panic several times. You feel guilty that you are going to college rather than getting a job to help your family financially. You feel sad but don't allow yourself to cry, feeling it's not manly.

Daughter: You are 17 and a senior in high school. Your father has died of cancer, just prior to the beginning of school. You feel the loss deeply but can't express your feelings. When your family wants to talk about your dad's death, you withdraw.

Daughter: You are 14 and in the last year of junior high school. Your dad has just died after a year-long bout with cancer. You want to rebel against your family and do your own thing but feel some guilt that you might be hurting your mother. You are annoyed with your older sister because she refuses to discuss things about your dad's death.

Mother: You are left with three children—a 19-year-old son, who is just entering college; a 17-year-old daughter; and a 14-year-old daughter. You are concerned about how you are going to make it financially and how you are going to cope emotionally without your husband. You are also in touch with some anger at your husband for dying and leaving you with all this responsibility. These feelings scare you. You are concerned about your son leaving home, your older daughter's inability to express her grief, and your younger daughter's alienation from your family.

Counselor: You have been asked by a mother, who recently lost her husband after a year-long bout with cancer, to sit down with her and her three children—a 19-year-old son, a 17-year-old daughter, and a 14-year-old daughter—and help them discuss their feelings and make realistic plans for the future. The mother feels overwhelmed by her situation. Your task is to facilitate the grief work and help them with whatever they ask for help with.

From *Grief Counseling and Grief Therapy* (4th ed.), by J. William Worden, PhD. Copyright © 2009 by Springer Publishing Company, LLC.

Grief Sketch 16

Husband: Six weeks ago your only child died in his sleep at the age of 3 months. The death was attributed to crib death. You were very attached to him and are angry that he left you but find it hard to express this openly. Your wife wants to get pregnant again soon, but you are reluctant. This has put stress on your sexual life.

Wife: You lost your 3-month-old child to crib death 6 weeks ago. You blame yourself for being asleep when the baby died. You believe that it wouldn't have happened had you been awake. You are eager to have another child, but your husband won't hear of this, and there is a resulting distance between you and your husband.

Counselor: You have been assigned by the hospital to follow up on a couple whose only child died suddenly of crib death 6 weeks ago at the age of 3 months. Your task is to assess how the couple is doing and see what resources they need at this time.

From *Grief Counseling and Grief Therapy* (4th ed.), by J. William Worden, PhD. Copyright © 2009 by Springer Publishing Company, LLC.

Grief Sketch 17

Widow: Your husband of 25 years died of cancer 2 years ago. You were close to him, but now, at age 51, you are thinking of finding a new partner. This idea causes you conflict. You feel disloyal to your dead husband, and you are afraid your friends will think you are crazy. Your children, who are in their late teens, are very much against the idea of you remarrying. You have sought counseling to help resolve this conflict.

Counselor: You have been approached by a 51-year-old widow who wants to find a new partner and possibly remarry. It's been 2 years since the death of her husband of 25 years. Assess where she is in the mourning process, help her deal with her conflicts about beginning a new relationship, and help her understand when grief is finished.

Minister: A 51-year-old widow in your parish is in conflict over seeking a new partner 2 years after the death of her husband. You knew her deceased husband. Your task is to help her resolve this conflict.

From *Grief Counseling and Grief Therapy* (4th ed.), by J. William Worden, PhD. Copyright © 2009 by Springer Publishing Company, LLC.

Grief Sketch 18

Boy: You are 9 years old and an only child. Your father died suddenly of a heart attack 3 months ago, and since then you have been having nightmares. The day your father died, you had an argument with him before leaving for school. You feel guilty about this but haven't told anyone.

School Counselor: You have been asked to see a 9-year-old boy whose father died 3 months ago of a heart attack. His teacher has noticed that he has become socially withdrawn and his grades have begun to slip. Your task is to assess what might be wrong and to see how his behavior might be related to his grief.

From *Grief Counseling and Grief Therapy* (4th ed.), by J. William Worden, PhD. Copyright © 2009 by Springer Publishing Company, LLC.

Appendix

THE TASKS OF MOURNING

I	To accept the reality of the loss	(Not believing)
II	To process the pain of grief	(Not feeling)
III	To adjust to a world without the deceased	
	A. External adjustments: Living daily without the person	(Not adjusting)
	B. Internal adjustments: Who am I now?	(Not growing)
	C. Spiritual adjustments: Reframe assumptive world	(Not understanding)
IV	To find an enduring connection with the deceased while embarking on a new life	(Not moving forward)

Table A.2

THE MEDIATORS OF MOURNING

Mediator 1   **Kinship (who died)**

Mediator 2   **Nature of the attachment**
            Strength/security
            Ambivalent/conflicted
            Dependency issues

Mediator 3   **Death circumstances**
            Proximity of death
            Expectedness of death
            Traumatic death
            Multiple losses
            Preventable death
            Ambiguous death
            Stigmatized death

Mediator 4   **Historical antecedents**
            Loss history
            Mental health history

Mediator 5   **Personality mediators**
            Age/gender
            Coping style
            Attachment style (secure, insecure)
            Cognitive style
            Ego strength (esteem, efficacy)
            Assumptive world (beliefs, values)

Mediator 6   **Social mediators**
            Support availability
            Support satisfaction
            Social role involvements
            Religious resources
            Ethnic expectations

Mediator 7   **Concurrent stresses (life-change events)**

Bibliography

Abraham, K. (1927). *Selected papers on psychoanalysis*. London: Hogarth.

Addington-Hall, J., & Karlsen, S. (2000). Do home deaths increase distress in bereavement? *Palliative Medicine, 14,* 161–162.

Ainsworth, M., Blehar, M., Waters, E., & Wall, S. (1978). *Patterns of attachment*. Hilldale, NJ: Erlbaum.

Ainsworth, M., Blehar, M., Waters, E., & Wall, S. (1978). *Patterns of attachment: A psychological stud y of strange situations*. Hillsdale, NJ: Erlbaum.

Akiyama, H., Holtzman, J., & Britz, W. (1986). Pet ownership and health status during bereavement. *Omega, 17,* 187–193.

Aldrich, C. K. (1963). The dying patient's grief. *Journal of the American Medical Association, 184,* 329–331.

Alexy, W. D. (1982). Dimensions of psychological counseling that facilitate the growing process of bereaved parents. *Journal of Counseling Psychology, 29,* 498–507.

Allumbaugh, D., & Hoyt, W. (1999). Effectiveness of grief therapy: A meta-analysis. *Journal of Counseling Psychology, 46,* 370–380.

American Psychiatric Association. (2000). *Diagnostic and statistical manual of mental disorders* (4th ed.). Washington, DC: Author.

Aronson, S. (1995). Five girls in search of a group: A group experience for adolescents of parents with AIDS. *International Journal of Group Psychotherapy, 45,* 223–235.

Attig, T. (1996). *How we grieve: Relearning the world*. New York: Oxford University Press.

Attig, T. (2004). Disenfranchised grief revisited: Discounting hope and love. *Omega, 49,* 197–215.

Barbato, A., & Irwin, H. J. (1992). Major therapeutic systems and the bereaved client. *Australian Psychologist, 27,* 22–27.

Barrett, D. (2002). The "royal road" becomes a shrewd shortcut: The use of dreams in focused treatment. *Journal of Cognitive Psychotherapy, 16,* 55–64.

Bauer, J., & Bonanno, G. A. (2001). I can, I do, I am: The narrative differentiation of self-efficacy and other self-evaluations while adapting to bereavement. *Journal of Research in Personality, 35,* 424–448.

Beck, A. T., Rush, J., Shaw, B., & Emery, G., et al. (1979). *Cognitive therapy of depression*. New York: Guilford Press.

Beckwith, B. E., Beckwith, S. K., Gray, T., Micsko, M. M., Holm, J. H., Plummer, V. H., et al. (1990). Identification of spouses at high risk during bereavement: A preliminary assessment of Parkes and Weiss' Risk Index. *Hospice Journal, 6,* 35–46.

Begley, M., & Quayle, E. (2007). The lived experience of adults bereaved by suicide. *Crisis, 28,* 26–34.

Belicki, K., Gulko, N., Ruzycki, K., & Aristotle, J. (2002). Sixteen years of dreams following spousal bereavement. *Omega, 47,* 93–106.

Belitsky, R., & Jacobs, S. (1986). Bereavement, attachment theory, and mental disorders. *Psychiatric Annals, 16,* 276–280.

Bell, J. P. (1988). AIDS and the hidden epidemic of grief: A personal experience. *American Journal of Hospice Care, 5,* 25–31.

Benight, C., Flores, J., & Tashiro, T. (2001). Bereavement coping self-efficacy in cancer widows. *Death Studies, 23,* 97–125.

Bennett, K. M., & Bennett, G. (2000). "And there's always this great hole inside that hurts": An empirical study of bereavement in later life. *Omega, 42,* 237–251.

Bennett, L., Kelaher, M., & Ross, M. W. (1994). The impact of working with HIV/AIDS on health care professionals: Development of the AIDS Impact Scale. *Psychology and Health, 9,* 221–232.

Beresford, L. (1993). *The hospice handbook.* Boston: Little, Brown.

Beutel, M., Deckardt, R., von Rad, M., & Weiner, H. (1995). Grief and depression after miscarriage: Their separation, antecedents, and course. *Psychosomatic Medicine, 57,* 517–526.

Blechner, M. J. (1993). Psychoanalysis and HIV disease. *Contemporary Psychoanalysis, 29*(1), 61–80.

Bloch, S. (1991). A systems approach to loss. *Australian & New Zealand Journal of Psychiatry, 25,* 471–480.

Boelen, P. A., & van den Bout, J. (2002). Positive thinking in bereavement: Is it related to depression, anxiety, or grief symptomatology? *Psychological Reports, 91,* 857–863.

Boelen, P. A., & van den Bout, J. (2005). Complicated grief, depression and anxiety as distinct postloss syndromes. A confirmatory factor analysis study. *American Journal of Psychiatry, 162,* 2175–2177.

Boelen, P. A., van den Bout, J., & de Keijser, J. (2003). Traumatic grief as a disorder distinct from bereavement-related depression and anxiety. *American Journal of Psychiatry, 160,* 1339–1341.

Boelen, P. A., van den Hout, M. A., & van den Bout, J. (2006). A cognitive-behavioral conceptualization of complicated grief. *Clinical Psychology: Science & Practice, 13,* 109–128.

Bonanno, G. (2001). Introduction: New directions in bereavement research and theory. *American Behavioral Scientist, 44,* 718–725.

Bonanno, G. A. (2004). Loss, trauma, and human resilience. *American Psychologist, 59,* 20–28.

Bonanno, G. A., & Kaltman, S. (1999). Toward an integrative perspective on bereavement. *Psychological Bulletin, 125,* 760–776.

Bonanno, G. A., Moskowitz, J. T., & Papa, A. (2005). Resilience to loss in bereaved spouses, bereaved parents, and bereaved gay men. *Journal of Personality and Social Psychology, 88,* 827–843.

Bonanno, G. A., & Papa, A. (2003). The social and functional aspects of emotional expression during bereavement. In P. Philippot (Ed.), *Nonverbal behavior in clinical settings* (pp. 145–170). London: Oxford University Press.

Bonanno, G. A., Papa, A., & O'Neill, K. (2002). Loss and human resilience. *Applied & Preventive Psychology, 10,* 193–206.

Bonanno, G. A., Wortman, C., Lehman, D., Tweed, R., Haring, M., Sonnega, J., et al. (2002). Resilience to loss and chronic grief: A prospective study from preloss to 18-months postloss. *Journal of Personality and Social Psychology, 83,* 1150–1164.

Bowen, M. (1978). *Family therapy in clinical practice.* New York: Aronson.

Bowlby, J. (1960). Grief and mourning in infancy and early childhood. *Psychoanalytic Study of the Child, 15,* 9–52.

Bowlby, J. (1977). The making and breaking of affectional bonds: I. Aetiology and psychopathology in the light of attachment theory. *British Journal of Psychiatry, 130,* 201–210.

Bowlby, J. (1977). The making and breaking of affectional bonds: II. Some principles of psychotherapy. *British Journal of Psychiatry, 130,* 421–431.

Bowlby, J. (1980). *Attachment and loss: Vol. 3. Loss, sadness, and depression.* New York: Basic Books.

Boykin, F. F. (1991). The AIDS crisis and gay male survivor guilt. *Smith College Studies in Social Work, 61*(3), 247–259.

Brice, C. W. (1991). Paradoxes of maternal mourning. *Psychiatry, 54*(1), 1–12.

Brier, N. (1999). Understanding and managing the emotional reaction to a miscarriage. *Obstetrics & Gynecology, 93,* 151–155.

Broen, A. N., Moum, T., Bodtker, A. S., & Ekeberg, O. (2004). Psychological impact on women of miscarriage versus induced abortion: A 2-year follow-up study. *Psychosomatic Medicine, 66,* 265–271.

Brooks-Harris, J. E. (2001). Saying goodbye ten years later: Resolving delayed bereavement. *Journal of College Student Psychotherapy, 16,* 119–134.

Brown, J. C. (1990). Loss and grief: An overview and guided imagery intervention model. *Journal of Mental Health Counseling, 12*(4), 434–445.

Bugen, L. A. (1977). Human grief: A model for prediction and intervention. *American Journal of Orthopsychiatry, 47,* 196–206.

Byrne, G., & Raphael, B. (1999). Depressive symptoms and depressive episodes in recently widowed older men. *International Psychogeriatrics, 11,* 67–74.

Cain, A. C. (Ed.). (1972). *Survivors of suicide.* Springfield, IL: Thomas.

Callahan, J. (2000). Predictors and correlates of bereavement in suicide support group participants. *Suicide & Life-Threatening Behavior, 30,* 104–124.

Carr, D., House, J. S., Kessler, R., Nesse, R., Sonnega, J., & Wortman, C. (2000). Marital quality and psychological adjustment to widowhood among older adults: A longitudinal analysis. *Journals of Gerontology, 55B,* S197–S207.

Carr, D., Nesse, R., & Wortman, C. (Eds.). (2006). *Spousal bereavement in late life.* New York: Springer Publishing.

Caserta, M. S., & Lund, D. A. (1992). Bereavement stress and coping among older adults: Expectations versus the actual experience. *Omega, 25,* 33–45.

Castle, J., & Philips, W. L. (2003). Grief rituals: Aspects that facilitate adjustment to bereavement. *Journal of Loss & Trauma, 8,* 41–71.

Cerney, M. S., & Buskirk, J. R. (1991). Anger: The hidden part of grief. *Bulletin of the Menninger Clinic, 55*(2), 228–237.

Cherney, P. M., & Verhey, M. P. (1996). Grief among gay men associated with multiple losses from AIDS. *Death Studies, 20,* 115–132.

Clark, S. E., & Goldney, R. D. (1995). Grief reactions and recovery in a support group for people bereaved by suicide. *Crisis, 16,* 27–33.

Cleiren, M., & Diekstra, R. (1995). After the loss: Bereavement after suicide and other types of death. In B. Mishara (Ed.), *The impact of suicide* (pp. 7–39). New York: Springer Publishing.

Cohen, M. (2000). Bereavement groups with the elderly. *Journal of Psychotherapy in Independent Practice, 1,* 33–41.

Compassionate Friends. (1999). *When a child dies: A survey of bereaved parents.* Author.

Constantino, R. E., & Bricker, P. L. (1996). Nursing postvention for spousal survivors of suicide. *Issues in Mental Health Nursing, 17,* 131–152.

Cook, J. A. (1988). Dad's double binds: Rethinking fathers' bereavement from a men's studies perspective. *Journal of Contemporary Ethnography, 17,* 285–308.

Currier, J., Holland, J., & Neimeyer, R. (2007). The effectiveness of bereavement interventions with children: A meta-analytic review of controlled outcome research. *Journal of Clinical Child & Adolescent Psychology, 36,* 253–259.

Cvinar, J. G. (2005). Do suicide survivors suffer social stigma: A review of the literature. *Perspectives in Psychiatric Care, 41,* 14–21.

Darwin, C. (1872). *The expression of emotions in man and animals.* London: Murray.

Davies, B., Gudmundsdottir, M., Worden, J. W., Orloff, S., Sumner, L., & Brenner, P. (2004). "Living in the dragon's shadow": Fathers' experiences of a child's life-limiting illness. *Death Studies, 28,* 111–135.

Davies, B., Spinetta, J., Martinson, I., & Kulenkamp, E. (1986). Manifestations of levels of functioning in grieving families. *Journal of Family Issues, 7,* 297–313.

Davies, R. (2004). New understandings of parental grief: Literature review. *Journal of Advanced Nursing, 46,* 506–513.

Davis, C., Wortman, C., Lehman, D., & Silver, R. (2000). Searching for meaning in loss: Are clinical assumptions correct? *Death Studies, 24,* 497–540.

Demi, A. S., & Miles, M. S. (1987). Parameters of normal grief: A Delphi study. *Death Studies, 11,* 397–412.

Demmer, C. (2000). Grief and survival in the era of HIV treatment advances. *Illness, Crisis & Loss, 8,* 5–16.

Deutsch, H. (1937). Absence of grief. *Psychoanalytic Quarterly, 6,* 12–22.

Didion, J. (2005). *The year of magical thinking.* New York: Knopf.

Doka, K. (Ed.). (1989). *Disenfranchised grief: Recognizing hidden sorrow.* Lexington, MA: Lexington Books.

Doka, K. (2002). *Disenfranchised grief: New directions, challenges, and strategies for practice.* Champaign, IL: Research Press.

Donnelly, E. F., Field, N. P., & Horowitz, M. J. (2000). Expectancy of spousal death and adjustment of conjugal bereavement. *Omega, 42,* 195–208.

Dorpat, T. L. (1973). Suicide, loss, and mourning. *Suicide & Life-Threatening Behavior, 3,* 213–224.

Drenovsky, C. K. (1994). Anger and the desire for retribution among bereaved parents. *Omega, 29,* 303–312.

Ehlers, A. (2006). Understanding and treating complicated grief: What can we learn from posttraumatic stress disorder. *Clinical Psychology: Science and Practice, 13,* 135–140.

Engel, G. L. (1961). Is grief a disease? A challenge for medical research. *Psychosomatic Medicine, 23,* 18–22.

Erikson, E. H. (1950). *Childhood and society.* New York: Norton.

Farberow, N. L., Gallagher, D. E., Gilewski, M. J., & Thompson, L. W. (1987). An examination of the early impact of bereavement on psychological distress in survivors of suicide. *Gerontologist, 27,* 592–598.

Farberow, N. L., Gallagher-Thompson, D. E., Gilewski, M. J., & Thompson, L. W. (1992). Changes in grief and mental health of bereaved spouses of older suicides. *Journals of Gerontology, 47,* 357–366.

Feely, N., & Gottlieb, L. N. (1980). Parents' coping and communication following their infant's death. *Omega, 19,* 51–57.

Feld, S., & George, L. K. (1994). Moderating effects of prior social resources on the hospitalizations of elders who become widowed. *Journal of Aging and Health, 6,* 275–295.

Field, N. P., & Bonanno, G. A. (2001). The role of blame in adaptation in the first five years following the death of a spouse. *American Behavioral Scientist, 44,* 764–781.

Field, N. P., Gal-Oz, E., & Bonanno, G. A. (2003). Continuing bonds and adjustment at 5 years after the death of a spouse. *Journal of Consulting & Clinical Psychology, 71,* 110–117.

Field, N. P., Gao, B. I., & Paderna, L. (2005). Continuing bonds in bereavement: An attachment theory based perspective. *Death Studies, 29,* 277–299.

Field, N. P., Nichols, C., Holen, A., & Horowitz, M. J. (1999). The relation of continuing attachment to adjustment in conjugal bereavement. *Journal of Consulting & Clinical Psychology, 67,* 212–218.

Fielden, J. M. (2003). Grief as a transformative experience: Weaving through different lifeworlds after a loved one has completed suicide. *International Journal of Mental Health Nursing, 12,* 74–85.

Flavell, J. H. (1977). *Cognitive development.* Englewood Cliffs, NJ: Prentice-Hall.

Fleming, S., & Robinson, P. (2001). Grief and cognitive-behavioral therapy: The reconstruction of meaning. In M. S. Stroebe, R. O. Hansson, W. Stroebe, & H. Schut (Eds.), *Handbook of bereavement research: Consequences, coping, and care.* Washington, DC: American Psychological Association.

Foilart, D., Clausen, M., & Siljestraum, C. (2001). Bereavement practices among California hospices. *Death Studies, 25,* 461–467.

Folkman, S. (2001). Revised coping theory and the process of bereavement. In M. S. Stroebe, R. O. Hansson, W. Stroebe, & H. Schut (Eds.), *Handbook of bereavement research: Consequences, coping, and care* (pp. 563–584). Washington, DC: American Psychological Association.

Folkman, S., Chesney, M., Collette, L., Boccellari, A., & Cooke, M. (1996). Postbereavement depressive mood and its prebereavement predictors in HIV+ and HIV– gay men. *Journal of Personality and Social Psychology, 70,* 336–348.

Folta, J., & Deck, E. (1976). Grief, the funeral, and the friend. In V. Pine, A. H. Kutscher, D. Peretz, & R. Slater (Eds.), *Acute grief and the funeral.* Springfield, IL: Thomas.

Fraley, R. C. (2002). Attachment stability from infancy to adulthood: Meta-analysis and dynamic modeling of developmental mechanisms. *Personality and Social Psychology Review, 6,* 123–151.

Fraley, R. C., & Bonanno, G. A. (2004). Attachment and loss: A test of three competing models on the association between attachment-related avoidance and adaptation to bereavement. *Personality & Social Psychology Bulletin, 30,* 878–890.

Freud, S. (1957). Mourning and melancholia. In J. Strachey (Ed. & Trans.), *The standard edition of the complete psychological works of Sigmund Freud* (Vol. 14, pp. 237–260). London: Hogarth. (Originally published 1917)

Freud, S. (1961). *Letters of Sigmund Freud* (E. L. Freud, Ed.). New York: Basic Books.

Freudenberger, H. (1974). Staff burnout. *Journal of Social Issues, 30,* 159–165.

Frey, W. H. (1980). Not-so-idle-tears. *Psychology Today, 13,* 91–92.

Frost, M., & Condon, J. T. (1996). The psychological sequelae of miscarriage: A critical review of the literature. *Australian & New Zealand Journal of Psychiatry, 30,* 54–62.

Fry, P. (2001). The unique contribution of key existential factors to the prediction of psychological well-being of older adults following spousal loss. *Gerontologist, 41,* 69–81.

Furman, E. (1974). *A child's parent dies: Studies in childhood bereavement.* New Haven, CT: Yale University Press.

Gaines, J., & Kandall, S. R. (1992). Counseling issues related to maternal substance abuse and subsequent sudden infant death syndrome in offspring. *Clinical Social Work Journal, 20,* 169–177.

Gajdos, K. C. (2000). The intergenerational effects of grief and trauma. *Illness Crisis & Loss, 10,* 304–317.

Gamino, L. A., Hogan, N. S., & Sewell, K. W. (2002). Feeling the absence: A content analysis from the Scott and White grief study. *Death Studies, 26,* 793–813.

Gamino, L. A., & Sewell, K. W. (2004). Meaning constructs as predictors of bereavement adjustment: A report from the Scott & White grief study. *Death Studies, 28,* 397–421.

Gamino, L. A., Sewell, K. W., & Easterling, L. (2000). Scott and White grief study— phase 2: Toward an adaptive model of grief. *Death Studies, 24,* 633–660.

Gardiner, A., & Pritchard, M. (1977). Mourning, mummification, and living with the dead. *British Journal of Psychiatry, 130,* 23–28.

Garfield, C. A., & Jenkins, G. J. (1981). Stress and coping of volunteers counseling the dying and th e bereaved. *Omega, 12,* 1–13.

Geller, J. L. (1985). The long-term outcome of unresolved grief: An example. *Psychiatric Quarterly, 57,* 142–146.

Gilbert, K. R. (1996). "We've had the same loss, why don't we have the same grief?" Loss and differential grief in families. *Death Studies, 20,* 269–283.

Goalder, J. S. (1985). Morbid grief reaction: A social systems perspective. *Professional Psychology: Research & Practice, 16,* 833–842.

Goldsmith, B., Morrison, R., Vanderwerker, L., & Prigerson, H. (2008). Elevated rates of prolonged grief disorders in African Americans. *Death Studies, 32,* 352–365.

Gorer, G. D. (1965). *Death, grief, and mourning.* New York: Doubleday.

Greaves, C. C. (1983). Death in the family: A multifamily therapy approach. *International Journal of Family Psychiatry, 4,* 247–259.

Greeff, A., & Human, B. (2004). Resilience in families in which a parent has died. *American Journal of Family Therapy, 32,* 27–42.

Greenberger, D., & Padesky, C. (1995). *Mind over mood: Change now you feel by changing the way you think.* New York: Guilford.

Grimby, A. (1993). Bereavement among elderly people: Grief reactions, post-bereavement hallucinations and quality of life. *Acta Psychiatrica Scandinavica, 87,* 72–80.

Guarnaccia, C., Hayslip, B., & Landry, L. P. (1999). Influence of perceived preventability of the death and emotional closeness to the deceased: A test of Bugen's model. *Omega, 39,* 261–276.

Gundel, H., O'Connor, M. F., Littrell, L., Fort, C., & Lane, R. D. (2003). Functional neuroanatomy of grief: An fMRI study. *American Journal of Psychiatry, 160,* 1946–1953.

Hackett, T. P. (1974). Recognizing and treating abnormal grief. *Hospital Physician, 10,* 49–50, 56.

Hagemeister, A., & Rosenblatt, P. (1997). Grief and the sexual relationship of couples who have experienced a child's death. *Death Studies, 21,* 231–252.

Haine, R. A., Ayers, T. S., Sandler, I. N., Wolchik, S., & Weyer, J. (2003). Locus of control and self-esteem as stress-moderators or stress-mediators in parentally bereaved children. *Death Studies, 27,* 619–640.

Harwood, D., Hawton, K., & Hope, T. (2002). The grief experiences and needs of bereaved relatives and friends of older people dying through suicide: A descriptive and case-control study. *Journal of Affective Disorders, 72,* 185–194.

Havinghurst, R. J. (1953). *Developmental tasks and education.* New York: Longmans.

Hawton, K., & Simkin, S. (2003). Helping people bereaved by suicide. *British Medical Journal, 327,* 177–178.

Hayes, J. A., Yeh, Y., & Eisenberg, A. (2007). Good grief and not-so-good grief: Countertransference in bereavement therapy. *Journal of Clinical Psychology, 63,* 345–355.

Hays, J. C., Gold, D. T., & Peiper, C. F. (1997). Sibling bereavement in late life. *Omega, 35,* 25–42.

Herrmann, N., & Eryavec, G. (1994). Delayed onset post-traumatic stress disorder in World War II veterans. *Canadian Journal of Psychiatry, 39,* 439–441.

Hershberger, P. J., & Walsh, W. B. (1990). Multiple role involvements and the adjustment to conjugal bereavement: An exploratory study. *Omega, 21,* 91–102.

Hodkinson, P. E. (1982). Abnormal grief: The problem of therapy. *British Journal of Medical Psychology, 55,* 29–34.

Hogan, N., Greenfield, D. B., & Schmidt, L. A. (2001). Development and validation of the Hogan Grief Reaction Checklist. *Death Studies, 25,* 1–32.

Hogan, N., Morse, J., & Tason, M. (1996). Toward an experiential theory of bereavement. *Omega, 33,* 43–65.

Hogan, N., & Schmidt, L. A. (2002). Testing the grief to personal growth model using structural equation modeling. *Death Studies, 26,* 615–634.

Hogan, N., Worden, J. W., & Schmidt, L. (2004). An empirical study of the proposed Complicated Grief Disorder criteria. *Omega, 48,* 263–277.

Hogan, N. S., Worden, J. W., & Schmidt, L. A. (2005). Considerations in conceptualizing complicated grief. *Omega, 52,* 81–85.

Horowitz, M. J. (1990). A model of mourning: Change in schemas of self and other. *Journal of the American Psychoanalytic Association, 38,* 297–324.

Horowitz, M. J. (2005). Meditating on complicated grief disorder as a diagnosis. *Omega, 52,* 87–89.

Horowitz, M. J., Wilner, N., Marmar, C., &, Krupnick, J. (1980). Pathological grief and the activation of latent self images. *American Journal of Psychiatry, 137,* 1157–1162.

Horowitz, N. H. (1978). Adolescent mourning reactions to infant and fetal loss. *Social Casework, 59,* 551–559.

Houck, J. (2007). A comparison of grief reactions in cancer, HIV/AIDS, and suicide bereavement. *Journal of HIV/AIDS & Social Services, 6,* 97–112.

Hoy, W. (2007). *Guiding people through grief: How to start and lead bereavement support groups.* Dallas, TX: Compass Press.

Hughes, C., & Fleming, D. (1991). Grief casualties on skid row. *Omega, 23,* 109–118.

Hutton, C. J., & Bradley, B. S. (1994). Effects of sudden infant death on bereaved siblings: A comparative study. *Journal of Child Psychology and Psychiatry and Allied Disciplines, 35,* 723–732.

Ingram, K. M., Jones, D. A., & Smith, N. G. (2001). Adjustment among people who have experienced AIDS-related multiple loss: The role of unsupportive social interactions, social support, and coping. *Omega, 43,* 287–309.

Irion, P. (1991). Changing patterns of ritual responses to death. *Omega, 22,* 159–172.

Irwin, H. J. (1991). The depiction of loss: Uses of clients' drawings in bereavement counseling. *Death Studies, 15,* 481–497.

Jacobs, S. (1999). *Traumatic grief: Diagnosis, treatment, and prevention.* Philadelphia: Brunner/Mazel.

Jacobs, S., Hansen, F., Berkman, L., Kasl, S., & Ostfeld, A. (1989). Depressions of bereavement. *Comprehensive Psychiatry, 30,* 218–224.

Jacobs, S., Hansen, F., Kasl, S., Ostfeld, A., Berkman, L., & Kim, K. (1990). Anxiety disorders during acute bereavement: Risk and risk factors. *Journal of Clinical Psychiatry, 51,* 269–274.

Jacobs, S., & Kim, K. (1990). Psychiatric complications of bereavement. *Psychiatric Annals, 20,* 314–317.

Jacobs, S., Nelson, J., & Zisook, S. (1987). Treating depression of bereavement with antidepressants: A pilot study. *Psychiatric Clinics of North America, 10,* 501–510.

Janis, I. L. (1958). *Psychological stress.* New York: John Wiley.

Janoff-Bulman, R. (1992). *Shattered assumptions: Towards a new psychology of trauma.* New York: Free Press.

Jellinek, M. S., Goldenheim, P., & Jenike, M. (1985). The impact of grief on ventilatory control. *American Journal of Psychiatry, 142,* 121–123.

Johnson, S. (1984). Sexual intimacy and replacement children after the death of a child. *Omega, 15,* 109–118.

Jordan, J. (2001). Is suicide bereavement different? A reassessment of the literature. *Suicide & Life-Threatening Behavior, 31,* 91–102.

Jordan, J., & McMenamy, J. (2004). Interventions for suicide survivors: A review of the literature. *Suicide & Life-Threatening Behavior, 34,* 337–349.

Jordan, J., & Neimeyer, R. A. (2003). Does grief counseling work? *Death Studies, 27,* 765–786.

Joy, S. S. (1985). Abortion: An issue to grieve? *Journal of Counseling and Development, 63,* 375–376.

Kaslow, N., & Aronson, S. (2004). Recommendations for family interventions following a suicide. *Professional Psychology: Research & Practice, 35,* 240–247.

Kastenbaum, R. (1969). Death and bereavement in later life. In A. H. Kutscher (Ed.), *Death and bereavement* (pp. 27–54). Springfield, IL: Thomas.

Kato, P., & Mann, T. (1999). A synthesis of psychological interventions for the bereaved. *Clinical Psychology Review, 19,* 275–296.

Katz, R., & Johnson, T. (2006). *When professionals weep: Emotional and countertransference responses in end-of-life care.* New York: Routledge.

Kemeny, M. E., Weiner, H., Taylor, S. E., Schneider, S., Visscher, B., & Fahey, J. L. (1994). Repeated bereavement, depressed mood, and immune parameters in HIV seropositive and seronegative gay men. *Health Psychology, 13,* 14–24.

Kerr, P. (1989, March 2). As murder case drags on, the mourning never ends. *New York Times.* Retrieved April 14, 2008, from http://query.nytimes.com/gst/fullpage. html?res=950DE0D7113CF931A35750C0A96F948260

Kilburn, L. H. (1988). *Hospice operations manual.* Arlington, VA: National Hospice Organization.

Kissane, D., & Bloch, S. (2002). *Family focused grief therapy.* Birmingham, UK: Open University Press.

Kissane, D., McKenzie, M., McKenzie, D. P., Forbes, A., O'Neill, I., & Bloch, S. (2003). Psychosocial morbidity associated with patterns of family functioning in palliative care: Baseline data from the family focused grief therapy controlled trial. *Palliative Medicine, 17,* 527–537.

Klass, D. (1986–1987). Marriage and divorce among bereaved parents in a self-help group. *Omega, 17,* 237–249.

Klass, D. (1988). *Parental grief: Solace and resolution.* New York: Springer Publishing.

Klass, D. (1999). *The spiritual lives of bereaved parents.* Philadelphia: Brunner/ Mazel.

Klass, D., & Marwit, S. J. (1988–1989). Toward a model of parental grief. *Omega, 19,* 31–50.

Klass, D., Silverman, P., & Nickman, S. (Eds.). (1996). *Continuing bonds: New understandings of grief.* Washington, DC: Taylor & Francis.

Klein, M. (1940). Mourning and its relationship to manic-depressive states. *International Journal of Psychoanalysis, 21,* 125–153.

Klerman, G., & Weissman, M. (1986). The interpersonal approach to understanding depression. In T. Millon & G. Klerman (Eds.), *Contemporary directions in psychopathology: Toward the DSM IV.* New York: Guilford.

Krupp, G., Genovese, F., & Krupp, T. (1986). To have and have not: Multiple identifications in pathological bereavement. *Journal of the American Academy of Psychoanalysis, 14,* 337–348.

Kübler-Ross, E. (1969). *On death and dying.* New York: Macmillan.

Kuhn, J. S. (1977). Realignment of emotional forces following loss. *Family, 5,* 19–24.

Lamberti, J., & Detmer, C. (2003). Model of family grief assessment and treatment. *Death Studies, 17,* 55–67.

Lang, A., Gottlieb, L. N., & Amsel, R. (1996). Predictors of husbands' and wives' grief reactions following infant death: The role of marital intimacy. *Death Studies, 20,* 33–57.

Larson, D., & Hoyt, W. (2007). What has become of grief counseling: An evaluation of the empirical foundations of the new pessimism. *Professional Psychology: Research & Practice, 38,* 347–355.

Lattanzi, M., & Hale, M. E. (1984). Giving grief words: Writing during bereavement. *Omega, 15,* 45–52.

Lazare, A. (1979). *Outpatient psychiatry: Diagnosis and treatment.* Baltimore: Williams and Wilkins.

Lazare, A. (1979). Unresolved grief. In A. Lazare (Ed.), *Outpatient psychiatry: Diagnosis and treatment* (pp. 498–512). Baltimore: Williams and Wilkens.

Lazarus, R., & Folkman, S. (1984). *Stress, appraisal, and coping.* New York: Springer Publishing.

Lebow, J. L. (Ed.). (2005). *Handbook of clinical family therapy.* Hoboken, NJ: John Wiley.

Legg, C., & Sherick, I. (1976). The replacement child: A developmental tragedy. *Child Psychiatry & Human Development, 7,* 113–126.

Lehman, D. R., Ellard, J. H., & Wortman, C. B. (1986). Social support for the bereaved: Recipients' and providers' perspectives on what is helpful. *Journal of Consulting & Clinical Psychology, 54,* 438–446.

Lensing, V. (2001). Grief support: The role of funeral service. *Journal of Loss & Trauma, 6,* 45–63.

Levine, C. (1995). Orphans of the HIV epidemic: Unmet needs in six US cities. *AIDS Care, 7*(Suppl. 1), S57–S62.

Lewis, C. S. (1961). *A grief observed.* London: Faber & Faber.

Lindemann, E. (1944). The Symptomatolgy and management of acute grief. *American Journal of Psychiatry, 101,* 141–148.

Lindemann, E., & Greer, I. M. (1953). A study of grief: Emotional responses to suicide. *Pastoral Psychology, 4,* 9–13.

Littlewood, J. L., Cramer, D., Hoekstra, J., & Humphrey, G. B. (1991). Gender differences in parental coping following their child's death. *British Journal of Guidance and Counselling, 19,* 139–148.

Lloyd, M. (1992). Tools for many trades: Reaffirming the use of grief counseling by health, welfare and pastoral workers. *British Journal of Guidance and Counselling, 20,* 150–163.

Lopata, H. Z. (1996). *Current widowhood: Myths and realities.* Thousand Oaks, CA: Sage.

Lorenz, K. (1963). *On aggression.* London: Methuen.

Lund, D. A. (2001). *Men coping with grief.* Amityville, NY: Baywood.

Lund, D. A., Dimond, M. F., & Juretich, M. (1985). Bereavement support groups for the elderly: Characteristics of potential participants. *Death Studies, 9,* 309–321.

Maciejewski, P. K., Zhang, B., Block, S. D., & Prigerson, H. G. (2007). An empirical examination of the stage theory of grief. *Journal of the American Medical Association, 297,* 716–723.

Main, M., & Hesse, E. (1990). Parents' unresolved traumatic experiences are related to infant disorganized attachment status: Is frightened and/or frightening parental behavior the linking mechanism? In M. T. Greenberg, D. Cicchetti, & E. M. Cummings (Eds.), *Attachment in the preschool years: Theory, research, and intervention* (pp. 161–182). Chicago: University of Chicago Press.

Main, M., & Solomon, J. (1990). Procedures for identifying infants as disorganized/disoriented during the Ainsworth strange situation. In M. Greenberg, D. Cicchetti, & E. M. Cummings (Eds.), *Attachment in the preschool years: Theory, research, and intervention* (pp. 121–160). Chicago: University of Chicago Press.

Malkinson, R. (2007). *Cognitive grief therapy. Constructing a rational meaning to life following loss.* New York: Norton.

Marris, P. (1974). *Loss and change.* London: Routledge & Kegan Paul.

Martin, J. L., & Dean, L. (1993). Effects of AIDS-related bereavement and HIV-related illness on psychological distress among gay men: A 7-year longitudinal study, 1985–1991. *Journal of Consulting & Clinical Psychology, 61,* 94–103.

Martin, T., & Doka, K. (1996). Masculine grief. In K. Doka (Ed.), *Living with grief: After sudden loss* (pp. 161–171). Washington, DC: Taylor & Francis.

Maslach, C. (1982). *Burnout: The cost of caring.* Englewood Cliffs, NJ: Prentice-Hall.

McBride, J., & Simms, S. (2001). Death in the family: Adapting a family systems framework to the grief process. *American Journal of Family Therapy, 29,* 59–73.

McCallum, M., Piper, W. E., Azim, H. F., & Lakoff, R. S. (1991). The Edmonton model of short-term group therapy for loss: An integration of theory, practice and research. *Group Analysis, 24,* 375–388.

McIntosh, J. L., & Kelly, L. D. (1992). Survivors' reactions: Suicide vs. other causes. *Crisis, 13,* 82–93.

McKeogh, M. (1995). Dementia in HIV disease: A challenge for palliative care? *Journal of Palliative Care, 11,* 30–33.

McNiel, D. E., Hatcher, C., & Reubin, R. (1988). Family survivors of suicide and accidental death: Consequences for widows. *Suicide & Life-Threatening Behavior, 18,* 137–148.

Melges, F. T., & DeMaso, D. R. (1980). Grief-resolution therapy: Reliving, revising, and revisiting. *American Journal of Psychotherapy, 34,* 51–61.

Middleton, W., Raphael, B., Burnett, P., & Martinek, N. (1997). Psychological distress and bereavement. *Journal of Nervous & Mental Disease, 185,* 447–453.

Middleton, W., Raphael, B., Burnett, P., & Martinek, N. (1998). A longitudinal study comparing bereavement phenomena in recently bereaved spouses, adult children and parents. *Australian & New Zealand Journal of Psychiatry, 32,* 235–241.

Mikulincer, M., & Shaver, P. (2003). The attachment behavioral system in adulthood. In M. Zanna (Ed.), *Advances in experimental social psychology* (pp. 53–152). Washington, DC: American Psychological Association.

Miles, M. S., & Crandall, E. K. B. (1983). The search for meaning and its potential for affecting growth in bereaved parents. *Health Values, 7,* 19–23.

Miles, M. S., & Demi, A. S. (1991–1992). A comparison of guilt in bereaved parents whose children died by suicide, accident, or chronic disease. *Omega, 24,* 203–215.

Miller, M., Frank, E., Cornes, C., Imber, S., Anderson, B., Ehrenpreis, L., et al. (1994). Applying interpersonal psychotherapy to bereavement-related depression following loss of a spouse in late life. *Journal of Psychotherapy Practice and Research, 3,* 149–162.

Mitchell, A. M., Gale, D. D., Garand, L., & Wesner, S. (2003). The use of narrative data to inform the psychotherapeutic group process with suicide survivors. *Issues in Mental Health Nursing, 24,* 91–106.

Monahan, J. R. (1994). Developing and facilitating AIDS bereavement support groups. *Group, 18,* 177–185.

Moore, M. M., & Freeman, S. J. (1995). Counseling survivors of suicide: Implications for group postvention. *Journal for Specialists in Group Work, 20,* 40–47.

Morgan, J. H., & Goering, R. (1978). Caring for parents who have lost an infant. *Journal of Religion and Health, 17,* 290–298.

Moss, M. S., Moss, S. Z., & Hansson, R. O. (2001). Bereavement and old age. In M. S. Stroebe, R. O. Hanssen, W. Stroebe, & H. Schut (Eds.), *Handbook of bereavement research: Consequences, coping, and care* (pp. 241–260). Washington, DC: American Psychological Association.

Murphy, S. (2000). The use of research findings in bereavement programs: A case study. *Death Studies, 24,* 585–602.

Muse, S., & Chase, E. (1993). Healing the wounded healers: "Soul" food for clergy. *Journal of Psychology and Christianity, 12,* 141–150.

Nadeau, J. W. (1998). *Families making sense of death.* Thousand Oaks, CA: Sage.

Nadeau, J. W. (2001). Meaning making in family bereavement. In M. S. Stroebe, R. O. Hansson, W. Stroebe, & H. Schut (Eds.), *Handbook of bereavement research: Consequences, coping, and care* (pp. 329–347). Washington, DC: American Psychological Association.

Neimeyer, R. (1999). Narrative strategies in grief therapy. *Journal of Constructive Psychology, 12,* 65–85.

Neimeyer, R. (2000). Searching for the meaning of meaning: Grief therapy and the process of reconstruction. *Death Studies, 24,* 541–558.

Neimeyer, R. (Ed.). (2001). *Meaning reconstruction and the experience of loss.* Washington, DC: American Psychological Association.

Neimeyer, R. (2003). *Lessons of loss: A guide to coping.* New York: Routledge.

Neimeyer, R., Prigerson, H. G., & Davies, B. (2002). Mourning and meaning. *American Behavioral Scientist, 46,* 235–251.

Nesbitt, W. H., Ross, M. W., Sunderland, R. H., & Shelp, E. (1996). Prediction of grief and HIV/AIDS-related burnout in volunteers. *AIDS Care, 8,* 137–143.

Neugebauer, R., Rabkin, J. G., Williams, J. B., Remien, R. H., Goetz, J., & Gorman, J. M. (1992). Bereavement reactions among homosexual men experiencing multiple losses in the AIDS epidemic. *American Journal of Psychiatry, 149,* 1374–1379.

Nolen-Hoeksema, S. (2001). Ruminative coping and adjustment to bereavement. In M. S. Stroebe, R. O. Hansson, W. Stroebe, & H. Schut (Eds.), *Handbook of bereavement research: Consequences, coping, and care* (pp. 545–562). Washington, DC: American Psychological Association.

Nolen-Hoeksema, S., McBride, A., & Larson, J. (1997). Rumination and psychological distress among bereaved partners. *Journal of Personality and Social Psychology, 72,* 855–862.

Nolen-Hoeksema, S., & Morrow, J. (1991). A prospective study of depression and post-traumatic stress symptoms after a natural disaster: The 1989 Loma Prieta earthquake. *Journal of Personality and Social Psychology, 61,* 115–121.

Nord, D. (1996). Issues and implications in the counseling of survivors of multiple AIDS-related loss. *Death Studies, 20,* 389–413.

O'Connor, M., Nikoletti, S., Kristjanson, L. J., Loh, R., & Willcock, B. (2003). Writing therapy for the bereaved: Evaluation of an intervention. *Journal of Palliative Medicine, 6,* 195–204.

O'Neill, B. (1998). A father's grief: Dealing with stillbirth. *Nursing Forum, 33,* 33–37.

Ott, C. (2007). Spousal bereavement in older adults: Common, resilient, and chronic grief with defining characteristics. *Journal of Nervous and Mental Disease, 195,* 332–341.

Papadatou, D. (2000). A proposed model of health professionals' grieving process. *Omega, 41,* 59–77.

Papadatou, D. (2006). Caregivers in death, dying, and bereavement situations. *Death Studies, 30,* 649–663.

Parkes, C. M. (1972). *Bereavement: Studies of grief in adult life.* New York: International Universities Press.

Parkes, C. M. (1975). Determinants of outcome following bereavement. *Omega, 6,* 303–323.

Parkes, C. M. (1980). Bereavement counselling: Does it work? *British Medical Journal, 281,* 3–6.

Parkes, C. M. (1986). Orienteering the caregiver's grief. *Journal of Palliative Care, 1,* 5–7.

Parkes, C. M. (1992). Bereavement and mental health in the elderly. *Reviews in Clinical Gerontology, 2,* 45–51.

Parkes, C. M. (1993). Psychiatric problems following bereavement by murder or manslaughter. *British Journal of Psychiatry, 162,* 49–54.

Parkes, C. M. (1998). Editorial. *Bereavement Care, 17,* 18.

Parkes, C. M. (2001). *Bereavement: Studies of grief in adult life* (3rd ed.). Philadelphia: Taylor & Francis.

Parkes, C. M. (2001). A historical overview of the scientific study of bereavement. In M. S. Stroebe, R. O. Hansson, W. Stroebe, & H. Schut (Eds.), *Handbook of bereavement research: Consequences, coping, and care* (pp. 25–45). Washington, DC: American Psychological Association.

Parkes, C. M. (2002). Grief: Lessons from the past, visions for the future. *Death Studies, 26,* 367–385.

Parkes, C. M. (2006). *Love and loss: The roots of grief and its complications.* New York: Routledge.

Parkes, C. M., Laungani, P., & Young, B. (1997). *Death and bereavement across cultures.* London: Routledge.

Parkes, C. M., & Stevenson-Hinde, J. (Eds.). (1982). *The place of attachment in human behavior.* New York: Basic Books.

Parkes, C. M., & Weiss, R. (1983). *Recovery from bereavement.* New York: Basic Books.

Parrish, M., & Tunkle, J. (2003). Working with families following their child's suicide. *Family Therapy, 30,* 63–76.

Paterson, G. W. (1987). Managing grief and bereavement. *Primary Care, 14,* 403–415.

Paul, N. L. (1986). The paradoxical nature of the grief experience. *Contemporary Family Therapy, 8,* 5–19.

Paul, N. L., & Grosser, G. H. (1965). Operational mourning and its role in conjoint family therapy. *Community Mental Health Journal, 1,* 339–345.

Pearlman, R. A., Hsu, C., Starks, H., Back, A. L., Gordon, J. R., Bharucha, A. J. et al. (2005). Motivations for physician-assisted suicide. *JGIM: Journal of General Internal Medicine, 20,* 234–239.

Peterson, G. (1994). Chains of grief: The impact of perinatal loss on subsequent pregnancy. *Pre- and Perinatal Psychology Journal, 9,* 149–158.

Piaget, J., & Inhelder, B. (1969). *The psychology of the child.* New York: Basic Books.

Pincus, L. (1974). *Death and the family: The importance of mourning.* New York: Pantheon.

Polatinsky, S., & Esprey, Y. (2000). An assessment of gender differences in the perception of benefit resulting from the loss of a child. *Journal of Traumatic Stress, 13,* 709–718.

Polombo, J. (1978). *Parent loss and childhood bereavement.* Paper presented at the Conference on Children & Death, University of Chicago.

Polster, E., & Polster, M. (1973). *Gestalt therapy integrated.* New York: Brunner/Mazel.

Powers, L. E., & Wampold, B. E. (1994). Cognitive-behavioral factors in adjustment to adult bereavement. *Death Studies, 18*, 1–24.

Poznanski, E. O. (1972). The replacement child: A saga of unresolved parental grief. *Journal of Pediatrics, 81*, 1190–1193.

Prigerson, H. G., Bierhals, A., Kasl, S., & Reynolds, C. (1996). Complicated grief as a disorder distinct from bereavement-related depression and anxiety: A replication study. *American Journal of Psychiatry, 153*, 1484–1486.

Prigerson, H. G., Frank, E., Kasl, S. V., Reynolds, C. F., Anderson, B., Zubenko, G. S., et al. (1995). Complicated grief and bereavement-related depression as distinct disorders: Preliminary empirical validation in elderly bereaved spouses. *American Journal of Psychiatry, 152*, 22–30.

Prigerson, H. G., & Jacobs, S. (2001). Traumatic grief as a distinct disorder. In M. S. Stroebe, R. O. Hansson, W. Stroebe, & H. Schut (Eds.), *Handbook of bereavement research: Consequences, coping, and care* (pp. 613–645). Washington, DC: American Psychological Association.

Prigerson, H. G., & Maciejewski, P. K. (2005–2006). A call for sound empirical testing and evaluation of criteria for complicated grief proposed for *DSM-V. Omega, 52*, 9–19.

Prigerson, H. G., Shear, M. K., Jacobs, S. C., Reynolds, C. F., III, Maciejewski, P. K., Davidson, J. R., et al. (1999). Consensus criteria for traumatic grief: A preliminary empirical test. *British Journal of Psychiatry, 174*, 67–73.

Randall, L. (1993). Abnormal grief and eating disorders within a mother-son dyad. *British Journal of Medical Psychology, 66*, 89–96.

Rando, T. A. (1993). *Treatment of complicated mourning.* Champaign, IL: Research Press.

Rando, T. A. (Ed.). (2000). *Clinical dimensions of anticipatory mourning.* Champaign, IL: Research Press.

Rando, T. A. (2003). Public tragedy and complicated mourning. In M. Lattanzi-Licht & K. Doka (Eds.), *Living with grief: Coping with public tragedy* (pp. 263–274). New York: Brunner-Routledge.

Range, L. M., & Calhoun, L. G. (1990). Responses following suicide and other types of death: The perspective of the bereaved. *Omega, 21*, 311–320.

Raphael, B. (1977). Preventive intervention with the recently bereaved. *Archives of General Psychiatry, 34*, 1450–1454.

Raphael, B., & Middleton, W. (1990). What is pathologic grief? *Psychiatric Annals, 20*, 304–307.

Raphael, B., Minkov, C., & Dobson, M. (2001). Psychotherapeutic and pharmacological intervention for bereaved persons. In M. S. Stroebe, R. O. Hansson, W. Stroebe, & H. Schut (Eds.), *Handbook of bereavement research: Consequences, coping, and care* (pp. 587–612). Washington, DC: American Psychological Association.

Redinbaugh, E., Schuerger, J., Weiss, L., Brufsky, A., & Arnold, R. (2001). Health care professionals' grief: A model based on occupational style and coping. *Psycho-Oncology, 10*, 187–198.

Reed, M. D. (1993). Sudden death and bereavement outcomes: The impact of resources on grief symptomatology and detachment. *Suicide & Life-Threatening Behavior, 23*, 204–220.

Reich, J., & Zautra, A. (1991). Experimental and measurement approaches to internal control in at-risk older adults. *Journal of Social Issues, 447*, 143–158.

Reid, M. (1992). Joshua—life after death: The replacement child. *Journal of Child Psychotherapy, 18,* 109–138.

Reilly, D. M. (1978). Death propensity, dying, and bereavement: A family systems perspective. *Family Therapy, 5,* 35–55.

Reilly-Smorawski, B., Armstrong, A. V., & Catlin, E. A. (2002). Bereavement support for couples following death of a baby: Program development and 14-year exit analysis. *Death Studies, 26,* 21–37.

Riley, L. P., LaMontagene, L. L., Hepworth, J. T., & Murphy, B. A. (2007). Parental grief responses and personal growth following the death of a child. *Death Studies, 31,* 277–299.

Robinson, M., Baker, L., & Nackerud, L. (1999). The relationship of attachment theory and perinatal loss. *Death Studies, 23,* 257–270.

Robinson, P. J., & Fleming, S. (1992). Depressotypic cognitive patterns in major depression and conjugal bereavement. *Omega, 25,* 291–305.

Robinson, T., & Marwit, S. J. (2006). An investigation of the relationship of personality, coping, and grief intensity among bereaved mothers. *Grief Studies, 30,* 677–696.

Rosen, E. J. (1990). *Families facing death.* Lexington, MA: Lexington Books.

Rosenblatt, P. C., Walsh, R. P., & Jackson, D. A. (1976). *Grief and mourning in cross-cultural perspective.* New Haven, CT: HRAF Press.

Rosenman, S. J., & Tayler, H. (1986). Mania following bereavement: A case report. *British Journal of Psychiatry, 148,* 468–470.

Rotheram-Borus, M. J., Weiss, R. S., Alber, S., & Lester, P. (2005). Adolescent adjustment before and after HIV-related parental death. *Journal of Consulting & Clinical Psychology, 73,* 221–228.

Rotter, J. (2000). Family grief and mourning. *Family Journal of Counseling & Therapy for Couples & Families, 8,* 275–277.

Rubin, S. S. (1990). Treating the bereaved spouse: A focus on the loss process, the self and the other. *Psychotherapy Patient, 6,* 189–205.

Rynearson, E. K. (1994). Psychotherapy of bereavement after homicide. *Journal of Psychotherapy Practice and Research, 3,* 341–347.

Rynearson, E. K., & McCreery, J. M. (1993). Bereavement after homicide: A synergism of trauma and loss. *American Journal of Psychiatry, 150,* 258–261.

Sahakian, B. J., & Charlesworth, G. (1994). Masked bereavement presenting as agoraphobia. *Behavioural and Cognitive Psychotherapy, 22,* 177–180.

Saldinger, A., Porterfield, K., & Cain, A. (2005). Meeting the needs of parentally bereaved children: A framework for child-centered parenting. *Psychiatry, 67,* 331–352.

Sanders, C. (1979). A comparison of adult bereavement in the death of a spouse, child, and parent. *Omega, 10,* 303–322.

Sanders, C. (1989). *Grief: The mourning after.* New York: Wiley.

Sanders, C. (1999). *Grief, the mourning after: Dealing with adult bereavement* (2nd ed.). New York: John Wiley.

Sandler, I., Wolchik, S., & Ayers, T. (2008). Resilience rather than recovery: A contextual framework on adaptation following bereavement. *Death Studies, 32,* 59–73.

Saunders, J. M., & Valente, S. M. (1994). Nurses' grief. *Cancer Nursing, 17,* 318–325.

Schnider, K. R., Elhai, J. D., & Gray, M. J. (2007). Coping style use predicts posttraumatic stress and complicated grief symptom severity among college students reporting a traumatic loss. *Journal of Counseling Psychology, 54,* 344–350.

Schumacher, J. D. (1984). Helping children cope with a sibling's death. In J. C. Hansen & T. Frantz (Eds.), *Death and grief in the family* (pp. 82–94). Rockville, MD: Aspen.

Schut, H., de Keijser, J., van den Bout, J., & Stroebe, M. S. (1996). Cross-modality group therapy: Description and assessment of a new program. *Journal of Clinical Psychology, 52,* 357–365.

Schut, H., Stroebe, M. S., de Keijser, J., & van den Bout, J. (1997). Intervention for the bereaved: Gender differences in the efficacy of grief counseling. *British Journal of Clinical Psychology, 36,* 63–72.

Schut, H., Stroebe, M. S., & van den Bout, J. (2001). The efficacy of bereavement interventions: Determining who benefits. In M. S. Stroebe, R. O. Hansson, W. Stroebe, & H. Schut (Eds.), *Handbook of bereavement research: Consequences, coping, and care* (pp. 705–737). Washington, DC: American Psychological Association.

Schutz, W. (1967). *Joy: Expanding human awareness.* New York: Grove.

Schwab, R. (1996). Gender differences in parental grief. *Death Studies, 20,* 103–113.

Schwartzberg, S., & Halgin, R. (1991). Treating grieving clients: The importance of cognitive change. *Professional Psychology, 22,* 240–246.

Schwartzberg, S. S., & Janoff-Bulman, R. (1991). Grief and the search for meaning: Exploring the assumptive worlds of bereaved college students. *Journal of Social and Clinical Psychology, 10,* 270–288.

Schwartz-Borden, G. (1986). Grief work: Prevention and intervention. *Social Casework,* 499–505.

Schwartz-Borden, G. (1992). Metaphor: Visual aid in grief work. *Omega, 25,* 239–248.

Sedney, M. A., Baker, J. E., & Gross, E. (1994). "The story" of a death: Therapeutic considerations with bereaved families. *Journal of Marital and Family Therapy, 20,* 287–296.

Shear, K. (2006). Adapting imaginal exposure to the treatment of complicated grief. In B. O. Rothbaum (Ed.), *Pathological anxiety: Emotional processing in etiology and treatment* (pp. 215–226). New York: Guilford Press.

Shear, K., Frank, E., Houck, P. R., & Reynolds, C. F. (2005). Treatment of complicated grief: A randomized controlled trial. *Journal of the American Medical Association, 293,* 2601–2608.

Shear, M. K., Zuckoff, A., & Melhem, N. (2006). The syndrome of traumatic grief and its treatment. In L. A. Schein, H. I. Spitz, G. M. Burlingame, P. R. Muskin, & S. Vargo (Eds.), *Psychological effects of catastrophic disasters: Group approaches to treatment* (pp. 287–333). New York: Haworth Press.

Sheldon, A., Cochrane, J., Vachon, M., Lyall, W., Rogers, J., & Freeman, S. (1981). A psychosocial analysis of risk of psychological impairment following bereavement. *Journal of Nervous & Mental Disease, 169,* 253–255.

Sherkat, D. E., & Reed, M. D. (1992). The effects of religion and social support on self-esteem and depression among the suddenly bereaved. *Social Indicators Research, 26,* 259–275.

Shoor, M., & Speed, M. N. (1963). Delinquency as a manifestation of the mourning process. *Psychiatric Quarterly, 37,* 540–558.

Shuchter, S. R., & Zisook, S. (1986). Treatment of spousal bereavement: A multidimensional approach. *Psychiatric Annals, 16,* 295–305.

Shuchter, S. R., & Zisook, S. (1987). The therapeutic tasks of grief. In S. Zisook (Ed.), *Biopsychosocial aspects of bereavement.* Washington, DC: American Psychiatric Association.

Shuchter, S. R., & Zisook, S. (1988). Widowhood: The continuing relationship with the dead spouse. *Bulletin Menninger Clinic, 52,* 269–279.

Sikkema, K. J., Hansen, N. B., & Ghebremichael, M. (2006). A randomized controlled trial of a coping group intervention for adults with HIV who are AIDS bereaved: Longitudinal effects of grief. *Health Psychology, 25,* 563–570.

Silverman, P. R. (1986). *Widow to widow.* New York: Springer Publishing.

Silverman, P. R. (2000). *Never too young to know: Death in children's lives.* New York: Oxford University Press.

Silverman, P. R., Nickman, S., & Worden, J. W. (1992). Detachment revisited: The child's reconstruction of a dead parent. *American Journal of Orthopsychiatry, 62,* 494–503.

Simos, B. G. (1979). *A time to grieve.* New York: Family Service Association.

Smilansky, S. (1987). *On death: Helping children understand and cope.* New York: Peter Lang.

Smith, P. C., Range, L. M., & Ulmer, A. (1991–1992). Belief in afterlife as a buffer in suicidal and other bereavement. *Omega, 24,* 217–225.

Sobel, H., & Worden, J. W. (1982). *Helping cancer patients cope.* New York: Guilford Press.

Solomon, R., & Rando, T. (2007). Utilization of EMDR in the treatment of grief and mourning. *Journal of EMDR Practice & Research, 1,* 109–117.

Speckhard, A., & Rue, V. (1993). Complicated mourning: Dynamics of impacted post abortion grief. *Pre- and Perinatal Psychology Journal, 8,* 5–32.

Sprang, G. (2001). The use of EMDR in the treatment of traumatic stress and complicated mourning: Psychological and behavioral outcomes. *Research on Social Work Practice, 11,* 300–320.

Steele, D. W. (1975). *The funeral director's guide to designing and implementing programs for the widowed.* Milwaukee, WI: National Funeral Directors Association.

Stroebe, M. S. (1992–1993). Coping with bereavement: A review of the grief work hypothesis. *Omega, 26,* 19–42.

Stroebe, M. S., Hansson, R. O., & Stroebe, W. (2001). Introduction: Concepts and issues in contemporary research on bereavement. In M. S. Stroebe, R. O. Hansson, W. Stroebe, & H. Schut (Eds.), *Handbook of bereavement research: Consequences, coping, and care* (pp. 3–22). Washington, DC: American Psychological Association.

Stroebe, M. S., Hansson, R. O., Stroebe, W., & Schut, H. (Eds.). (2001). *Handbook of bereavement research: Consequences, coping, and care.* Washington, DC: American Psychological Association.

Stroebe, M. S., & Schut, H. (1999). The dual process model of coping with bereavement: Rationale and description. *Death Studies, 23,* 197–224.

Stroebe, M. S., & Schut, H. (2001). Meaning making in the dual process model of coping with bereavement. In R. A. Neimeyer (Ed.), *Meaning reconstruction and the experience of loss* (pp. 55–73). Washington, DC: American Psychological Association.

Stroebe, M. S., & Schut, H. (2001). Models of coping with bereavement: A review. In M. Stroebe, R. Hansson, W. Stroebe, & H. Schut (Eds.), *Handbook of bereavement research* (pp. 375–403). Washington, DC: American Psychological Association.

Stroebe, M. S., & Schut, H. (2005). Complicated grief: A conceptual analysis of the field. *Omega, 52,* 53–70.

Stroebe, M. S., & Schut, H. (2005). To continue or relinquish bonds: A review of consequences for the bereaved. *Death Studies, 29,* 477–494.

Stroebe, M. S., Schut, H., & Finkenauer, C. (2001). The traumatization of grief: A conceptual framework for understanding the trauma-bereavement interface. *Israel Journal of Psychiatry and Related Sciences, 38,* 185–201.

Stroebe, M. S., Schut, H., & Stroebe, W. (2005). Attachment in coping with bereavement: A theoretical integration. *Review of General Psychology, 9,* 48–66.

Stroebe, M. S., Schut, H., & Stroebe, W. (2006). Who benefits from disclosure? Exploration of attachment style differences in the effects of expressing emotions. *Clinical Psychology Review, 26,* 133–139.

Stroebe, W., Schut, H., & Stroebe, M. S. (2005). Grief work, disclosure and counseling: Do they help the bereaved? *Clinical Psychology Review, 25,* 395–414.

Stroebe, W., & Stroebe, M. S. (1987). *Bereavement and health: The psychological and physical consequences of partner loss.* Cambridge: Cambridge University Press.

Stroebe, W., Stroebe, M. S., & Abakoumkin, G. (1999). Does differential social support cause sex differences in bereavement outcome? *Journal of Community & Applied Social Psychology, 9,* 1–12.

Stroebe, W., Stroebe, M. S., Abakoumkin, G., & Schut, H. (1996). The role of loneliness and social support in adjustment to loss: A test of attachment versus stress theory. *Journal of Personality and Social Psychology, 70,* 1241–1249.

Summers, J., Zisook, S., Atkinson, J. H., Sciolla, A., Whitehall, W., Brown, S., et al. (1995). Psychiatric morbidity associated with acquired immune deficiency syndrome–related grief resolution. *Journal of Nervous & Mental Disease, 183,* 384–389.

Taylor, S., & Rachman, S. J. (1991). Fear of sadness. *Journal of Anxiety Disorders, 5,* 375–381.

Telonidis, J. S., Lund, D. A., Caserta, M. S., Guralnik, J. M., & Pennington, J. L., Jr. (2005). The effects of widowhood on disabled older women. *Omega, 50,* 217–235.

Traylor, E., Hayslip, B., Jr., Kaminski, P., & York, C. (2003). Relationships between grief and family system characteristics: A cross lagged longitudinal analysis. *Death Studies, 27,* 575–601.

Tubbs, C., & Boss, P. (2000). An essay for practitioners: Dealing with ambiguous loss. *Family Relations, 49,* 285–286.

Turetsky, C. J., & Hays, R. (2003). Development of an art psychotherapy model for the prevention and treatment of unresolved grief during midlife. *Art Therapy, 20,* 248–256.

Vachon, M. L. S. (1979). Staff stress in the care of the terminally ill. *Quality Review Bulletin, 251,* 13–17.

Vachon, M. L. S. (1987). *Occupational stress in the care of the critically ill, the dying, and the bereaved.* Washington, DC: Hemisphere.

Vaillant, G. E. (1985). Loss as a metaphor for attachment. *American Journal Psychoanalysis, 45,* 59–67.

Valsanen, L. (1998). Family grief and recovery process when a baby dies. *Psychiatria Fennica, 29,* 163–174.

Van Baarsen, B., Van Duijn, M., Smit, J., Snijders, T., & Knipscheer, K. (2001). Patterns of adjustment to partner loss in old age: The widowhood adaptation longitudinal study. *Omega, 44,* 5–36.

Van der Hart, O. (1988). An imaginary leave-taking ritual in mourning therapy: A brief communication. *International Journal of Clinical and Experimental Hypnosis, 36,* 63–69.

Vess, J., Moreland, J., & Schwebel, A. (1985–1986). Understanding family role reallocation following a death: A theoretical framework. *Omega, 16,* 115–128.

Volkan, V. (1972). The linking objects of pathological mourners. *Archives of General Psychiatry, 27,* 215–221.

Volkan, V. (1985). Complicated mourning. *Annual of Psychoanalysis, 12,* 323–348.

Wade, T., & Wade, D. (2001). Integrative psychotherapy: Combining ego-state therapy, clinical hypnosis, and Eye Movement Desensitization and Reprocessing (EMDR) in a psychosocial developmental context. *American Journal of Clinical Hypnosis, 43,* 233–245.

Wagner, B., Knaevelsrud, C., & Maercker, A. (2005). Internet-based treatment for complicated grief: Concepts and case study. *Journal of Loss & Trauma, 10,* 409–432.

Wagner, K. G., & Calhoun, L. G. (1991). Perceptions of social support by suicide survivors and their social networks. *Omega, 24,* 61–73.

Wakefield, J. C. (2007). Extending the bereavement exclusion for major depression to other losses: Evidence from the National Comorbidity Study. *Archives of General Psychiatry, 64,* 433–440.

Walliss, J. (2001). Continuing bonds: Relationships between the living and the dead within contemporary Spiritualism. *Mortality, 6,* 127–145.

Walsh, F., & McGoldrick, M. (1991). *Living beyond loss: Death in the family.* New York: Norton.

Weisman, A. D. (1972). *On dying and denying.* New York: Aronson.

Weisman, A. D., & Hackett, T. P. (1961). Predilection to death. *Psychosomatic Medicine, 23,* 232–255.

Weisman, A. D., & Worden, J. W. (1980). *Psychological screening and intervention with cancer patients.* Boston: Massachusetts General Hospital.

Werth, J. (1999). The role of the mental health professional in helping significant others of persons who are assisted in death. *Death Studies, 23,* 239–255.

Wheeler, I. (2001). Parental bereavement: The crisis of meaning. *Death Studies, 25,* 51–66.

White, R. W. (1952). *Lives in progress.* New York: Holt, Rinehart, & Winston.

Wijngaards-de Meij, L., Stroebe, M. S., & Schut, H. (2005). Couples at risk following the death of their child: Predictors of grief versus depression. *Journal of Consulting & Clinical Psychology, 73,* 617–623.

Wilson, R. (2001). Parents' support of their other children after a miscarriage or perinatal death. *Early Human Development, 61,* 55–65.

Winnicott, D. (1953). Transitional objects and transitional phenomena. *International Journal of Psychoanalysis, 34,* 89–97.

Wolfenstein, M. (1966). How is mourning possible? *Psychoanalytic Study of the Child, 21,* 93–123.

Worden, J. W. (1976). *Personal death awareness.* Englewood Cliffs, NJ: Prentice-Hall.

Worden, J. W. (1996). *Children & grief: When a parent dies.* New York: Guilford Press.

Worden, J. W. (2000). Towards an appropriate death. In T. Rando (Ed.), *Clinical dimensions of anticipatory mourning* (pp. 267–277). Champaign, IL: Research Press.

Worden, J. W., Davies, B., & McCown, D. (2000). Comparing parent loss with sibling loss. *Death Studies, 23,* 1–15.

Worden, J. W., & Kübler-Ross, E. (1977–1978). Attitudes and experiences of death workshop attendees. *Omega, 8,* 91–106.

Worden, J. W., & Monahan, J. (2001). Caring for bereaved parents. In A. Armstrong-Daily & S. Goltzer (Eds.), *Hospice care for children* (2nd ed., pp. 137–156). New York: Oxford University Press.

Worden, J. W., & Silverman, P. R. (1993). Grief and depression in newly widowed parents with school-age children. *Omega, 27,* 251–260.

Wortman, C. B., & Silver, R. C. (1989). The myths of coping with loss. *Journal of Consulting & Clinical Psychology, 57,* 349–357.

Wortman, C. B., & Silver, R. C. (2001). The myths of coping with loss revisited. In M. S. Stroebe, R. O. Hansson, W. Stroebe, & H. Schut (Eds.), *Handbook of bereavement research: Consequences, coping, and care* (pp. 405–429). Washington, DC: American Psychological Association.

Zaiger, N. (1985–1986). Women and bereavement. *Women and Therapy, 4,* 33–43.

Zerbe, K. J. (1994). Uncharted waters: Psychodynamic considerations in the diagnosis and treatment of social phobia. *Bulletin Menninger Clinic, 58*(2, Suppl. A), A3–A20.

Zisook, S., & DeVaul, R. A. (1977). Grief-related facsimile illness. *International Journal of Psychiatry in Medicine, 7,* 329–336.

Zisook, S., & Kendler, K. S. (2007). Is bereavement-related depression different than non-bereavement-related depression? *Psychological Medicine, 37,* 779–794.

Zisook, S., Paulus, M., Shuchter, S. R., & Judd, L. L. (1997). The many faces of depression following spousal bereavement. *Journal of Affective Disorders, 45,* 85–94.

Zisook, S., & Shuchter, S. R. (1993). Uncomplicated bereavement. *Journal of Clinical Psychiatry, 54,* 365–372.

Index